A Sousa Reader

Essays, Interviews, and Clippings

Edited by Bryan Proksch

Also available from GIA Publications

John Philip Sousa's America: The Patriot's Life in Images and Words
by John Philip Sousa IV with Loras John Schissel
G-8161
G-8161DVD (book with DVD)

Marching Along: Reflections of Men, Women and Music
An Autobiography
by John Philip Sousa
A reprint of the original edition with a dedication by John Philip Sousa IV
G-8620

A Sousa Reader

Essays, Interviews, and Clippings

Edited by Bryan Proksch

GIA Publications, Inc.
Chicago

G-9278
ISBN: 978-1-62277-212-4

GIA Publications, Inc.
7404 Mason Ave.
Chicago, IL 60638
www.giamusic.com

Cover design by Martha Chlipala.
Layout design by Paul Burrucker.

Printed in the United States of America.

To George Foreman, Vince DiMartino, and the Advocate Brass Band

Acknowledgments

I wish to acknowledge a number of individuals and institutions that helped make this volume possible. Lamar University provided me with research funding to visit the Sousa Archives on more than one occasion. I am grateful to Kurt Gilman and Brian Shook—chairs of Lamar's Mary Morgan Moore Department of Music—and to Derina Holtzhausen, dean of Lamar's College of Fine Arts and Communication for their support. The book's existence is a tribute to the staff of the Sousa Archives, especially to archivist Scott Schwartz, whose assistance was invaluable. Patrick Warfield graciously offered suggestions for improvement of an early draft, which I greatly appreciate. Sheila MacKay kindly compared my transcriptions to the original publications to improve accuracy, a tedious job but one at which she excelled. John Philip Sousa IV unhesitatingly granted permission to reproduce those few post-1922 items still under the author's copyright and volunteered to write the foreword. The staff of GIA Publications has been a pleasure to work with, especially Alec Harris, president, who approved the project almost before it began and Kirin Nielsen, who worked on typesetting and proofreading. Permissions editor Michael Boschert was instrumental in determining which of Sousa's post-1922 writings could be included and which required permissions beyond our budgetary capabilities. Finally I wish to thank my wife Kari and my sons Max and Sam for their patience as I worked on the project.

Bryan Proksch
Editor

Table of Contents

Foreword by John Philip Sousa IV xiii

Editorial Preface xv

Introduction xix

1880–1893: The Marine Band 1

"Mr. Sousa's Estimation of the Distin Band Instruments"
(May 1883) 1

American Composers on Benjamin Harrison's
Inaugural Ball Program (early 1889) 2

"John Philip Sousa on Bands: Some Remarks by the
Marine Band Leader on a Recent Controversy" (March 1889) 5

Excerpts from "Not One National Song" (August 1889) 7

"Band Tournament" (November 1889) 9

"Music for the People, as Interpreted by the Famous Leader
of a Famous Band" (September 1890) 11

"Music We Must Have" (November 1890) 16

"Mr. Sousa and His Band" by P. S. Gilmore (March 1892) 21

1894–1905: The Bandmaster and the New Century 23

On the Use of Subdominant Trio Sections in Marches
(August 1898) 23

"A Century of Music" (December 1899) 24

"The Ideal Band" (January 1900) 25

"American Music in Paris: John Philip Sousa Says That It Is Well
Received" (May 1900) 30

"No State Aid for Art" (July 1900) 31

"What I Think of England" (December 1901) 38

"According to Sousa: Great March King Describes How He
    Controls His 'One-Man' Band" (January 1905) 41

1905–1906: Fighting the Music Industry 45

"Another Phrase of the Piracy Question:
    International Obligations" (February 1905) 45

"Mr. Sousa on Musical Pirates: Protest and a Parallel"
    (April 1905) 47

"Musical Piracy" (April 1905) 50

"The Business of the Bandmaster" (August 1905) 52

"Music in America: Its Progress as Viewed by the Famous
    March Composer, Sousa" (September 1905) 59

Testimony before the Congressional Committees on
    Patents (June 1906) 61

"The Menace of Mechanical Music" (September 1906) 70

"The Year in Music" (December 1906) 81

1908–1917: Opinions and Pastimes 89

"How I Earned My Musical Education" (November 1908) 89

"How I Built the Sousa Band" (September 1911) 90

"No Nationalism in Music" (October 1911) 94

Editorial Response to "No Nationalism in Music" (October 1911) 96

"Sousa's Views on Woman" (October 1911) 97

"Here's Sousa's First Self-Written Interview" (October 1911) 98

"Some Suggestions to Young Men" (December 1912) 103

"American Musical Taste" (1912) 104

"Ready! Pull! Dead!" (June 1914) 112

"A Horse, a Dog, a Gun and a Girl" (August 1916) 115

"If I Had to Begin All Over Again" (December 1916) 117

"Differences of Opinion as to Correct Metronomic
    Tempo Indications" (April 1917) 118

"The Symphony Orchestra and the Concert Band" (May 1917) 120

"The Xylophone" by Joe Green (November 1917) 126

1917–1918: Sousa at War 131

"Mrs. Sousa Aiding the Soldiers" (November 1917) 131

"Muck Should Get Out of U.S., Thinks Sousa" (November 1917) 132

"Parents of Patriotism are Mother and Music" (March 1918) 133

"'Don't Propose Until I Compose,' Sousa Warning" (May 1918) 138

"Sousa's Ridiculous Assignment" (June 1918) 140

"Leave German Music to Germans" (October 1918) 141

1919–1928: The Roaring Twenties 143

"Appreciations of Rachmaninoff from Famous Musicians
in America" (October 1919) 143

"All's Well with the Musical World" (1921) 144

"Success in Music and How to Win It." (1921) 145

"Music, an Ideal Christmas Present" (December 1921) 147

"Dry Law a Tragedy—Sousa" (August 1922) 152

"Sousa in Reply" and "In Reply to Sousa" (October 1922) 154

"Sousa on Prohibition" (October 1922) 157

"John Philip Sousa's Spaghetti Portuguese" (November 1922) 158

"No Effort Will Be Made to Stop Sousa Concert by Officials"
(November 1922) 159

"Ministers Oppose Sunday Band Concert; Marches Better than
Sermons, Says Sousa" (November 1922) 161

"Director Albert under Arrest for Staging Sousa Concert on Sunday;
5,000 Hear 'March King'" (November 1922) .161

"Magnificent to Be Broadminded as Well as Christian—Sousa"
(November 1922) 164

"The Sunday Issue" and "The Sousa Concert" (November 1922) 166

"'Good Music Waits an Inspiration', Says Sousa" (February 1924) 169

"Jazz, in Its Present State, May Develop National Style" (July 1924) 170

"Good Jazz is Good; But It Can Be Horrid—Sousa" (April 1928) 174

Bibliography 177

Index 179

About the Editor 185

Foreword

Now some eighty-five years after the death of the "March King," this wonderful, thoughtful, and informative publication delivers a unique perspective on the thoughts, ideas, and life of John Philip Sousa, my great-grandfather.

Prior his death, Sousa published his autobiography, *Marching Along*, and since that time Paul Bierley and others have expanded our knowledge of the style and the movement of Sousa and his Band. A few years ago Loras Schissel and I published *John Philip Sousa's America*, which looks at Sousa in words and pictures as never previously done.

Now a sensational publication takes a new and refreshing look at the "Pied Piper of Patriotism" in a novel way that will certainly help anyone who has an interest in John Philip Sousa or in marches and "military music" better understand the man and his dedication to music and to America.

A Sousa Reader offers fantastic insights into Sousa's thoughts about politics, competitive bands, the quality of his and others' music, other musicians of the time, his philosophy, the future of bands, live music, and more.

I am personally thrilled to have the honor of writing the foreword to this outstanding look inside my great-grandfather. I sincerely hope that both musicologists and the general reader use this marvelous resource, and I hope there will be a second volume to follow.

Enjoy,
John Philip Sousa IV

Editorial Preface

My overarching goal in gathering and editing this collection was to preserve as much as possible the items as originally printed. Small corrections to careless mistakes in grammar, punctuation, spelling, and omitted words (such as articles) have been made without comment. Outdated spellings (for instance, "to-day" and "Tschaikowsky") have been retained as have most of the idiosyncrasies of the original sources' style sheets (capitalization of words, apostrophes for plural possessives, various abbreviations, Oxford commas or lack thereof, British spellings for overseas publications, etc.).

Larger corrections, redactions, and editorial additions not in the original are indicated within square brackets. The only exception to this is Sousa's testimony before Congress, where the stenographer transcribed things like "[laughter]" in square brackets. For that item my editorial comments have been made in italics within square brackets to make the distinction clear. In cases where a correction would prove more intrusive than retaining the original error the original has been retained with a "[sic]" annotation to show that it has been rendered as in the original in spite of the problem. Titles for the essays and newspaper columns within quotation marks are those as written in the original. In those cases in which a title was missing, one has been provided by the editor without quotation marks. For the most part newspaper subheadings and pull quotes merely selected choice phrases already printed in the article that followed. These have been omitted except in the few cases where they seemed necessary as unique or to complete a title.

None of the original items used footnotes: all footnotes are my editorial insertions. I have inserted footnotes mostly to assist non-scholarly readers in understanding the broader context of Sousa's ideas and to make clear some of Sousa's more obscure references to then-current terms, events, figures, quotations, and musical works. I have also used them to direct readers to scholarly literature and germane information relating to dates and places.

The bulk of the material printed herein was taken from the *Sousa Press Books* (abbreviated as *SPB* throughout) as bound and housed at the Sousa Archives at the University of Illinois. The location of the original within the *SPB* is given under the source heading for each item. Depending on binding and pagination, the location is noted either as "volume, page" or "volume: sub-volume, page." Because the binding and pagination of the *SPB* follow preexisting groupings, there are many inconsistencies in numbering (some use both page numbers and letters, some volumes have many sub-volumes and some have none, etc.). One reason for including the original location is to confirm that Sousa knew of the item's existence (since he hired a press agent to gather them); another reason is to assist researchers seeking related readings in the *SPB* (the *SPB* is not currently indexed, but related items often appear in close proximity). Given the size and current state of the *SPB*, the absence of an *SPB* reference does not necessarily mean that the item is not contained in the press books, rather it indicates only that the editor located the source material elsewhere.

A cautionary word on dating is necessary: the *SPB* at best includes only the press agent's handwritten date and a newspaper name for the original clippings (never page or column numbers). This means the dates may not be entirely reliable in every case and become more problematic the further back one goes. The dates only indicate when an item was published, not when it was written, although letters written to editors often included the date they were written. With these potential inaccuracies and ambiguities in mind, it is noteworthy that each time the editor has found the original publication independently of the *SPB* the date written in the *SPB* has proved to be accurate. On the other hand, in some instances the *SPB* does not include a date or a specific source: in these cases a question mark (?) or circa (*ca.*) has been included and internal clues together with the clipping's placement within the *SPB* have been used in an effort to make as educated an estimate as possible.

Regarding copyright, every reasonable, good faith effort has been made to locate owners or administrators for those items originally printed after December 31, 1922 and possibly still under copyright. In future printings, the publisher will, if notified, acknowledge the omission of any bona fide copyright claims on the items in these pages. Sousa's business records have long since been destroyed; therefore, making definitive assessments has proven difficult—if not impossible—in some cases.

Bryan Proksch
Editor

Introduction

Who was John Philip Sousa? What did he think about music, politics, and the world? These are basic questions which this volume hopes to address. While Sousa's autobiography *Marching Along* gives us Sousa's own perspective, it was published in 1928 at the tail end of the bandmaster's half-century career. There is so much more information available, most of it recorded "in the moment" with an immediacy that presents Sousa in a different light. This is not to say that *Marching Along* is somehow inaccurate, but rather recognizes that one's perspective and opinions change and evolve. Put another way, reading Sousa talking about testifying before Congress twenty years after the fact is not quite the same as reading his actual testimony.

In presenting a variety of materials from throughout Sousa's career, *A Sousa Reader* allows the reader to witness his life and ideas from exciting new perspectives. Sousa was opinionated: frank and honest with the press and public in a way not often seen. He defended his views viciously when criticized, but changed his mind on occasion as well. His political views, at first blush brash and straightforward, demonstrate a nuance and evolution seldom seen in modern times: patriotic almost to a fault, staunchly conservative in his sense of the role of government, yet markedly liberal on social issues. He was savvy as a businessman and a bandmaster, innovative, forward-looking, and yet artistic and romantic in his views on the power of music. Despite consummate musicianship, Sousa struggled at times to navigate the increasing fissures between the classical and popular musical worlds. While he existed largely in the popular sphere from the public's perspective, he believed his genius placed him firmly in a classical lineage that included Wagner and the greats. In sum total he was a Teddy Roosevelt-like figure for the musical world, a brash, self-confident American leading the nation to a bright future through innovation and capitalism.

This is book born out of my own personal necessity. When trying to research Sousa's viewpoints on Joseph Haydn and the Classical era for a different book, it quickly became apparent to me that virtually none of Sousa's own writings was readily available outside of archival holdings. So I decided to quick collect his essays from the *Sousa Press Books* (housed at the University of Illinois's Sousa Archive) and be on my way. Little did I know that the *Sousa Press Books* are a bookcase-sized collection of thousands of pages gathering probably over ten-thousand items. These were initially gathered by Sousa's press agents and later photocopied and organized by Paul Bierley. Virtually none of their contents are known outside of those who have viewed them firsthand. There is nothing quick or concise about the collection—there is no index or table of contents, and the clippings are not in a reliable chronological order—and yet what a resource! *A Sousa Reader* was born.

One goal in my selection of items for *A Sousa Reader* has been to offer a taste of the variety of items held in this wonderful collection. Although this reader reproduces select writings and clippings from throughout Sousa's lengthy career, the sheer size of the *Sousa Press Books* means that it cannot hope to approach anything that might be termed complete. Such a vast undertaking seems unnecessary anyway, given the repetitive nature of some of his essays and that some were only lightly revised for his autobiography. At the same time, the *Sousa Press Books* present an irresistible gathering of interviews and other newspaper materials of great interest to the historian previously inaccessible even in the internet age. This volume, then, is designed to gather and make available in a user-friendly form a variety of Sousa's writings and interviews while avoiding duplication of items later recycled in his autobiography. Included are other noteworthy materials, such as essays and letters written by Sousa's wife and bandsmen, and even the occasional satirical essay or spaghetti recipe.

It is hoped that *A Sousa Reader* will open up Sousa's life and times to a broad spectrum of readers while encouraging further research into the life and times of one of the most important and fascinating figures in the history of American music.

1880-1893

The Marine Band and Chicago World's Fair

"Mr. Sousa's Estimation of the Distin Band Instruments"

Source: unknown Philadelphia newspaper, ca. May 8, 1883, in *SPB* 21:1, 29.

> *By 1883 Sousa had been the conductor of the U.S. Marine Band for three years. Operettas, including* The Smugglers *(1882) and* Désirée *(1883), were his primary compositional focus. Although his first million-copy march,* The Gladiator, *would not appear until 1886, this early endorsement letter (appended to the end of a page-long biography) demonstrates his increasingly visible stature among American musicians.*

Washington, D. C., May 8, 1883

Mr. Henry Distin

Dear Sir:– I will endeavor to reply briefly to your request for my opinion of your celebrated band instruments.

The name of Henry Distin was always familiar to me as being synonymous with superiority in the manufacture of brass band instruments, and my association with bands and bandsmen assures me of the universal estimation they are held in by discriminating performers.

On my recent visit to Philadelphia when I inspected the new steam factory erected for you by Mr. J. W. Pepper, I was greatly surprised at the magnitude and completeness of it. It is apparent that there is nothing lacking in its appointments for the production of the very best instruments. I was particularly pleased with your recent inventions for improving the tone and register of brass instruments. I have no doubt your thorough knowledge, both theoretically and practically, of the entire range of brass instruments enables you to produce a class of instruments which are unrivalled.

With the earnest wish that your endeavors will meet with complete success for yourself and Mr. Pepper,

I am, yours sincerely,
John Philip Sousa

American Composers on Benjamin Harrison's Inaugural Ball Program

Source: *The American Musician*, early 1889, in *SPB* 89, 70.

> *John Travis Quigg (d. 1893) edited a number of newspapers and music periodicals throughout his career.*[1] *In the 1870s he also composed a number of popular songs. He was an influential organizer of the 1876 Philadelphia Centennial Exposition, headlined by Theodore Thomas. The exposition commissioned Richard Wagner's* American Centennial March, *conducted by Simon Hassler to mixed reviews.*[2] *Presented is Quigg's initial essay critical of the selection of music by non-Americans for Benjamin Harrison's inaugural ball, Sousa's reply, and Quigg's response. The Marine Band and Beck's Orchestra played the* Presidential Polonaise *jointly, with Sousa conducting.*[3]

The musical programme of the Grand Inaugural Ball, which will be held in Washington on the evening of March 4, is in good hands: Prof. Sousa, of the U. S. Marine Band, and my esteemed friends, Mr. Simon Hassler and Mr. J. G. S. Beck, of Philadelphia. I was pained, however, on looking at the programme, to find that out of some twenty odd numbers of the

---

1   Further on Quigg see Mathews, ed., *Hundred Years*, 382–84. Quigg's date of birth has been listed variously as 1832, 1838 and 1839; his 1889 obituary in *The New York Times* mentions he was "about sixty years old."

2   Bierley, *American Phenomenon*, 38.

3   Details of the ball, including the titles of a number of the pieces performed, can be viewed on www.newspapers.com as published in *The Weekly Wisconsin*, March 9, 1889, 10. The report is contradictory on the size of Beck's ensemble, mentioning both 100 and 125 members. While the 1889 date for this entry is somewhat less than fully secure since Sousa played at a number of inaugural balls, the Wisconsin newspaper agrees with many of the composers and participants listed in Sousa's reply. Simon Hassler's presence and role are not mentioned there, however.

promenade and dance music, but two American composers are represented, and these happen to be Professor Sousa and Simon Hassler. This is to be a national affair, to celebrate the inauguration of an American President, and it is certainly fitting that American composers should find a place upon the programme of a national event. There is no good reason, either, why American composers should be boycotted by the maker of these programmes. I do not believe in boycotting the compositions of distinguished foreign composers, but I believe in giving our own countrymen a fair chance to have their compositions heard upon such an occasion. It is not only unjust to American composers, but to American publishers who pay for the American copyrights. If Mr. Sousa and Mr. Hassler will send for the catalogues of O. Ditson & Co., Wm. A. Pond & Co., the New York Music Publishing Co., or Carl Fisher, they will find therein the band and orchestral compositions of Gilmore, Wiegand, Puerner, Braham, Fohs, Lax, Meyrelles, Riezel, Müller, and many others whose names escape me at this writing, who have written compositions worthy to be placed upon any programme. American composers like Sousa and Hassler cannot better advance their own interests, then [sic] by cultivating a spirit of nationality, and giving, I do not say a preference, but a fair show to their brother composers in this country, thus making an American copyright more valuable, and encouraging American publishers to publish more original and less foreign reprint music. I say this in all good faith to Messrs. Sousa and Hassler both of whom I greatly esteem.

J. Travis Quigg

Since the first part of this Lounger was in print, I have received the following letter from Mr. John Philip Sousa, director of the United States Marine Band, dated Washington, D. C., February 20:

My Dear Mr. Quigg:

The pluck and persistency exhibited by you in espousing the cause of American music and musicians has always elicited my warmest admiration; but allow me to correct an error, unintentional, no doubt, but still an error, that appeared in the last issue of *The American Musician*. In an article relating to the Inaugural Ball programme, you say "I was pained, however, on looking at the programme to find that out of some twenty odd numbers of the programme and dance music, but two American composers are represented, and these happen to be Professor Sousa and Simon Hassler."

With your permission we will sit down in some quiet little nook and go over the programme together. We find that No. 6 is by Weingarten, a New Yorker; No. 9 by Zimmerman, a Philadelphian; No. 19 by Voelkler, a Richmond man; No. 21 by Downing, a New Yorker; No. 22 by Hoffman, a Chicagoan; No. 23 by Puerner, a New Yorker; Nos. 7 and 12 by your old friend Hassler, and Nos. 5 and 10 by your humble servant. The numbers, of music composed and copyrighted in this country, I think are a splendid showing, when you take into consideration that a programme-builder should never allow geographical lines to interfere with the selection of what he considers most suitable for the prospective performance.

One thing more: I would very gladly add to my library the works of such Americans as Paine, Buck, Chadwick, Bird, Whiting, Bristow, Timm, Kelley, Gilder, Gilchrist, Warren, and many others if it were possible to secure arrangements suitable for military band. The greater part of the music published in this country for wind instruments is arranged to meet the exigencies of the average American band, which as you are aware, runs largely to brass, and consequently is unsuited for an organization such as ours, where the wood-wind predominates.

Yours sincerely,
John Philip Sousa

Mr. Sousa adds in a postscript: "Please don't call me professor." I have no doubt that the American composers whom Mr. Sousa names will be glad to accept his generous offer, and be only too willing to have arrangements made for military band of selections from their works, and furnish Mr. Sousa with the parts. Performances are better than professions, and Mr. Sousa proves his earnestness by his liberal offer.

J. Travis Quigg

"John Philip Sousa on Bands: Some Remarks by the Marine Band Leader on a Recent Controversy"

Source: *Philadelphia Inquirer*, March 28, 1889, in *SPB 89*, 66.

> *Sousa increasingly wanted to take the Marine Band on tour, but money quickly became an unforeseen headache for him. Could a government band earn income from private engagements? If not, should the government bear the costs of the trips? An 1888 engagement in Philadelphia ended up cancelled after the National League of Musicians publically opposed it. Shortly thereafter questions arose about the employment of government musicians (who clearly were non-union) for paid performances. Sousa's frustration on both accounts is evident in his response.[4] In the longer term the issues led Sousa to quit the Marine Band in favor of leading a private ensemble.*

To the Editor of *The Inquirer*:

I have seen an article in *The Inquirer* of March 21, relative to a protest, emanating from certain Philadelphia musicians against allowing the Marine Band to perform in your city. As the protest follows so closely on the heels of the ensanguined warfare waged between two of your local bandmasters, as to who should perform at the Park concerts, the one with his five thousand dollars' worth of melodies, or the other with his four thousand seven hundred dollars' worth of tuneful pabulum, it strikes me, as a man up a tree, that your average Philadelphia Son of Harmony is never happy unless he is making discord.

It would appear from the frequent quotations from the National League of Musicians in your article, that they desire to place a stigma on the members of the musical profession who are employed by the government. A disinterested person would imagine that it is their wish that the liberties guaranteed us as citizens should be curtailed because we serve Uncle Sam in a musical capacity. It smells suspiciously like an attempt to build a Chinese wall around the nation's music-makers, so that no sound shall escape for the benefit of a music-hungry public.

---

4   Further see Warfield, *March King*, 172–73.

In my simple and untutored way, I cannot understand why it is wrong for us to exercise our professional skill when not conflicting with our official duties, more than a civilian musician to teach music in the morning, write music in the afternoon, and play music in the evening, receiving for each a separate stipend. I would be pleased to see, just for a curiosity, the member of the National League of Musicians who don't [sic] cast daily, into the sea of engagements at least four lines. Sometimes, it's true, he'll only get a nibble or two, but oftener he'll hook a fish on each line, and I can assure you he only throws away what he can't carry.

The public don't engage us because we are a government institution, but for the reason that, by persistent and arduous practice, we have reached that point where we are looked upon as a musical factor of more than ordinary importance. And as for prices paid for our services—why, if the average National Leaguer knew of some of the plums that come our way he would turn green with envy. Mr. Editor, we come high, but the public wants us.

There is another side to this question that is usually overlooked. It is not so much a controversy between the National League and the Marine Band as it is between the National League and the people at large. Our sixty-odd million people say: "We desire to engage the Marine Band, and are willing to pay liberally for them." Up pops this little Jack-in-the-box, and, in a voice tinged with the aroma of the brewery, exclaims: "You shan't do it; you must take us." "But," says the awfully-frightened sixty-odd million, "we don't want you." "That don't make any difference," vociferates this musical bully; "if you don't want us, you shan't have them!"

One word of brotherly advice to the National League, and I am done. If it is your wish to command the respect and admiration of your public, do it by legitimate means. Don't try to ride rough-shod over your competitors because you are strong and they are weak. Don't put a premium on idleness. Cultivate liberal-mindedness; try to believe a man has some rights, even if he is a government musician. Form yourselves into bands and orchestras, select your conductors, study hard, and out of your troubles will come recognition and tranquility —

> "And the night shall be filled with music,
> And the cares that infest the day

> Shall fold their tents like the Arabs,
> And as silently steal away."[5]

John Philip Sousa
Washington, March 26.

Excerpts from "Not One National Song"

Source: *New York Times, August 25, 1889, in SPB 89, 41.*

One of the passions consistently revealed in Sousa's essays and interviews was the idea that the United States needed an official national anthem. The process took decades and would not be resolved definitively until Herbert Hoover signed a law so designating The Star-Spangled Banner *in 1931. Interviewers frequently asked Sousa for his views on the topic, often hinting that* The Stars and Stripes Forever *should be a leading candidate. The always-flattered Sousa consistently replied in the negative. In 1917, the national crisis to which Sousa referred came to pass with the United States' entry into World War I. That same year a committee appointed by the Federal Bureau of Education (which counted Sousa, Walter Damrosch, and Oscar Sonneck among its members) crafted a standardized arrangement of* The Star-Spangled Banner. *The interview below makes frequent reference to Sousa's soon-to-be-published* National, Patriotic, and Typical Airs of All Lands *(1890).*

[...]

It was while discussing national music that Prof. Sousa made the startling statement that we have no national air. "But how about 'Hail Columbia,' 'The Star-Spangled Banner,' 'My Country,' and a few more of the same sort generally considered national airs?" he was asked.

"People confound a national air with a popular and a patriotic one," replied Prof. Sousa. "In Europe they have national airs because they have been made so either by the Government or by the people, and on all ceremonial occasions they are played as a matter of course. For example, England has 'God Save the Queen,' France 'La Marseillaise,' and so on. Now, in England, at an affair of state, whenever the Queen is present the bands play 'God Save the Queen,' and the bandmasters of the Life Guards

---

5   Sousa here quotes the last verse of "The Day is Done" (1844) by Henry Wadsworth Longfellow.

or the Coldstream Guards or any other good band do not have to ask what air they shall play. They know only one tune is admissible. And when an Englishman hears the air, no matter where he is, off comes his hat and he remains standing until the last note. Children are taught it at school, and they think it as sacred as a hymn. But with us, when the President takes part in any ceremony, one band may play 'America' and another 'The Star-Spangled Banner,' according to the taste of the conductor."

"Then Congress by an act could create a national air?"

"Well hardly. Congress can do a great many things, but it cannot do that. The national air of a people must come from some great event in the life of the Nation, perhaps some crisis. It must be spontaneous; it must appeal to national pride and the national sentiment, and then, when it does that, the country takes it up and clings to it as jealously as it does to its other traditions. [...]"

"Wasn't the civil war a great enough crisis to inspire the best efforts of musicians?"

"Undoubtedly, but you must remember the people were divided, and the work of a Northern composer would not have been acceptable to the people of the South. If, however, the country had risen against a foreign foe[,] any song composed at that time would have fired the national heart, and if of the right kind would have been accepted by the people. It is true we went through a crisis in the early days of the Republic, but I guess in those days our ancestors were too busy fighting to pay much attention to music. 'Hail Columbia' belongs to the last century, but it was composed by a German, the leader of the John-Street Theatre, in New York, in compliment to Gen. Washington, and for many years it was known as 'The President's March.' We ought not to adopt as our national air the work of a foreigner. The words of the 'Star-Spangled Banner' are American, but the music is English."[6]

[...]

"There are plenty of men in this country who are capable of writing a national air," Prof. Sousa remarked, "but, as I said before, the occasion must develop the music. Every week I receive two or three pieces of music which their authors fondly imagine may become the national air [... but] they do not seem to 'catch on.' Besides, when the national air is written, I hope it will be

---

6   John Stafford Smith wrote the music to *The Star-Spangled Banner.*

the outcome of some national event. At the present time foreigners devote more attention to the writing of our national air than do our own people."

[...]

"Band Tournament"

Source: *The Leader*, ca. November 2, 1889, in *SPB 89*, 70.

> *Sousa's comments on "test pieces" and the sizes of bands at the time are insightful, even as his "classes" and "scoring" of bands predict the ways in which high school bands and drum corps would later be evaluated. It is less apparent why the drums are not itemized after the "first class" bands and why the largest ensemble lacks a piccolo.*

Washington, D.C., Nov. 2, 1889

Editor of *The Leader*:—

Dear Sir,—In answer to your request of the 31st ultimo I beg leave to submit the following plan in classifying bands. I have placed the bands of the first class at fifty wind instruments, and while bands of that size are few and far between at present time, I believe the day is not distant when they will be more plentiful than bands of thirty are now. The military band appeals more strongly to popular taste than any other musical body, with, perhaps, the exception of the mixed choir.

As the possibilities of the military band are more clearly understood by our people, I believe it will increase in numerical strength and widen in scope.

Genial and whole-souled Pat. Gilmore is the father of the military band in this country. All honor to him! May he live to see his progeny multiply a thousandfold!

I desire to state in connection with the classification I submit that I do not look upon a band of fifty performers as a complete organization, by any means; but, as bands of that size are not remote possibilities, I suggest that number for the first class.

Very sincerely,
John Philip Sousa

Dir. of Band of the U. S. Marine Corps

First Class

Instrumentation (50).—14 B-flat Clarinets (8 1st, 4 2d, 2 3d), 2 Flutes, 2 Oboes, 2 E-flat Clarinets, 2 Bassoons, 1 Alto-Clarinet, 2 1st Cornets, 2 2d Cornets, 2 Trumpets, 4 Horns, 3 Tenor-Trombones, 1 Bass-Trombone, 2 Alto-Horns in B-flat, 1 Euphonium, 3 E-flat Basses, 1 BB-flat Bass, 4 Saxophones, 2 Flugelhorns, and drums.

Points (marking or scoring).—1st, Intonation; 2d, Full control of the dynamics; 3d and 4th, Unity in rubato and "technique;" 5th, Brilliancy; 6th, Power and volume.

Test Pieces.— Overture—"Fingal's Cave," *Mendelssohn*; English ed. Overture—"Tannhäuser," *Wagner*; Godfrey's arr. in MSS. Rhapsody No. 2, *Liszt*; Schmidt's arr. in MSS. Unfinished Symphony, *Schubert*; Warelli's arr. Overture—"Ruy Blas," *Mendelssohn*; English ed.

Second Class

Instrumentation (30).—6 B-flat Clarinets (3 1st, 2 2d, 1 3d), 1 E-flat Clarinet, 1 Piccolo, 1 Oboe, 2 Bassoons, 1 Alto-Clarinet, 2 1st Cornets, 1 2d Cornet, 1–2 Trumpets, 3 Horns, 3 Trombones, 1 Euphonium, 1 Alto-Horn in B-flat, 1 E-flat Bass, 1 BB-flat Bass, 1 Bass-Drum, 1 Small Drum, 1 Cymbals.

Points (marking or scoring).—1st, Intonation; 2d, Absence of "brassy quality of tone;" 3d and 4th, Brilliancy and power in execution; 5th, Observance of marks of expression.

Test Pieces.— Overture—"William Tell," *Rossini*; arr. by Reeves. "Mosaic," Overture *Riniere*; Eng. ed. "Kunstler Poppourri," *Kuhner*; Eng. ed. "Reminiscences of Meyerbeer," *Godfrey* or *Henicke*. Overture— "Domino Noir," *Auber*; French ed.

Third Class

Instrumentation (22).—3 B-flat Clarinets (2 1st, 1 2d), 1 Piccolo, 1 E-flat Clarinet, 1 E-flat Cornet, 2 1st B[-flat] Cornets, 1 2d Cornet, 2 Trumpets, 3 Horns, 2 Trombones, 1 Euphonium, 2 E-flat Basses, 1 Bass Drum, 1 Small Drum, 1 Cymbals.

POINTS (marking or scoring).—1st, Intonation; 2d, Sonorous quality of tone; 3d, Uniform observance of marks and expression; 4th, Brilliancy of execution; 5th, Power of tone.

TEST PIECES.— Selection—"Les Huguenots;" [*Meyerbeer*,] arr. by Henicke. "Ein Marcher," *Bach*. Selection— "Nabucco;" [*Verdi*,] arr. by Claus. Finale from Opera "Ariel;" arr. by Reeves.[7] Overture—"Militarie," *Puerner*.

Fourth Class
INSTRUMENTATION (18). 2 E-flat Cornets, 1 1st B-flat Cornet, 1 Flugelhorn, 1 2d B[-flat] Cornet, 2 Trumpets, 3 Altos, 2 Trombones, 1 Euphonium, 2 Basses, 1 Bass Drum, 1 Small Drum, 1 Cymbals.

POINTS (marking or scoring).—1st, Intonation; 2d, Unity in quality of tone; 3rd, Brilliancy in execution; 4th, Softness of tone; 5th, Power of tone.

TEST PIECES.— Am not familiar with purely brass-band music.

"Music for the People, as Interpreted by the Famous Leader of a Famous Band"

Source: unknown newspaper, signed "R.J.W.," September 5, 1890 (?), in *SPB* 89, 69.[8]

> *This lengthy interview provides insight into Sousa's approach to concert programming, repertoire, and rehearsal standards. A relatively early interview, he would maintain many of the opinions expressed here for the rest of his career. Sousa's reference to Michael Nolan's "Little Annie Rooney," the song which inspired the comic strip* Little Orphan Annie, *is striking in that he refers to it as an overplayed "wall flower" even though it was composed in 1889.*

---

7   Sousa may be referring to a section by that title within Jules Massenet's *Scènes dramatiques* (1874).
8   The exact year of publication is uncertain. This article seems to match the font and editorial style of another dated 1890 on the same page of the *SPB*, but these early press clippings are not as well documented or as chronologically organized as the later volumes. Clippings on the previous page date to 1889, but the reference to Michael Nolan's "Little Annie Rooney" (1889)—which had to be imported from England—makes 1889 less likely than 1890 as the publication date for this interview.

Washington, September 5.—(*Special.*)—

There are no military marches so popular in the United States to-day as those of John Philip Sousa, leader of the Marine Band. There is no band master whose concerts are better attended than those given under the leadership of this gentleman. He is a thoroughly educated musician, as his operatic writings show, being trained to the art from childhood with an experience embracing the entire range of all that is known on the subject. There could therefore be no better authority on what constitutes popular music than he. Mr. Sousa was at the Barracks today in fatigue uniform, directing a rehearsal of his famous organization. When he had finished his duties for the morning, Mr. Sousa was asked to give his views on "music for the people." He complied readily, and among many other interesting things said:

"My theory is that all professional people, actors, doctors, lawyers and newspaper men, as well as musicians, fear the criticism of their brother professionals more than they do that of the outside public. For that reason many of the conductors of bands make their programmes of music out of classical material. They feel that if they selected light matter their brother musicians would think their taste and education not above it. It is a sort of

Professional Cowardice,

and there are a very few men of eminence in the musical profession who have the courage to face this odd idea.

"This should not be," continued Mr. Sousa, "for with this fear in their hearts many very ordinary, but ambitious conductors attempt to perform music far beyond the abilities of themselves and the organizations they misdirect. I have seen a conductor wrestle with the intricacies of a symphony, leading his poor musicians into the wilderness of despair, whose knowledge was not sufficient to make an instrumentation of the much despised McGinty, but to play anything less than so-called classical music would be an acknowledgment of musical weakness, so he'll probably wrestle with Beethoven et al. until he mounts the golden stairs, and poor Beethoven and a long suffering public will have to stand it.[9]

9	The "much despised McGinty" seems to be a reference to a number of Irish folksongs (or quasi-folksongs) popular around the turn of the century that use "McGinty" as a stock character. Instances include "Down Went McGinty," "Up went McGinty," "McGinty's First Love," and "Paddy McGinty's Goat."

"As a general thing, the poorer a band is and the more incompetent its leader, the higher the class of music they attempt. It is not very long ago that the fourth-rate conductor of a fifth-rate band told me he played Tannhaeuser's Overture with twelve mouthpieces, but when I heard it, I thought it would have been better if that conductor had practiced a few scales with his twelve 'mouthpieces' for a decade or two before attempting any composition.

Popular Music Must be Well Presented

"In regard to the proficiency of a band, I hold that it is not so much the class of music it plays as it is the manner in which it presents a piece. Any one must admit that it is certainly more enjoyable to hear a comic opera, pot-pourri or melange of popular songs played with delicacy and brightness, than it is to hear classical music butchered. A great many eminent musicians at the head of bands or orchestras will take an immense amount of pains rehearsing a piece by a great composer, however simple it may be, while the so-called popular music is, as a general thing, thrown at the public without a bit of study. So that, where the higher class of music gets every advantage through laborious rehearsals, the lighter pieces, being regarded as beneath the notice of performers, are slighted. As an illustration of the point I am making, I once heard a crack organization play a piece by Mendelssohn in a magnificent manner to great applause. The applause was persistent enough to demand an encore, and for an encore the conductor played 'Good-bye, Sweetheart'—one of the so-called popular pieces.[10] The latter was roundly hissed, not because it was of a lower order than the composition which had been applauded, but because it was 'vamped.' The hissing was not at the piece, but at the manner of its rendering. Where one had been studied carefully the other was left to the chance of each man being familiar enough with the 'old-timer' to get through with it."

Mixed Programmes Necessary

"In making my programme," Mr. Sousa went on, "I try to cater to all tastes. Every one of my programmes will have one or two pieces of a high character, then three or four of a lighter character, and the rest is of the intensely

---

10   This appears to be a reference to John Liptrot Hatton's "Good-bye" (1863). On the dating of this
      song and its early publication history see Abel, *Confederate Songs*, 712.

popular order. The result, so far as I know, or have heard, is a success. I do not think that a programme of all popular music would do, any more than I believe that a programme [of] all classical [music] would be satisfactory for a public concert. My friend Gilmore, the famous bandmaster, holds this same view. When playing with the Strauss Orchestra here lately his band played the Tannhaeuser overture, and for an encore the 'Red, White and Blue.'[11] Both pieces were finely rendered and heartily applauded by the same audience, and Strauss' Orchestra giving but one class of music was rather obscured. At a recent concert of the Marine Band in Philadelphia I played to an audience that I could tell was well up in music of the highest class. My first piece was the 'Walkuere,' by Wagner. It was a tremendous success. 'Annie Rooney' at that time had not become a wall-flower, and I played it for an encore. It had been orchestrated with care, and the band had carefully rehearsed it. Never in my experience did I hear such applause as greeted the second piece. This shows that people who can appreciate Wagner will appreciate 'Annie Rooney,' provided both are well rendered. There is one thing to remember, however, in regard to popular music, and that is the fact that most band arrangements of popular melodies are very poor. This tends to drag them down. Instead of presenting 'Annie Rooney,' which we will use for an illustration, frowsy-headed and unadorned, she should be dressed up in pleasing style by proper orchestral arrangement, and her good points brought out."

The Classical Humbug

"There is a good deal of humbug about this classical music," continued the Professor. "With the majority it is a fad, pure and simple. People will turn up their noses at a piece with John Jones' name attached as a composer, who would appear to be filled with ecstatic rapture were the same piece labeled Beethoven.

"Some years ago I was invited to conduct an orchestra composed of semi-professionals and amateurs, who, like most of such people, prided themselves on the classical order of their programme. They met once a week. On this particular occasion they were to play a symphony by Beethoven and another by Schubert, a piano concerto by Beethoven, one [each] of Wagner's

---

11   Edward A. Berg composed the *Red, White and Blue March* in 1861.

and Gluck's productions, and David's 'Desert.'[12] This was supposed to be played offhand by the classical dilettanti, who worshiped that sort of thing. There were perhaps fifty of a select audience, and an orchestra of forty members. When I saw the programme I ventured mildly to suggest that there should be a waltz or something inserted to brighten the thing up, but the gentleman who had charge of the affair held his hands up in horror at the idea and informed me contemptuously that 'We never play waltzes.' Well, I thought I was hired to drill the orchestra, and although there was a small audience present, I did not know it was to be what I would call a performance. During the first piece, in the first twelve measures, I believe I stopped that orchestra fifty times to make it repeat, and I could not understand the apparent uneasiness, if not consternation, exhibited by the members of the orchestra and their friends, until I was informed by one of the gentlemen present that I was making a mistake; they did not want any criticism or rehearsal, they simply wanted me to conduct the performance. I put down my baton and fled.

"The selections that this so-called classical crowd had made to play offhand would have taken two months to drill any orchestra in.

The Public Need Educating
"I believe in educating the public in music," said Mr. Sousa, "but not by heroic methods. There is no doubt the standard of music among the masses has improved very much in late years, but to give them a surfeit of classical music will always be tiresome, and sometimes objectionable, to the average audience. All audiences are necessarily of mixed musical taste, and it is necessary to mix the programme. There is one thing that has always struck me in considering this subject," mused Mr. Sousa, "and that is that most people like comedy in music, as well as in literature, and all great writers have known this and catered to it. Shakespeare in his heaviest tragedies always introduces a thread of comedy. I therefore, can not understand why the great orchestra leaders can not put a little light matter into their programmes without feeling that they are degrading art. Where an orchestra is engaged to play before a promiscuous audience, it should always be remembered by the conductor that the majority of people care more for

---

12   Félicien David composed *Le desert* in 1844.

comedy than for tragedy, more for humor than for sermons, and a musical director should have a goodly part of his music [be] of a light character. There are ten comedy companies to one of tragedy, on the stage to-day, and this bears out my idea. There is no class of people so quick to understand the wants of the public as the theatrical managers, and if tragedies were demanded there would be ten tragedy companies to one of comedy. The people who know the Marine Band, and know its repertoire, know it plays as high a class of compositions as is played by any organization in the world. But at the same time it would never think of slighting or ignoring light pieces because the band is drilled on heavy work.

"Without setting myself up as an authority," said Mr. Sousa in conclusion, "I think that if most conductors had the courage of their convictions they would act up to them, instead of tearing [down] the opinion of their brother professionals. If they did I am sure they would get along better with the public. These views of mine you will remember, and be careful to state, are applicable solely to organizations playing for the people and not for a select class. If an organization travels on its own pecuniary responsibility, and gives four symphonies at each concert, that is a matter that concerns its management and the people who want to hear that kind of music." R. J. W.

"Music We Must Have"

Source: *Chicago Tribune*, November 23, 1890, 26.

> *The World's Columbian Exposition (also known as the Chicago World's Fair) of 1893 was a seminal event both for the city and the nation at the close of the century. Total attendance was over 26 million, including some 750,000 fairgoers on "Chicago Day" alone. Structures built for the so-called White City remain in active use to this day as museums.*
>
> *Music played no small role in the festivities, especially as national pavilions featured exhibits and performers from around the world. Much thought went into the planning of music, as Chicagoans took an active interest in all of the ways in which their city and nation would be represented. The title is not Sousa's; instead the Tribune editor collected the opinions of a number of prominent musical figures about planning the music to be played with just over two years left before the doors opened.*

Sousa's views were quite different from those of more classically oriented writers, but in the end the Exposition followed Sousa's suggestions to a larger extent than those of Damrosch or Thomas. Dvořák conducted his Eighth Symphony, Scott Joplin introduced the world to ragtime, and the Mormon Tabernacle Choir performed as part of its first national tour. Freshly separated from the Marine Band, Sousa brought his newly formed private band (temporarily dubbed the "World's Fair Band") for two weeks of concerts, including a joint performance with Theodore Thomas and his orchestra.[13]

Music We Must Have.

Without It All Agree the Fair Will be Sadly Marred.

But the Questions Are: How Much Shall We Pay for It? What Kind of Music Shall It Be? and, Shall American[s] or Foreigners Write It?—Letters from Theodore Thomas, Walter Damrosch, and Others on the Subject.

> [...] Some time ago *The Tribune* touched on the subject lightly. Since then a few of the prominent musicians of Chicago and elsewhere have given their opinions in reply to the letters from this office and have answered part of the questions. Theodore Thomas writes:

In reply to your questions regarding American composers and the production of their works at the coming World's Fair in Chicago I would say:

1. The best way to bring forward American compositions is to commission some of the composers born in America who are known and acknowledged to have the ability and the scholarship necessary for such an undertaking to compose suitable orchestra and choral works for the occasion and give them a reasonable pecuniary remuneration over and above the expenses of preparing the works for performance. In the case of vocal works texts written for the occasion might be submitted to the composers or the composers should submit the texts they preferred, before writing the music, to a committee appointed for the purpose.

---

13   Further see Bierley, *American Phenomenon*, 58–60, which includes a picture of the band from St. Louis just after their time at the Exposition. On the formation of Sousa's Band see Warfield, "Making the Band," 30–66.

2. It would not be advisable to give a similar commission to the foreign composers of the present day. In 1876, Richard Wagner was commissioned to write a composition for the Centennial at Philadelphia, and the result was not satisfactory, although in my opinion the march he wrote for that occasion has been underrated.[14] At present there are no composers in Europe who would be likely to send even as good a work for such an occasion as the one obtained from him then. The American composers have progressed so much since that time that an attractive program might be arranged from their compositions. As a popular demonstration the celebration might close with a performance of national airs by a combination of military bands.[15]

Mr. Walter Damrosch departs somewhat from Mr. Thomas' stand. He says:

The theme you suggest in your favor of Nov. 8 is so great and the subject of such importance that a more careful consideration of it seems to me to be necessary than my time will at present permit. But in brief outline my idea is as follows:

An invitation should be sent to all composers living in America to compete for a prize composition. Capable judges should be appointed, and the composition which, in their opinion is considered the best, should be performed in a fitting manner some time during the Exposition, and at the expense of the Exposition. It might be found practical to offer prizes for a variety of compositions, orchestral, choral, or a combination of both. The prize to be awarded may consist of anything from a wreath to an embellished silver cup, but in my opinion it need not consist of money. I do not think that there is a single composer of serious aims and ambitions who would be tempted to compete because of a possible pecuniary gain. The occasion is so important, the honor conferred so great, that these should be incentive enough, and it certainly seems to me that the absence of the commercial

---

14 Thomas was one of the most prominent musicians involved in the Philadelphia festival, and so his views on Wagner's composition could be perceived as biased. Further on that event see the above source on Benjamin Harrison's Inaugural Ball.

15 This could be an oblique reference to Sousa's *National, Patriotic, and Typical Airs of All Lands*, which had just been published.

element from this[,] the artistic side of the Exposition[,] can only add to its dignity and importance. As few restrictions as possible should be placed upon the competitors in regard to the choice of subject for the choral compositions, and its poetic treatment. It might be sufficient to announce that the words must be on some theme which shall have a poetic connection with the discovery of America and its subsequent development, but giving the composer full scope in his choice of subject within the restrictions mentioned above.[16] Composers do not like to have the inspiration from within too much fettered by restrictions from without, and it is as well to give them the opportunity to try their strength in the direction for which they have the greatest inclination.

Your question as to "whether we should allow foreigners to compete on this occasion" I am not prepared to answer. It depends a good deal on what we desire. If the idea is to foster and encourage American composers I should say no, as I am afraid that an American composer would stand but a poor chance of winning the prize if brought into competition with such men as Brahms, Tschaikowsky, Saint-Saens, and other great composers now living in Europe. The old countries have the advantage of us in their centuries of musical development, and it is in no way befitting the courageous efforts of our young composers if we admit the superiority of the Old World over the New in this respect. In regard to the place for the performance of the prize compositions I could not suggest a better [one] than the Auditorium, a hall of magnificent proportions and ideal acoustics. During my professional visits to Chicago I have had every opportunity of observing the restless, untiring energy of its citizens in art and education as well as in business, and I am convinced that the gentlemen in charge of the Exposition will succeed in making its artistic side a worthy illustration of the great progress which music has been making in this country. Examples should be given of every department of music, and the great lesson thereby taught to our own people of the necessity of art in our lives.

John Philip Sousa, the leader of the famous Marine Band, has perhaps another view-point on music than that of Mr. Thomas and

---

16   The Exposition was initially scheduled for 1892 to coincide with the 400th anniversary of Columbus's discovery of America. In the end the schedule fell behind to where it did not open until 1893.

Mr. Damrosch, but as a Government official and the director of the most noted military band in America his opinion carries great weight. Mr. Sousa contributes an interesting statement of what he thinks should be done. He says:

The subject of music at the World's Columbian Fair is one of more than ordinary importance, and should command every possible attention. For some reason both instrumental and vocal music in its instructive sphere received very little recognition at the [1876 Philadelphia] Centennial Exposition, but as the art has made such wonderful progress in our land during the last decade, and is now firmly established in the affections of the people, any attempts to entail [sic] its possibilities or limit its resources at the coming Fair will call down the condemnation of the whole country. The educational as well as the entertaining side of the subject should be thoroughly considered.

The tastes of three classes must be consulted: The music student, the music lover, and the common auditor. The first should be furnished with food for reflection[17] and material for enlightenment; for the second the program should embrace every variety of pure musical literature, while the third should be served with dainty bits of sentiment and brightness. Among the latter class will be many who have not risen above the smock-frock days of the country brass band or the nurse-bottle epoch of the cotillon orchestra. They should be amused—educated if possible—but amused by all means. How can this be done? By organizing three distinct musical bodies. An orchestra, a chorus, and a military band, each full and complete in every detail. These bodies should give daily concerts and on certain occasions be massed for the performance of special works. In addition to these permanent bodies[,] famous organizations should be engaged from time to time to add to the musical luster of the Fair, as well as to awaken sectional interest.

American compositions, everything else being equal, should be given the preference on all official days, but no composition should be performed simply because it is American.

If compositions are to be entered for competition the judges should be selected from five musical nations, the one from America being a native-

---

17   The word "reflection" as printed here is not clearly legible and has been inferred.

born and not a naturalized citizen. A naturalized citizen might unwittingly favor a composition embracing the characteristics of the music of his fatherland without considering the intrinsic value of the work, and thereby creating a balance of power and a biased judgment. The acceptance of the work, together with the cost of publication and the control of the copyright, is sufficient reward to bestow upon the successful competitors. All works meeting the approbation of the judges, besides the successful compositions, should be placed in the library of the Fair and performed at suitable times.

Much has been said about excluding foreign compositions. I contend that if we are to admit foreign machinery, why not foreign music? German sausages are welcomed[,] why not German symphonies? If French fashions, why not French fantasies? If Italian oils, why not Italian odes? If British merchandise, why not British madrigals? No, Mr. Editor, we cannot conscientiously extend an invitation to our friends across the way to visit us and then restrict them to the hog pen and the kitchen. We are too proud to say we can surpass your hardware, but not your harmony; your cutlery, but not your counterpoint; your mutton, but not your melody. No doubt an ode will be written for the opening of the Fair. Let the competition be open to the world, and let the laurel-wreath bedeck the brow of him who rises to the sublimity of the occasion, whether he calls his home Senegambia or Sioux City, Pumpkintown or Patagonia.

> Other prominent musicians add other suggestions which may be of value to the men who will have to do with the Fair's music. [Opinions shorter in length by George E. Whiting, John James Hattstaedt, and Adam Golbel follow.]

"Mr. Sousa and His Band" by P. S. Gilmore

Source: unknown newspaper, early March 1892, in *SPB 89*, 64.

> *Earmarked as Gilmore's heir apparent in the realm of "military music" from virtually the outset of his appointment as the conductor of the Marine Band, Sousa consistently cited Gilmore as a strong influence on the development of band music broadly and on his own practices specifically. Here Gilmore publicly crowns Sousa as his successor, even if he attributes some of that success to the*

perks of steady government funding. Gilmore had only some six months left to live: he died in St. Louis, the same city to which he addressed this letter, on September 24.

The following letter from Mr. P. S. Gilmore is in reply to one received from the chairman of a committee of prominent business men of St. Louis interested in the concerts soon to be given in that city by the United States Marine Band:

New York, March 1, 1892

My Dear Sir:

I am frequently asked, as you now ask, my opinion of the Marine Band of Washington. Well, the band cannot help being a splendid band, for three reasons. First, its permanent location in Washington is a great inducement for first-class musicians to join the band, musicians who could not be induced to join the regular army, fearing that frontier life might be their fate. Second, the members of the Marine Band are obliged to attend a long rehearsal almost every day in the year, which alone is sufficient to make them play splendidly together. Third, they are under a director, Mr. John Philip Sousa, who is a most accomplished musician, whose own compositions, as also his admirable arrangements of other composers' works, give abundant evidence of his genius, originality, and artistic ability.

With such a leader, whose aim is perfection, and with the beauty, the culture, and the brain of the nation at the Capitol for his audiences—enough to inspire both him and his men to bring forth the most charming effects of which the divine art of music is capable—is it not to be expected that the Marine Band of Washington should stand peerless and unrivaled on the American continent? Go, then, and hear them play when you have an opportunity, and you will doubtlessly be convinced that Uncle Sam has a band of which the Government and the people ought to feel, and do feel, justly proud.

Very sincerely yours,
P. S. Gilmore

1894-1905

The Bandmaster and the New Century

On the Use of Subdominant Trio Sections in Marches

Source: *The Etude* 16, August 1898, 231.

> *Ending a work off-tonic is striking in classical music but taken for granted in marches. Today bandsmen of every age know to "add a flat" for the trio section. Sousa here explains the genesis of this convention based on his personal experiences.*

Some months ago *The Etude* received a letter from a subscriber making inquiry as to the propriety of closing a march with the trio, instead of repeating the first movement [strain] before closing. The letter was forwarded to Mr. Sousa, who was the author of the innovation. His reply follows:

"Your letter of February 9th last became mislaid in the hurry and bustle of the travel attendant upon our prolonged concert tours, and for that reason has remained unanswered until now. In reply to your question, 'Is it proper that a two-step ending in a trio should end in a key foreign to the one it begins in,' permit me to say this:

"In the accepted form of compositions of march order it was always customary to make the third part go to the subdominant, the most usual, and the dominant, the most unusual form. In my childhood in Washington I noticed that the bands parading with the regiments in nearly every instance, although the composition called for da capo, would finish playing on the last strain of the march; therefore, if it was done practically in the use of the march I could not understand why it should not be done theoretically in the writing of the march. Accordingly, in composing my marches I ignored the old established rule and wrote with the idea of making the last strain of the march the musical climax, regardless of the tonality.

Yours truly,
John Philip Sousa

"A Century of Music"

Source: *New York World*, December 31, 1899, in *SPB* 9:2, 34.[18]

> *This short essay appeared within a special supplement to the* New York World *entitled the* End of the Century Book *with the subtitle "A Record and Review of Human Endeavor and Achievement in the Most Wonderful Century Earth Has Known." Contributions to the special section included views on theology, manufacturing, criminology, and even "sanitary science." Sousa wrote on music; other notables included Susan B. Anthony and poet Julia Ward Howe on "Woman," Daniel Frohman on theatre and New York University chancellor Henry MacCracken on education. Sousa's list of composers shows a marked bias towards popular figures and operatic composers, an indication of his self-image within the larger history of music.*

To one standing on the threshold of the century now drawing to a close a cursory glance over the political field of the world must have clearly shown that old ideas and institutions were being swept away and the world was starting in with a grand sweep for newer and better conditions. As music is the most potent of all the arts to move and excite the emotions, it was natural that the revolution in the body politic should have been accentuated in the sphere or musical art. Nations just emerging from revolution, from tyranny, from oppression and national degradation, looking into the sunlight of liberty and freedom, could find no better means of expressing their thoughts than in heroic measures and loud acclaim of musical sounds.

Perhaps the first of the writers of this century to impress his genius and to leave the imprint of his talent in the world of popular music was Rossini. When it is realized that he was born in 1792 and that one of the most

---

18   This essay was published in two forms, the one reproduced here and another slightly abridged in an unknown newspaper in *SPB* 9:2, 39.

popular[,] if not the most popular pieces of music in the world to-day[,] is his "William Tell" overture, it speaks volumes for the brilliant opening of this century.

To-day the master minds of music have their own types; express their feelings both as nationalists and as individuals, and impart to their compositions the typical characteristics of their nations, whereas before this century even men as great as Handel, Gluck and Mozart wrote in the style belonging to a nation the antipodes of their own. While all these masters, and especially Mozart, made reforms or changes in operatic treatment, either the musical tyranny of the people would not permit them to depart so radically from the fashionable forms of their art as did their great successors, Weber and Wagner, or else they were unable to gain such a clear insight into the possibilities of the lyric drama as those later masters of the art. The great achievements of Beethoven's life, who was born in 1770, were made during the present century.

Of the great figures of the century in opera I should name Wagner first, Verdi second, Meyerbeer third, Weber fourth, Rossini fifth, and then in places of honor among composers Auber, Donizetti, Bellini, Herold, and Flotow. The latter, while charged with being an imitator of other national schools, has written two works that still hold the stage of the world—"Martha" and "Stradella." The century has developed a Schubert, a Schumann, a Mendelssohn, a Wagner, a Verdi, a Liszt, a Tschaikowsky, a Rubinstein, a Berlioz, a Chopin, a Brahms, a Gounod, a Massenet, a Saint-Saens, and a countless array of wonderful instrumental performers.

"The Ideal Band"

Source: *The Independent* (New York City), January 25, 1900, in *SPB* 9:2, 54.

Sousa's Band made three European tours between 1900 and 1905 and undertook a world tour in 1910–11. A wide-ranging essay, "The Ideal Band" was published prior to the 1900 tour and shows Sousa preparing for direct comparison to European bands for the first time in his career. Notice how he calls the Garde Républicaine the best band in Europe, not the best in the world! The paragraph on "normal pitch" refers to problems encountered in Britain as "low pitch" (A=439 Hz.) and "high pitch" (A=452 Hz.) vied for dominance. British bands would finally adopt "low pitch" in the 1960s.

The ideal band does not exist, never has existed and most likely never will exist, because all things human are imperfect. But if we could conceive it as a reality we would be more justified in looking for it in this country than in any other, since here music is most cosmopolitan and most progressive. Musicians from all over the world come to us, not merely to visit, but to settle down and add what they can to our artistic life. They bring with them the musical traditions, the skill and the instruments of their countries. Contact with representatives of other schools of musical thought and culture broadens them and brings out their best qualities and in the swirl of competition here the best of art forms, methods and men are apt to survive.

America has not, as yet, a great native musical literature, but that will come in time if the progress of the past twenty years may be taken as a fair indication of what the future will bring forth. We are certainly developing a great number of fine native musicians. I doubt if there can be found in all the world men better versed in harmony and structure than McDowell, Paine, Dudley Buck, Geo. Chadwick and other Americans, and it is certain that the great spread of musical culture now going on in our land will result in giving the world a new race of composers who, starting with the initial advantage of cosmopolitanism and being at the same time more free from traditional trammels than others, should produce work that is aspiring, broad, fresh and worthy. To attain the ideal in the band and orchestra we must have perfection of leadership, perfection of players and perfection of instruments.

The possibilities of the instruments are being increased by better construction and new mechanical devices, great players of wind instruments are multiplying, and their skill enables them to cover up imperfections that were formerly apparent, so that now the outlook is very hopeful. If a wind instrument could be invented that combined the sustained and sympathetic qualities of the violin with the brilliancy of the flute we might consider that the possibility of attaining the ideal standard for a band would be nearer than now were the clarinet family to occupy the leading position.

The nearest we come to the ideal now is with a band that has more than the orchestral proportion of flutes, hautboys, clarinets, bassoons, trumpets, horns and trombones, and the usual orchestral battery added to instruments that belong more to the wind band family, such as cornets, euphoniums, fluegelhorns, saxophones and bass-tubas.

Having assembled the best possible instruments and players in this attempt to approach the ideal, the next step is to secure unanimity—which comprehends tonal and phrasing relationship. When that has been secured there is the dynamic quality to develop, which may be compared to the oratorical quality, and after that has been brought to its highest point there must be developed the ability of the mass of instruments to interpret the music from the standpoint of the leading spirit—who should be the conductor. Thus the power is gained to be by turns gay, sad, strong, boisterous; one moment indulging in all the wild abandonment of the Bacchante, and the next revealing the calm purity of the lullaby.

The ideal leader's dominance must be complete. He must have no doubts that can communicate themselves to those over whom he sways the baton. Each artist has his own conception of the score committed to his care, and it is a psychological impossibility for him to forsake these unless the leader can inspire absolute confidence in his own portrayal, which may, to the artist's mind, be absolutely a new revelation. The leader, therefore, must combine great technical knowledge with convincing power. He must be instant, he must be absolute. He must know the capability of every man and instrument before him and must be able to evoke sympathetic response that is immediate and unanimous. Such qualities are rare, and, therefore, in looking over musical history we find that we can count the really great leaders on our fingers.

I do not believe that Congress can do anything to aid in the development of the ideal band. I am absolutely opposed to the idea of Government subsidy for art in any of its forms. Art, when under Government control, is apt to be conservative, and tho[ugh] conservatism may be a very good thing for the office holders and salary drawers, it is likely to be a bad thing for progress and originality. As an instance of this tendency of the subsidized organizations to stand still may be noted the fact that when the best bands and orchestral leaders throughout the civilized world adopted the Normal Pitch, the English Government bands refused to move forward with the others on the ground that conforming would necessitate the purchase of new instruments. Thus we now have the spectacle, in England, of the grand opera and orchestras like that at Covent Garden using the Normal Pitch, while the Government bands continue the High Pitch.

Competition is healthy, and the fact that our bands and orchestras depend on the public at large for their very existence makes them alert and anxious to improve. The struggle for the elusive dollar that is going on here will produce more substantial musical returns in the future than will be contributed by the subsidized bands of Europe, among which the "has been" is good enough for the present.

Even under the best of circumstances there are difficulties in the way of instrumental progress. Although the saxophone was invented in 1846 many governmental bands throughout the world still do without it. New instruments are only mastered by means of careful study and much patient practice; it is very important that they should be introduced because some of them, combining the qualities of wood and brass, give tone improvement and make easily possible a register which was before extremely difficult. Therefore, it is not good for art that the artists should be so comfortable and safe that they do not need to struggle and use every means for improvement.

The band that I will take with me to Paris this year at the invitation of Commissioner General Peck, of the United States Commission to the Paris Exposition, will be representative of this country. The band contains many men born here, owing all they have of education and training to this country. Our programs will probably be found broader in scope than those of the other bands, as the French are apt to play French music only, the Germans German music only and so forth. Our uniform will be of dark blue, richly braided, turned up at the cuffs with velvet and having the American shield at the collar. This shield and the gold cord on the cap are the only touches of bright color. It is quietly elegant, and will form quite a contrast to the gorgeous uniforms of the other bands that will take part with us in the *fêtes*.

During the time that we are over there we will tour all Europe and go to England, if the Transvaal War is ended before we return home.[19]

---

19   In an editor's error, a period precedes "if" (which is not capitalized). The Second Boer War (the Transvaal War) was only three months old at the time of publication, but would continue until 1902. Sousa's band did not travel to England in 1900.

Sousa's Band in Mitchell, South Dakota, during the 1907 tour, wearing the "quietly elegant" uniforms referred to in 1900.

The last great international band competition took place in Paris in the year 1867. All the countries of Europe were invited to compete and all took part with the exception of England. The jury consisted of Ambroise Thomas, Hans Von Bulow, Felician David, Leo Delibes, [Albert] Grisar and [Eduard] Hanslick.

Three first prizes were awarded, as follows: Band of the Garde du Corps (German), [class] A, Band of the Garde Republicaine (French), [class] B, and 73d Regiment Band of Austria, [class] C. These led the crack bands of Holland, Russia, Spain, Baden, Bavaria, etc. I believe that at the present time the Band of the Garde Republicaine is considered the best in Europe.

As we shall play every day at the fair, and as we shall take a very prominent part in the *fêtes*, such as the unveiling of the Lafayette Statue on July 4th, and the French national *fête* on July 14th, we are going to a place and an occasion that will subject our American artists, instruments, music and methods to a rigid, but I trust fair, criticism.

New York City

"American Music in Paris: John Philip Sousa Says That It Is Well Received"

Source: *St. Louis Republic*, May 13, 1900, part 2, pg. 1.

> *The Sousa Band's 1900 European tour revolved around the Exposition Universelle in Paris. Similar in scope to the 1893 World's Columbian Exposition in Chicago and a successor to the famous 1889 Exposition Universelle, the 1900 fair featured musical performances from around the world. In this widely printed W. R. Hearst wire-service article Sousa describes his experiences first-hand. The Salle des Fêtes mentioned by Sousa was a massive hall constructed for the 1889 exhibition that could seat over 15,000 fairgoers.*

The Salle des Fêtes, one of the Sousa Band's venues at the Exposition Universelle in 1900. The band also performed a number of open-air concerts in a bandstand on the Esplanade des Invalides.

Special by Cable

Paris, May 12

The condition of music at the exhibition brings to my mind very vividly the music of the Columbian Exposition. At Chicago[,] Thomas's Orchestra was in evidence; at Paris it is a Cologne [Colonne] orchestra which discourses sweet music.

Numerous national villages at the Columbian exhibition had their orchestras or bands of more or less importance. These represented their respective countries. Here, too, different nations have their bands, ours [i.e., the Sousa Band] being the official band of the United States Committee. We are here to expound military music as we understand it in America. I am glad to say that our interpretation of American military music made such a strong impression that the French Government put at our disposal the Salle des Fêtes, where we will give concerts under the patronage of the French and American commissions.

When we give Massenet's music, naturally it is well received. I am glad also to say that our own music is as well received here as in the United States.

An exhibition such as this is musically valuable, as it leads away from conservativism, and individual genius has an opportunity of exploiting itself for the benefit of art. I have no doubt that the musical pabulum furnished during the exhibition will be of great value to the world. All of us who are here working in the musical vineyard will profit by the association.

"No State Aid for Art, Says Mr. John Philip Sousa"

Source: *New York Herald* (Paris edition), early July 1900, in *SPB* 87, 9.[20]

The above items demonstrate that state-sponsored musical ensembles were on his mind while in Paris, but the following interview, in particular, caused a controversy. It is apparent from the opening sentences that the unnamed interviewer likely did his best to frame Sousa's words in a more inflammatory

---

20 Although this newspaper report includes a concert program at the end and a location, the exact date of publication is not certain. Sousa's Band played at the Esplanade des Invalides almost daily from July 3–19, 1900. When combined with the July 15 date for the reader's response letter and the quickness of Sousa's response to that letter, one of those concerts early in the month as documented by Bierley (*Incredible Band*, 158) seems most likely. The band played at the same venue in May, so that month is also possible. The band spent June touring Germany.

way than Sousa likely intended, but he nevertheless caught the bandmaster in a particularly irascible mood! Perhaps the interviewer dealt with Sousa in a more direct (and literal) way than Sousa was likely used to in the United States, where he was already a celebrity. This is one of the few instances in which Sousa was recorded using a foul word before publishing Marching Along *in 1928.*

In the wake of this interview, an incensed reader wrote such a strongly worded letter to the editor of the newspaper that Sousa felt compelled to defend his points in a remarkably inflammatory follow-up letter of his own. Although the reader's letter and Sousa's response are faithfully transcribed in Marching Along *(and therefore not included in this volume), the initial spark for the controversy as seen below only appears in abridged form in the autobiography.[21]*

Opposed to the Idea of National Theatres, National Bands and Similar Subsidized Organizations. Discourages Original Work. Impressions of Military Bands in France and Germany Through American Spectacles. Play Few Foreign Works. Does Not Approve of the Use of Stringed Instruments in a Military Band.

"Although at a certain period of my life I rather favored the idea of 'National' theatres, 'National' orchestras, 'National' bands, and 'National' conservatories, I have been converted completely by a comparison of the superior results produced by individual effort over those due to a governmentally- subsidized art."

Down with State aid for art!

Such a motto will probably be found engraved on Sousa's heart one day—may it be far off—much as "Calais" was popularly supposed to be written on Queen Mary's.

Time after time yesterday his conversation returned to the kindly unkindness of keeping music in swaddling clothes by means of governmental subsidies.

For instance:—

"I think French military bands are wonderfully good—considering the care the State devotes to them.

---

21   For the responses see Sousa, *Marching Along*, 200–205.

"An artistic organization that is fostered by State aid is like a hardy plant brought up in a hot house. It may keep on living, and that's all you can say about it, for it will always be sickly.

"The reputation of a band that is not based exclusively on public favor resembles the reputation for military genius earned by some generals in time of peace, and that melt like snow in July in the first weeks of actual warfare.

"If a musician, a writer, or a painter has anything in him, he will dig it out of himself if the State will only let him starve long enough.

"When a bandmaster has nothing to pay his bandsmen with save what the public thinks he deserves, he must do good work or go to the wall. But if he has the Government behind him it is merely in human nature that he will quote the famous saying: 'The public be d——d!'"

"Any emphasis lacking in these and many similar phrases that starred Sousa's long talk with me upon French and German military bands was supplied by an ironical glimmer that stole into his dark eyes every time he referred to governmental help in any form, a twinkle that bore most eloquent testimony to the small space occupied in his organism by reverence for the services rendered to art by the powers that be.

An engaging personality is this swarthy American musician, whose fame has swept the whole length and breadth of the United States, down into Mexico, and whose concerts in Paris have become one of the most popular features of the Exhibition.

Always Crowded Near the Band

No matter how deserted other points may be, you are certain to find a dense crowd gathered round the bandstand in the Esplanade des Invalides every afternoon between the hours of half-past three and five o'clock. During that space of time you will be lucky if you can find an unoccupied seat. You will see people standing in a truly infernal blaze of sunshine, fanning themselves, mopping their faces, and cooling themselves by frantically applauding some particularly popular number, some well-executed solo by such favorites as Pryor, the trombone Paganini; Hell, a flugel-hornist, with a tone such as a contralto might envy; or Clarke and Rogers, cornettists "di primo cartello."

The enthusiasm displayed by the audiences at these open-air concerts is one of their most striking features to Parisians, accustomed to the discreet applause that will follow an appreciated number played by such a popular organization as, say, the Garde Républicaine. A musician who attended one of the concerts with me was astounded to note the effect produced by a Wagner excerpt upon people who had just been frantically greeting one of Sousa's stirring marches, which he alone seems to hold the secret of composing.

"It's odd," said my friend, "that such widely different compositions should be equally well appreciated for, after all, you need to know Wagner to enjoy him."

"That's just it. You see Wagner is not a new-comer in America as he is, comparatively speaking, here. And Sousa has done a great deal to make him known there."

Sousa, in discussing the same point, referred with a shade of disapproval to the conservative tendency evidenced by French bandmasters, as demonstrated in the programmes which he had heard.

"It is an old saying," he remarked, "that love and art have no frontiers. There seems, however, to be a predilection for French music in French bandmasters. Other things being equal, they appear to prefer music by a native composer to music by a foreigner. I could understand this were they arranging programmes to be played outside their own country, when a desire to show the wealth of their nation from a musical point of view might justifiably warrant them in giving the preference to works written by their fellow-countrymen. But, it seems to me a wider range of selection might easily be permitted for concerts in Paris, where Saint-Saëns, Massenet, Gillet, [and] Ganne are likely to run no danger of being eclipsed in popular affection were Wagner, Goldmark, Puccini, or other foreign composers drawn upon a little more generously.

Band Programmes in Paris
"I have the programmes of military-band concerts given in the Luxembourg, the Palais-Royal and other places. At the Luxembourg, Massenet contributes two numbers out of five, Delahaye one, Saintis one, and Weber is represented by a selection from his 'Freischutz.' At the Palais-Royal there is not a foreign work on the programme. Yet there must be some number in international musical literature that might have been dropped into the concert, if only to flavor it with the spice of exoticism, as it were.

"This, again, I attribute to the evil influence of Governmental support, which always creates a tendency to work in a groove, to stop in a rut. As it does not matter financially whether the public is pleased or indifferent, why should the bandmaster waste the gray matter of his brain in building programmes that will arouse interest, why should he grow old in going through veritable public libraries of musical works in the hope—alas! too seldom rewarded—of finding some new or unknown gem with which to feed the insatiable repertory that a concert organization such as my own is compelled to possess?

"I am convinced that military bands in France could be made something really marvelous. The evident artistic taste of the nation is displayed in the high average standard of excellence attained by executants who are not professional musicians, and who are in the military bands merely because they are doing their military service. The precision of their playing is soldier-like, if not particularly telling, for elasticity of 'tempo' is the life of a musical composition.

"It must also be admitted that military bands, both in Germany and France, are not perfectly adapted to the purposes for which they are used. In Germany their instrumental composition is admirable for military work, that is, for parades, marches and other purely professional duties of a regimental band. They are, thus, badly equipped for concert playing, as the nice shades of tone-color are absolutely beyond their capabilities.

"In France, on the other hand, greater care is devoted to the composition of military bands for concert use, which naturally destroys to a certain extent their effectiveness for military work, owing to their delicate instrumentation. In addition, the French bands are not shown at their best, even when heard in concert, as they so frequently play in the open air without a sounding-board to reinforce and concentrate the sound, and thus many of the nuances that would be wonderfully effective under proper acoustic conditions are lost.

An Artistic Atmosphere

"I have been impressed by the artistic atmosphere of France and Germany. Not only are the musicians brilliantly gifted, but the audiences are also very critical, discriminating, and intelligent. At the same time Governmental aid is a drawback rather than an assistance, as, although it may facilitate in the routine of artistic production, it is an impediment to the development of true artistic genius. If you look over the field of musicians, conductors and composers, you cannot fail to be struck with the fact that those who are most famous, most popular with the people, and whose reputation has passed the frontiers of their respective countries[,] are precisely those who have been left untrammeled by Governmental or official bonds, and who have been compelled to put forward the best that was in them by the beneficent law of the survival of the fittest, which has forced them to be ever upon the alert to conquer competition.

"I am convinced that many of the occupants of official positions in France and Germany would discover original genius of a high order in themselves were they to be left entirely to their own resources, while some who are first in the race might be limping in the rear. For the Juggernaut of public opinion and support soon crushes out the life of him who has nothing but Governmental influence to justify his occupancy of a given position in the artistic world.

"I have heard during my visit here several of the military bands. As I said before, I have been impressed by the excellent artistic results obtained as a general rule, a detail that proves the genuine musical nature of the people. The Garde Républicaine band, for instance, is admirable, and others would be better under more favorable conditions.

"As far as specific criticism is concerned, I do not care for the use of a string contra-bass in a military band. If a string-bass, why not a 'cello? And once granted the 'cello, why not the viola and divided violins? In fact, why not become a symphony orchestra at once? There is no room in a military band for stringed instruments. The bass tuba does all and more than a contra-bass can do, is richer, gives fuller and sounder harmonic basis for the volume of tone, and can be played on the march—which a contra-bass cannot!

Might be Improved

"I think, too, that French military bands would be improved if the alto-horn and valve-trombone were abandoned. They are only concessions to the laziness of instrumentalists, and are a poor substitute for the warm, effective and beautiful tone of the French horn and trombone.

"Another thing; I fancy musicians still entertain a vague idea that a military band is inferior to the symphony orchestra. Inferior it is not; it is simply different. There is no hierarchy in art. The artistic effect produced is the sole criterion of value. A simple folk-song may be a greater living musical truth than a symphony that calls for the united resources of all the musical instruments to perform. The melody that touches the heart of both the trained musician and the uneducated public is a musical thought that has been lying dormant in the hearts and minds of the people, and to which the composer has given expression at last. The form in which that thought is presented is of no importance. Yet composers will write for the symphony orchestra willingly, and for the military band with a certain sense of doing a humbler work.

"This feeling is absurd, and is rather a proof of ignorance, or indolence, upon the part of the writers than anything else, for it shows either that they have not realized all the resources of the wood and brass wind, or that they do not care to take the immense trouble necessitated in trying to reproduce the musical effect of some well-known orchestral work with the military band.

"It is curious that this prejudice does not exist with regard to the orchestra. I attended one of Colonne's concerts today, and the second number on the programme was a transcription of Chopin's 'Funeral March,' an orchestration of a piano composition. I may add that it was well played and admirably conducted. The wood and brass wind are irreproachable, and the strings have an excellent quality of tone. In fact, I enjoyed the concert immensely. But if an orchestra may play transcriptions of piano works, why should not a military band play transcriptions of works for orchestra?

"It may be this feeling that causes French bandmasters to limit themselves to overtures and operatic selections with little 'genre' pieces instead of roaming over the entire world of music.

"And, I repeat, they probably would if the State left them entirely to their own resources. There is nothing that develops individual initiative so much as the necessity of scoring a success. Literature in France has been left without [a] 'prix de Rome,' yet it is flourishing, and will do so until it is given an annuity, when, like music and painting, it will become very conservative and tradition loving. For there is nothing that encourages conservatism more than a position under the Government. . . . ."

Sousa's Programme To-day

The following is the programme of the concert which will be given by Sousa's band on the Esplanade des Invalides, at 3:30 p.m. to-day:—

Overture, "Festival" [op. 42] . . . . Leutner

Symphonic poem, "Columbus" . . . . Leavitt

Gems from "The Belle of New York" . . . . Kerker

Bugle solo, "Werner's Farewell" . . . . .Nessler
    (By Mr. Frank Hell)

Patriotic Hymn, "Unto Thee, O the God of our Fathers" . . . . .Forsythe

Valse, "El Capitan" . . . . .Sousa

Euphonium solo, "Garden of Flowers" . . . . Gatti
    (By Mr. Simone Mantia)

Song, "All Souls' Day". . . . . Lassen

March, "Hail to the Spirit of Liberty" (new). . . . . .Sousa

Selection "Orphée aux Enfers". . . . . Offenbach

"What I Think of England"

Source: *London Daily Mail*, December 10, 1901, in *SPB* 87, 31.

> *In addition to his musical activities Sousa wrote works of fiction, including the novelette* The Fifth String *(1902) and the partly autobiographical* Pipetown Sandy *(1905).*[22] *His celebrity seems to have been the primary driving factor behind good sales numbers for these: critics generally attacked them. In the present essay, published just days before his three-month 1901 tour of England concluded, Sousa practices his wit on a London readership.*

A curious psychological phenomenon occurs when a man, plunged suddenly into some emergency or new surroundings, notices all the trifling things connected with his position, but disregards the all-important essentials.

That to a great extent has been my experience during my long and enjoyable visit to England, which visit is now practically at an end. I am afraid that I have neglected the study of your great institutions and the habits and characteristics of the people, and instead taken a keen interest in the less important matters which have come under my notice.

---

22   Further on these see Bierley, *Works*, 185–88.

And if I have viewed these things from a humorous standpoint, it is only the way of my fellow- countrymen; for Americans have an inborn love for looking at the light side of nature. We grow

More Real Humorists

in the States than the whole of Europe combined—including Scotland.

Even on such a solemn occasion as bidding good-bye to London I could not be serious, though I tried to get myself down to that key. My last audience at Covent Garden demanded a speech, and waited in breathless expectancy for my sad and eloquent farewell. Instead, I informed them that knowing they would want a speech, I wrote out a "star" one, calculated to occupy some five hours in delivery, but that, unfortunately, my favourite dog found the speech and swallowed it, and he was now suffering from intellectual indigestion. I may have been outraging the conventions, but these few flippant words seemed to go down all right.

Now, the thing that has impressed me most in Great Britain is the railway carriage foot-warmer.[23] It is not so big as St. Paul's Cathedral, nor so long as Regent Street, but nothing architectural in the whole country has made such a vivid impression on my mind as the foot-warmer.

In my contemplative moments your foot-warmer forces its way to the front. If I dream, it is of foot-warmers; and in the only nightmare I have had since I came to England I imagined that somebody had made a sort of Pharaoh of me and buried me under a pyramid of foot-warmers. I would advise you to invent a new kind of shock for your American visitors.

The first time I saw the foot-warmer something on wheels came into the railway station and men in uniform began to fling about what I thought were undergrown milk-churns. "Why is this cart coming down the station filled with tin cans?" I asked. The man refused to explain.

Then somebody put me into the "cart" and somebody else threw a can inside. At first I thought it was an infernal machine, but I was wearing the uniform of the United States and I swore to die bravely. All the way I kept one foot firmly pressed down on the can, which I believed would go off at any moment. Of course, it did nothing of the sort; but in three or four hours I began to experience a curious sensation in that foot.

---

23   Railway foot-warmers in England at this time were little more than rented jugs filled with hot water and placed on their side for the rider's comfort.

It tingled in a way that recalled a frostbite I had in North America when the thermometer was 28 deg. below zero. Growing worse, I took off my boot. The foot-warmer or refrigerator or whatever the machine was had given me chilblains![24]

At the next stopping-place I sent for rough towels, and by vigorous rubbing managed to restore circulation in the foot. I affirm that if your "tight little island" were big enough to take a long railway journey in, the whole nation would be laid up with chilblains.

Another thing that badly needs revising is your money system. There is an idea in America that things are very cheap in Great Britain, and visitors from the States work on that hypothesis. But it is all wrong—at least, for the simple-minded and trustful American; though no doubt it is all right for the tradesman. Let me illustrate my point.

The other evening I had just time to take exactly nine whiffs at a cigar before commencing the performance. I went into a cigar store—I mean a tobacco shop—and asked for a mild smoke.

"How much?" I said.

"Sixpence," was the reply.

"Cheap," said I, "wonderfully cheap," and giving him the nimble coin in a hurry lest he should change his mind I lit the cigar and proceeded to enjoy the nine whiffs. At the eighth I began to think.

"Sixpence," I said to myself, "is equivalent to our twelve cents. This cigar is sold in America at the rate of three for a quarter—fourpence, Geewiz! It's mighty dear after all."

I would suggest that for the guidance of guileless Americans in England the Mint should put a star after the word "Sixpence" on that coin and a corresponding footnote, "This sum equals twelve cents." A great deal more money is being spent by American visitors in buying things cheaply than they imagine.

Another snare and delusion is the guinea. There is no such coin in England outside museums, and yet you price goods at so many guineas. Many Americans think the guinea another word for sovereign and make their purchases accordingly. The laugh is the storekeeper's. The other day I bought

---

24 Chilblains is approximately the opposite of frostbite—skin inflammation and irritation due to exposure to heat.

thirty guineas' worth of clothes, and after a long sum in mental arithmetic discovered that I had paid thirty shillings more than I thought I had paid. "Why do you call them guineas," I asked the attendant, "instead of pounds?"

"In dealing with gentlemen we always call them guineas," the nice man explained.

Having figured the whole thing out, I said:

"Well, in future I shall receive money as a gentleman and pay it as the other thing. It seems to me that is the only way to trade on profitable lines in this country."[25]

"According to Sousa: Great March King Describes How He Controls His 'One-Man' Band"

Source: *Daily Express* (United Kingdom), January 11, 1905, in *SPB* 20:3, 256.

> *Sousa rarely addressed his conducting methods as directly and specifically as he does in this essay. A number of cartoon drawings of his conducting gestures found their way into the press, and these indicate that he was as compelling a conductor as he here implies. The few surviving video clips of him in action are fascinating, but they show the master as more passive on the podium than might be imagined. Perhaps the later dates of those clips (one from 1916 and another from the late 1920s) was a factor.*

To ask that I should write of how I conduct my band is a little hurtful to my estimate of the modesty of a public man, inasmuch as I must strew the personal pronoun with a lavish hand throughout this column. Still, as this is none of my seeking, I trust that I may be forgiven if there are any inter alia paragraphs, especially as my instructions do not permit of my being anything but brutally frank.

---

25   These jokes, dealing as they do with British currency before it was decimalized, require a bit of explanation for the modern reader. Sixpence, his price for a single cigar, was half a shilling (itself 1/20 of a pound). While an American would have thought of it as six "pennies" casually, sixpence was really 1/40 of a pound (hence not really six "cents" but more than double that). Further confusing the matter, coined guineas were not minted after 1816, but the term continued to be used colloquially well into the twentieth century. The pricing was based on one's class, as noted by Sousa. A guinea was 21 shillings whereas a pound was only 20 shillings, therefore charging in guineas added a 5% gratuity. As a gentleman Sousa was expected to do business in guineas, whereas tradesmen usually dealt with pounds.

When I went to Germany one of the critics likened my band to a "living organ." Now, to my thinking, that was a discerning critic, because the effect I am always striving after is "homogeneity."

During many years critics and others have discussed my methods of conducting from every point of view. The austere, goggle-eyed individual who has sawdust in his veins has fixed his gaze coldly upon me, and said that my "Delsarte" was for effect only, while the man who had rich corpuscles racing through his anatomy has not hesitated to say that it was just right, and then proceeded to prove it.[26]

For instance, while conducting the strongly-marked rhythms of Spanish music, I have been said to suggest the sinuous movement of an Andalusian dancing girl. Now, that is just what I strive to do.

And why not?

The Conductor's Business

Is it not the business of the conductor to convey to the public in its most dramatic form the central idea of a composition? And how can he convey that idea successfully if he does not enter heart and soul into the life and story of the music? How, otherwise, can he give to the performers of his band the spirit they require? When I am directing the alluring, passionate music of Spain and Hungary I feel the warm Southern blood tingling in my veins, and it is my aim to give that life blood to my musicians and my listeners.

Many and many a time some poor fellow with an angularity and awkwardness—which certainly among all well-meaning people should be counted unpardonable sins—has seen fit to sneer at the theory I follow in conducting. The movements I make I cannot possibly repress, because at the time I am actually the thing that I am conducting, and naturally imagine my players and auditors are the same.

I have it said to me, "When you are conducting, Sousa, it seems natural, but in another it would appear incongruous."

One of the most laughable, yet perhaps one of the truest, things that has been said of me is that I resemble one of those strolling players who carry

---

26   This references François Delsarte (1811–1871), an influential French vocalist who argued that singers (or in this case conductors) should use facial expressions to depict musical emotions more clearly for their audiences. While he never wrote a method book of his own, Genevieve Stebbins's *The Delsarte System of Expression* (1885) popularized his ideas in the United States.

a drum on their backs, cymbals on their heads, a cornet in one hand and a concertina in the other—who is, in fact, a little band all to himself. That is what I am endeavouring to do all the time—to make my musicians and myself a one-man band.

Magnetic Wires

Only, instead of having actual metallic wires to work the instruments, I strike after magnetic ones. I have to work so that I feel every one of my fifty-eight musicians is linked up with me by a cable of magnetism. Every man must be as intent upon and as sensitive to every movement of my baton, or my fingers, as I am myself. For my part—though I do not claim to be possessed of supernatural powers—I know precisely what every one of my musicians is doing every second or fraction of a second that I am conducting. I know this because every single member of my band is doing exactly what I make him do.

Thus, when I stretch out my hand in the direction of some player, I give him the music I feel, and as I beckon to him the music leaps back to me. Again, if I hold up my baton to still the brasses, they are stilled as instantaneously and effectively as though they were mechanical instruments from which, by the pressure of an electric button, I had cut off the current.

It will be seen that to get together a band which is so utterly a part of myself is not an easy matter. I ransack the earth for the exact musicians I require[.] I will pay almost any money to get the right man in the right place, and nationality is of no account.

One may get a clever man, a really fine musician, who does not fit, and that one man is ruinous to my band. He sticks out as prominently and as painfully as "a sore thumb." Nor can he be made part of the whole without the exercise of great patience and kindness, if ever; and when he does not fit—out he goes. My main idea is to give each performer the conviction that his efforts are indispensable to the success of the band. As a matter of fact, they are.

Success of Sympathy

But the element which welds us all into one harmonious whole is sympathy—my sympathy for them and theirs for me. When that has been established I have the force to make each man play according to Sousa.

The vital necessity for the qualities of inspiration, reality, and magnetism were brought home to me when I was a schoolboy fiddling at college functions. I saw speakers who came forward, and who—well, just spoke so many words. Then would come an orator[,] a man who acted the part, who lived the part, who was the part because he believed it, and so swept the people off their feet.

Now this inspiration is even more necessary to the conductor than to the orator.

It is just the same with the composition of music. Millions of pieces have been written, but none of them lived or will live unless they have genuine inspiration at the back of them. Of all my marches that have succeeded, "The Stars and Stripes Forever" easily holds first place in the hearts of the public, and if ever there was a piece of music born of real inspiration it is this self-same march.

I was returning to America in 1896 from a tour through Europe, and I was dreadfully homesick. I paced the deck of the [S. S.] Teutonic while strain after strain of a march unfolded itself to me and even as I hummed it mentally and came to the following notes in the first strain:—

the words "Death to the enemy, death to the enemy," would spring to my mind, and they have never departed from me.[27]

And now to epitomize the principle upon which I conduct I must indulge in paradox. It is that by the utter effacement of self I force my personality upon the public through my band.

---

27   This excerpt (from the Solo B-flat Cornet part, mm. 15–16, concert pitch) is in Sousa's hand in the essay, but the quality of the original is not sufficient to reproduce here. The text underlay for *The Stars and Stripes Forever* was a part of the march as originally conceived, but for publication the phrase was dropped and the eighth-note motive ended up as an accompanimental figure to the words "protect" and "tyrant crew" in the phrase "The emblem of the brave and true, Its folds protect no tyrant crew." For a detailed assessment of the compositional process of this march see Smart, "Genesis."

1905–1906

Fighting the Music Industry

"Another Phrase of the Piracy Question: International Obligations"

Source: *The Times* (London), ca. February 25, 1905, in *SPB* 87 "Extra Clippings," 7.

> *Intellectual property rights were one of Sousa's long-term causes, and would eventually lead him to testify before Congress in 1906 and to help found ASCAP in 1914.[28] With this letter he began what might today be termed a "media blitz." In short order Sousa penned additional letters to the major London newspapers, publically lobbying Parliament to change the status quo. They passed the Musical Copyright Act of 1906 one year later.*
>
> *In this, the first of those letters, he directly challenges British enforcement of international copyright law. A March 19 reprinting begins by mentioning "While British authors are complaining that the copyright laws work to their disadvantage and to the profit of American writers, in music the copyright arrangements seem to afford less protection in Great Britain than elsewhere. There is something like a chronic warfare over the piracy of songs..."[29] Clearly enforcement was a challenge everywhere.*

To the editor: *The Times.*

Sir,—

The question of music piracy has been so fully exploited that it is not my desire to enter upon any general discussion of the case; but, if you will

---

28   Further on the topic see Chessum, "Salaried Warriors."
29   "Musical Piracy in England" in illegible newspaper, in *SPB* 21:1, 9.

permit me to encroach upon your valued columns, I should like to invite your attention to the international aspects of the question. The British government participated in the Berne conferences of 1885 and 1887, and the International Copyright Convention which resulted was adopted in full by English orders in council, which were intended to afford foreign authors and composers protection for their works in Great Britain in return for reciprocal advantages for British authors and composers in the other countries parties to said agreement. In 1891 the United States of America agreed upon terms of international copyright with the countries comprising the Berne convention, including Great Britain. As far as Great Britain is concerned, this international copyright agreement has proved a delusion and a snare, because no foreign author or composer is protected in his rights here.

To the best of my belief, music piracy does not exist in any country where there is an international copyright law in force, except Great Britain.[30] Certainly it has been unknown in the United States since 1891, and when a British subject has complied with the copyright laws of my country he is immediately clothed with clearly defined legal rights which are protected for him by the strong arm of the American law. I know that my compositions, after having been entered for copyright in Germany, France, Belgium, &c., are not stolen, and only in Great Britain do I fail to receive the complete protection for my music which was clearly the intent of the Berne convention and the subsequent copyright agreement with the United States. Reciprocity is of no value if it does not reciprocate.

I have before me a pirated edition of my latest composition, which was printed and hawked about the streets of London within a few days of the authorised publication of this march, at a price at which my publishers could not afford to print it. And this has been the case with all my compositions in England for several years. Piracy has had the effect of practically stopping the sale of my genuine publications, thus depriving me of the substantial income from that source that the popularity of my music in this country gives me every reason to expect.

---

30   Note the omission of Italy, another signee to the Berne Convention, from his discussion. He had already witnessed the piracy of his music there firsthand during an 1896 vacation: the "Giovanni Filipo Sousa" incident became one of his most oft-repeated anecdotes. Further see Sousa, *Marching Along*, 158–59.

I am informed that the opposition of one of the law makers of this country has heretofore prevented the enactment of proper legislation to remedy this evil. Whatever reason this gentleman may have for refusing the British composer the legitimate return for the work of his brain, I certainly deny his right to say that the American composer must come under the same ban, when the international copyright treaty guarantees to the American composer the same protection in Great Britain that he enjoys at home. Is it reasonable to suppose that any country would have expended the time, trouble and money to establish an international copyright agreement with Great Britain except with the full belief that she would faithfully fulfil the terms of that agreement?

If, subsequently, Great Britain discovered that her laws were too lax to give the foreign composer the protection guaranteed him, I submit that it then became incumbent upon his majesty's government to enact such legislation as would protect the foreign composer in his rights under the Berne convention.

In short, when other countries are honourably carrying out the terms of a treaty to which Great Britain was a party, it seems to me that the national honour and pride demand that immediate steps be taken to fulfil the treaty obligations of this country in the matter of international copyright.

Yours, &c.,
John Philip Sousa
February 25, 1905

"Mr. Sousa on Musical Pirates: Protest and a Parallel"

Source: *The Daily Mail* (London), April 22, 1905, in *SPB* 22, 104

Perhaps emboldened by the coverage his letter of February 25 (above) received, Sousa expanded and clarified his position in a second letter, sent to a different major British newspaper. This letter hints that he read an article with an opposing viewpoint, perhaps explaining his more frank language in this letter when compared to the previous one. Sousa tended to rely on alliteration when confronting opposing views, perhaps nowhere as evident as it is here.

To the editor of the *Daily Mail*

Sir,—

With an avidity worthy the cause, I have read during my sojourn in these tight little islands everything that has come my way which has borne on the subject of music piracy.

Because of the laxity of your laws, and because of the perseverance of your music pirates, my royalties have gone a-glimmering. To use an anatomical expression current in the picturesque occident of my country, I have been "getting it plump in the jugular."

One or two of the arguments I have noted, which were in opposition to the publisher and composer, have not struck me as hilariously humorous, or even as faintly facetious.

To elucidate—I read in your journal some days ago, a communication in which the writer places the blame for the deplorable condition of the music trade here on the publisher, and points with argumentative finger to the fact that if the publisher had heeded the cry of the masses—whoever that nebulous body may be—and had sold his wares for less money, the music pirate would never have budded into existence. Inter alia, it would appear that the music pirate was called into the arena of activity to fill a long-felt want—to supply music at a cheaper price than the one at which the publisher cared to sell it—whether he could afford to or not.

Twopenny Philanthropy

It would appear under those conditions that the music pirate had a philanthropic mission. This mysterious and mercenary Messiah, noticing the dire distress of the tune-starved masses—whoever they may be—said, "I will save them. I will fill their melodic 'little Marys' with music at 2d. a meal. I will gorge them with gavottes, build them up with ballads, and make muscle with marches. They shall become comely with comedy conceits, and radiantly rosy with rag-time rondos—and all at 2d. a throw."

And this beneficent pirate has waxed fat and saucy as he has hawked in the highways and byways spurious editions of him who is the favored of Melpomene and the boon companion of Orpheus. And I beg to ask, in words tinged with doubt and despair, where does the favored of Melpomene and the boon companion of Orpheus come in? The royalties of the "f. of M.," and the "b. c. of O." are like angels' visits—few and far between.[31]

Shall the sunlight depart from the soul of the sweet singer of melody? Shall the fount of the muse dry up, as it were? Is there no balm in Gilead? Is there no surcease from sorrow for royalties that never materialize? Behold, oh star-eyed Britannia, a suppliant at the bar of public opinion asking for justice, for your own and for your friends' own.

The Green Goods Man

It is not difficult to quote parallels, nor is it impossible to cite analogous conditions. For the moment we will drop the pirate, with his ill-gotten wealth—we will leave this land of hope and glory, and will cross over to my dear little old United States, the land of glory and hope.

Over there at times there has sprung into notice a gentleman who has said to his suffering fellow-citizens, "You poor, overworked, underwaged, downtrodden creatures, you have to pay too much for your money. Twenty shillings for a pound is outrageous!"[32] And forthwith he informs them in a carefully-worded circular, sent in the dark of the moon, that he will supply a thousand-dollar note beautifully printed on a press of his own, for the small sum of ten dollars, legal tender.

You see the deadly parallel? Your pirate offers to supply two shillings' worth of music for 2d. Our pirate offers to supply two shillings of money for 2d.

We call him the green goods man in my country, but we do not throw any bouquets at him. A hard-hearted but clear-headed policeman grabs him by the scruff of the neck, and yanks him before equally as hard-hearted and quite as clear-headed a judge, who sends him up for twenty years at hard labour. Then our department, corresponding with your Scotland Yard, noses around and gets the bracelets on all others who have any of the green goods man's queer stuff in their possession—and before you can say Jack Robinson the penitentiary shows an increase in the number of its inmates.

---

31   "F. of M." and "b. c. of O." abbreviate his turns of phrase "favored of Melpomene" and the "boon companion of Orpheus" respectively. Melpomene is the ancient Greek muse of singing and of tragedy.
32   On Sousa and the British monetary system see "According to Sousa" on page 40.

A Discouraging Effect

This process has a very discouraging effect on the green goods man and his satellites, and the bucolic victim, whether in or out of gaol, is suddenly face to face with the grim fact that it costs twenty shillings to get a pound.

I have never heard that the actions of the green goods man have been endorsed by our Houses of Congress, or by any branch of the Judiciary. Surely, if anybody is to be patted on the back, the man who can supply cheap money is of more consequence to the world than the fellow who can supply cheap music.

If the gentleman who makes a counterfeit presentment of my compositions can pursue the even tenor of his way unmolested, proud in the consciousness of a duty well done, I cannot help feeling that this sea- girt reservation of yours would be a harvest-home and a haven of rest for the American green goods man.

Sorrowfully,

John Philip Sousa

"Musical Piracy"

Source: *The Daily Telegraph* (London), April 27, 1905, in SPB 20:3, 271.

> *In another letter on British copyright problems, Sousa invokes a personal example to illustrate his point:* The Bride Elect *(1897). It seems likely that music piracy was not the only reason his London production of the operetta fell apart, given that* The Bride Elect *was less successful financially and critically in the United States than Sousa here intimates. As substantial as the $25,000 publication royalty figure he cites might seem, he later claimed to have turned down a $100,000 offer for exclusive production rights from the theater that produced the premier.*[33]

---

33   Further see Sousa, *Marching Along*, 168–69. Bierley (*Works*, 17) notes that the *New York Journal* offered $10,000 for exclusive publication rights to the music; apparently Sousa made a better decision in that case by declining it than he did with the six figures he left in Connecticut.

To the editor of *The Daily Telegraph*,

Sir—

When old Fletcher of Saltoun, in "An Account of a Conversation," said, "I knew a very wise man that believed if a man were permitted to make all the ballads, he need not care who made the laws of a nation," he evidently reckoned without the music pirate.[34] Those of us who love law and order, and go in for the eternal fitness of things, realise that the maker of laws in this kingdom of yours is a most imposing personage, and we see by his sins of omission that he can entail hardship and unhappiness on many. It may be a grand thing to write the music of the people, but if one's efforts meet with no recompense, and irresponsible hawkers profit by your creation, fame alone will not fill the measure of what should be inviolably your own.

This is by way of preliminary. There is one side of the music pirate's incursions into what should be prohibited territory that perhaps has not been touched upon or made as clearly understood as it should be; that is, the loss of the many who depend on the work of a composer for their livelihood. I will cite my own case to make clear this point.

A few years ago there followed in the chain of operas I have written one called "The Bride-Elect" which made a most substantial success in my own country. When I came to Great Britain some months ago I was approached by a well-known London manager, who desired to produce the piece here. I wrote to the owners of the stage rights in America, asking them to send [the] full score, prompt copy, orchestral parts, plates of costumes, and everything necessary for an opening in this metropolis. The owners had copies made of all these things at some considerable expense, and shipped them to me, but as my profit would necessarily depend on the success of my music, and as the music pirate could steal all the numbers, and I would be without redress, I reshipped the opera to America.

My publisher informs me that during the run of "The Bride-Elect" in America there were sold arrangements of the music to the extent of 314,994 copies, which brought in royalties a sum amounting to $25,000. If the work

---

34   Andrew Fletcher of Saltoun (1655–1716) opposed Scotland's incorporation into the United Kingdom (the subject of the 1703 book quoted by Sousa) and spent time in exile for plotting insurrection. Sousa used this quotation frequently throughout his career.

were to duplicate the success here, there would be no reason to suppose that the sale would be any smaller in England, and that would be much too large an amount of money for a composer to hand over to a music pirate. Judging by the interest exhibited by the pirate in regard to compositions of mine heretofore played here, I am very sure "The Bride-Elect" would get the endorsement of that delectable individual. I can hear the cynical and opulent brain-robber, surrounded by his champions and admirers, sneeringly remark, "Who cares whether he produces his opera or not?" and his henchmen echoing the sneer, "Who cares?" I will tell them who cares, leaving the composer, the publisher, and the producer entirely out of the question. The singers, actors, chorus people, orchestral players, costumiers, printers, advertising departments of newspapers, stage hands, sandwich men, the various theatrical advertising agents, &c.—they are the ones that will care. A production of the opera, such as I would have liked to make here, affects the well-being of at least 300 people, and they care. I believe I do not violate any confidence when I say the sooner the lawmakers of this United Kingdom protect the interests of the above-mentioned subjects of his Majesty the better it will be for everyone concerned. The music pirate does not add to the gaiety of nations, and the sooner he is effectually and eternally squelched, the sooner will happiness return to the soul of

John Philip Sousa.
Carlton Hotel, April 26

"The Business of the Bandmaster"

Source: *The Criterion*, August 1905, 19–21, in *SPB* 21:1, 27–31.

This wide-ranging essay provides insights into Sousa's methods for forming and leading a band. The parallels with modern music education—from the importance of rehearsal, discipline, and sight-reading skills to leadership skills, comradery, and the difficulty of becoming a professional—are striking. Still, Sousa betrays the mindset of his age later in the essay. His comments on African-American music and traditional Japanese music demonstrate a mindset at odds with a musical world increasingly interested in drawing connections across musical styles. In later years Sousa would confront jazz—the eventual national school of music he predicted, albeit not in the guise he expected—head on, reasserting his longstanding belief that music is either good or bad, not new or old. The issue seems not to have been one of musical style for Sousa: he heard all styles as connected to the Western classical tradition.

Many Called, but Few Chosen

The organizing and maintaining of a superior band I regard in the light of a calm, calculative, business proposition, as much a matter of practical consideration as the selection and training of men for banking or other commercial duties. Personal predilection and prejudice do not enter into the equation—only merit and adaptability to the individuality of the leader. As the head of a counting-house exercises powers of selection in gathering about him a staff as nearly perfect as possible, so is the bandmaster untiring in his search for the best available talent, and willing to give time and labor to its amalgamation in the general body. By hundreds, yes, thousands, the applicants come. One and all are given a hearing, but few, indeed, are chosen. Editors tell me that of manuscripts submitted to the magazines barely one per cent. ever achieve the dignity of cold type. The applicants for any one of the great bands are received in a like proportion, with like chances of success. Moreover, the principle of the survival of the fittest is strong. After twenty years of organization and hard training, entailing the personal examination of more than fifty thousand musicians and the training of perhaps five thousand of them, I have no hesitation in affirming that I have approached the ideal standard, and that my men rank in efficiency, unity, and those qualities which go to make individual genius second to none in the world.

The Ability to Read Music at Sight

There are many qualities of which the general public is little aware, that go to the making of the band musician. In the first place, no matter how brilliant a soloist a musician may be, if he has not the gift of sight-reading and a thorough training therein, he cannot be considered. Though many fall short on grounds of artistic excellence and still find acceptance, those that do not come up to the requirements in rapid sight-reading are ineligible. This seems like setting the mathematics of music above the aesthetics, yet there is good and sufficient reason for it. In the first place, the public taste is ever varying, and it has been found expedient to give a wide range of programme[s], particularly here in

America. Sectional tastes must be duly consulted. The Boston programme differs from that of Atlanta or New Orleans, the Milwaukee programme from that of Denver and the Coast. People who pay well for their repast have a right to dictate in a measure what shall be on the bill-of-fare. The programme is thus subject to change, and there lies the imperative demand for facility in reading music at sight.

Individuality in Musicians and Leader

As to individuality, the second consideration, I note that musicians of the strongest native idiosyncrasies are the most keenly susceptible to the individuality of the leader. After all, individuality is only the result of wide assimilative power combined with a keen sense of selection. Occasionally we find this individuality uncompromising, but, as a rule, the best men gradually merge into the manner of the aggregation, taking up and keeping the pace in the leader's own way, and by projecting their individual geniuses into the body politic, strengthen and enrich it. But it is the leader's individuality that is ever predominant. To people who hear difficult music played with the utmost ease, it often seems so easily done that it appears to have been easy from the beginning. Yet if the fifty best musicians in the world should meet and for the first time attempt some difficult composition, the result might be interesting, but it would be most incongruous and far from artistic; and the greater the individuality of each, the more inharmonious the whole. But let those fifty men go into training under a competent leader, and in a short time the very highest standard of musical excellence would be achieved. I have ever been on the lookout for men of the strongest individuality, yet not so set and confirmed in their idiosyncrasies as to become irreconcilable to the leader's own style. However excellent he may be, if a musician cannot seize upon and merge himself into the ruling spirit of the band as a whole, he must be withdrawn, sacrificed to the unity of the organization, which, after all, is the thing most to be desired.

Military Discipline Combined with Tact

Military training is of great value in preparing men for any difficult task requiring concerted effort. Yet men abhor the feeling of forced durance, and it is the cleverest officer that leads his men to any difficult task in such a way as completely to disarm this sentiment of restraint. Long conversance with military affairs has taught me that men of intelligence are naturally more easily led then driven; and whatever happens, either in practice or in public, I avoid personal reproof, in order that the musician may not lose a moiety of his self-confidence. Though the patience of the whole band, and most of all the leader's, may be tried to the utmost, there should ever be maintained a complete mastery of the situation. Let the commander once lose his firm grip, the men in the ranks discover it instantly and a virtual stampede follows, even as of men in battle whose leader wavers at some critical crisis. The old methods of discipline have fortunately passed away. It is realized now that a leader may treat his men with the utmost consideration, giving them reasonable scope, and yet accomplish great things by making each man feel an individual responsibility toward the organization. If a man begs to be excused from rehearsal and I refuse him with scant courtesy, he goes sullenly and half-heartedly to work. But if I say, "Very well, sir; but do you realize that this rehearsal is particularly for you?" he is put on his mettle and goes to his task with fine determination. Instilling a personal sense of honor and responsibility avails infinitely more than bullying and compulsion.

Good Treatment and Fair Compensation

It is one thing to get good men into an organization, another to hold them there. I have no hesitation in saying that the men who make up the Sousa Band feel themselves bound together by very strong ties, and take the lapses of any single member as a reflection upon the whole. I know that the applause bestowed upon the band is taken by every man as a personal tribute, and every adverse criticism as a personal charge. The success which comes after years of training belongs to the men as well as the leader. The first effort toward making a musician contented with his lot is to compensate him fairly for his services. When a man is being poorly paid, however glad he may be to belong to an organization which avowedly occupies a high place in the public estimation, he loses heart and is preoccupied with the problems which come with poverty. There is not a man in the band who receives less than thirty-five dollars a week, and there are many who receive a hundred. The wages that I have always insisted upon are higher than those of the union, and I do not know of more than a single instance where I have been called upon by that excellent organization to explain my position in a dispute with one of my men.

American Music and Musicians

In my choice of musicians I, of course, prefer Americans. I am proud to say that a large majority—probably ninety per cent.—of the band are natives of this country. I am an American myself, imbued to the core with things American, and have naturally a strong sense of fatherland. I find that American musicians are more eager, more adaptable and earnest in their work than foreigners; they are proud of the flag and of the fact that this country has produced one of the greatest bands of the world. I wish, however, it were as easy to find American music of great originality and excellence; alas, I do not know where to search for it. If only one in a hundred musicians is available, what shall be said of the compositions by American composers? In the face of congratulations upon finding characteristic music among the Southern negroes, I must confess that there is nothing original and certainly nothing of the negro in the music of the South. It is the emanation of the white sentiment, the product of the white intellect. I have found the same lack of native originality in studying the national airs of the world outside of Europe. Some years ago, in compiling a work for our Government on this subject, I collected the national and typical airs of various countries, from America to the South Seas. I must say that there is very little that may be called strictly original, or indeed even typical of the country whence it came. The Puerto Rican and the Philippine anthems, for instance, are Spanish, pure and simple. Even the supposedly characteristic music of Japan, remote as it is from Occidental moods and music, shows the influence of European method; the old music of Japan is without beauty, melody, or artistic worth.[35]

Nothing New in Music under the Sun

Originality in music is one of the rarest things to be found on earth. Looking back over the centuries you will see but few signal instances of actual originality that gives promise of lasting for all time. The reason is that, whereas many wonderful things may be accomplished by perseverance, long training, and talent of a high order, music is a matter of inspiration. If a great painter wishes to paint a battle or a sacred scene, he need only

---

35   Sousa here contrasts traditional Japanese music with that of the more Westernized Meji Restoration
     period, which began in 1868.

dwell upon the idea till he evolves something, then go to work and make the most perfect copy possible of something in nature. Musical art is exactly the opposite; for the nearer you copy nature, the further you are from expressing a high musical idea that shall interest the public. A thunder storm is inspiring and glorious; but an intimation of it would be laughable. There is no such thing as absolute realism in music; it is a matter of inspiration pure and simple. To produce a composition that is not merely reminiscent seems almost impossible in our time, and particularly in our country, where men assimilate with such ease and adapt themselves so readily to circumstances. Although I have several American compositions on every programme, I am constrained to say that there are no typical American songs that have come to my knowledge, and the man who writes one will be hailed as a prophet. Even our treasured airs are not national with us at all, and without the eternal wellsprings of the music of other countries and other times to draw upon, I fear that the little so-called American music that we have would never have come into existence. This may sound like treason to my profession, both as a composer and leader, but the keener critical sense is not to be deceived. A man unconsciously stores away in the pockets of the mind vast harmonies which may come out later in the throes of composition. He may believe them original, but upon closer scrutiny he finds that his subconscious memory has supplied his conscious sense with a motley of melody which he has placed in "pensive array" to suit his fancy. Of course the music may be copyrighted and sung throughout the land as original, but, considered according to the standard of the larger criticism, there is nothing new in music under the sun.

A Musician's Love of His Instrument

Musicians become used to their instruments with long association and learn to regard them as something almost human, as the trainer does his race-horse or the engineer his locomotive. I encourage this expression of musicianly interest and sensitiveness, and never attempt to force a new instrument upon a man, although I may know that his wood-wind instrument, let us say, may [go] sharp or flat with the variations of temperature. The musician is in love with his instrument, and will fight for it to the end. Every time I have endeavored to force a new instrument upon a musician the result has been failure. The more pleasing a musician's environment and the conditions of his work, the surer he is to forget self and bring out the best there is in him.

Society's Increased Respect for the Musician

A source of gratification to the lovers of music is that the public impression of musicians as a class has undergone a great revision within the past few years. Within my memory, to be a musician was to accept a place in the social scale a little lower than the mountebank. The dignity of the profession has been elevated, and infusion of new blood of the very best stock has brought about a sort of renaissance of the band and of band music. I have tried to contribute to this in my small way, and am pleased to have succeeded, with the help of an organization composed of men not only of consummate ability, but gentlemen in the highest sense of the word. With the establishment of schools and conservatories throughout this country, and with the education of the public taste to a higher standard of musical excellence, there has come about a regeneration of the sentiment toward music and musicians. The whole profession has received a stimulus never before known in this New World.

A Glorious Future for Music in America

And as a result of this stimulus, some of the rarest talent of the world may be produced—if not the music of the future. As soon as men turn their powers of invention from things commercial to things artistic, America will lead in art as it has in the practical inventions, for the constructive ability of the American is second to none on earth.

We have hitherto devoted our creative energies to the development of natural material resources, and making ourselves a power in the commercial and military world. But this era will produce another wherein the arts are to receive a greater degree of respect and of inventive energy. The refinements of life will take a more important place in our national perspective, and those administering them will be regarded as people occupying not a lower but a higher intellectual plane. An absolutely original national school of music may be evolved, and America may take her place in the front rank in the musical world as she has long maintained her foothold among the world-leaders of mechanical and industrial enterprise.

"Music in America: Its Progress as Viewed by the Famous March Composer, Sousa"

Source: unknown newspaper, ca. September 1905, in *SPB* 21:1.

> *Presumably home from his 1905 tour of Britain and Ireland, Sousa's comparison of musical taste abroad with that of America provided him with an opening to promote his own musical style as significant and "classical" in its own right. Even as he argues for the abandonment of America's longstanding worship of the symphony, the composers he mentions were, on the whole, working in exactly that genre. Note his closing sentence, where he mentions how "plantation songs and Sousa marches" are what Europeans respect most in American music.*

No nation today, in a commercial way, can reckon without America, and the time is not far distant when artistic America must also be reckoned with. A nation which in its short life has shown the genius of ours for progress in a material way certainly can and will in time show it along the lines of artistic development.

Perhaps the tide toward Americanism in art has heretofore been successfully held back by the absolute lack of insularity in our nation's life, for admittedly there are no people today who are so interested in other peoples of the world as the Americans. The cosmopolitan character of our population may have something to do with this, though I am inclined to the belief that it is due to our youth in the family of nations. With the child's curiosity, we allow ourselves to become interested and be entertained as well as instructed by our neighbors.

Owing to the fact that great numbers of the professional musicians in this country are foreigners, the world at large is ignorant of the wonderful love of music found in the American. New York vies with London as a musical Mecca, while city, town and village in our land show keenest interest in musical affairs. I fully believe that an unqualified indorsement of a player or a composition by an American audience would be duplicated and sincerely seconded in every country of the Old World, and I say this with a knowledge born of actual experience in the great art centers of Europe.

Perhaps the European has reached one stage that is not sufficiently thought of and appreciated here, viz.: Classification tending toward one standard. For example, to us Americans the writer of a symphony is held in reverential awe, while the writer of a master ballad is not looked on with equal importance. The European, on the other hand, has a standard for every form of composition, with the result that the composer of a trite, dry-as-dust symphony, is considered of less importance in the musical world, than he who creates a striking, original song. The European does not judge a composition by its complexity or simplicity, but solely by its merit in a particular class. For this reason we find that men like Johann Strauss, Offenbach, Suppe, Milloecker and others are the darlings of their respective nations, because they have accomplished that which is most meritorious in some special line. For this reason also it is not uncommon to hear played by a grand orchestra in Europe a Strauss waltz, a Sousa march, a Ganne mazurka, and a Gillet morceau in one and the same programme, or to find side by side the works of Wagner, Tschaikowsky and those of their compeers.

Along the purely technical side American music shows such perfection of scholarship that I question if any European country can produce seven greater technicians than Paine, MacDowell, Buck, Chadwick, Parker, Foote and Whiting. These men, in compositions such as "The Golden Legend," "The Light of Asia," "Judith," "The Columbian Ode," "In the Mountains," "The Indian Suite," "Hora Novissima," "The Haunted Forest," "Henry of Navarre" and "Azara," are thoroughly convincing in their magnificence of erudition.

Continuing the list of Americans who have made their mark as creative musicians, such men as Hadley, Herbert, Nevin, McCoy, Stewart, Bartlett and many others show there is no paucity of musical ideas in this country.

I have heard it said that we have no national school of music, but this statement I consider far from the fact. "National school of music" means "international imitation." That which is imitated in America and Europe today, and is as much admired as the national music of any other country, are the plantation songs and Sousa marches, both of which spring from American soil, and, like the shot at Bunker Hill, are heard around the world.

John Philip Sousa

Testimony before the Congressional Committees on Patents

Source: *Committees on Patents of the Senate and House of Representatives Conjointly of the Bills S. 6330 and H. R. 19853, to Amend and Consolidate the Acts Respecting Copyright, June 6, 7, 8, and 9, 1906* (Washington, D. C.: Government Printing Office, 1906), 23–25, 30, 108–09, 121, and 143.

> *Over the course of his lengthy career Sousa witnessed a technological revolution in music recording and playback. Existing copyright laws offered the composer no protection regarding recording rights and royalties. Sousa, Victor Herbert, and others testified before Congress in 1906 urging them to pass protections so that they could collect royalties on recordings of their compositions.*
>
> *The following testimony is probably the most reliably transcribed interview of Sousa ever held, and his wit and fire in defending his views while under close scrutiny come to the fore. Normally in favor of technological progress and the accessibility of audiences to music, on the issue of recordings and player pianos Sousa adopted a reactionary position. Congress eventually passed a law on mechanical copyrights in 1909 in which Sousa and Herbert mostly prevailed. Henceforth composers could deny permission to record and they would collect royalties on recordings they had licensed; however, once they had licensed a work for recording, they were required to license it to anyone upon request.[36] In this item brackets in roman font are in the original transcription, while all footnotes and bracketed text in italics are editorial insertions.*

[*Wednesday, June 6, 1906*]
Statement of John Philip Sousa

Mr. Sousa. Mr. Chairman, I would much rather have my brass band here. I think it would be more appreciated than my words will be. [Laughter.]

Mr. Chaney.[37] We would rather have you, just now.

Mr. Sousa. Thank you. Mr. Chairman,[38] I would like to quote Fletcher, of Saltoun, who said that he cared not who made the laws of the land if he

---

36   For a detailed discussion of Sousa's interaction with copyright law, and on his arguments in 1906 specifically, see Warfield, "Menace."

37   John C. Chaney, a Republican, represented Indiana's second congressional district from 1905–09.

38   The House committee was chaired by Frank D. Currier, a Republican, who represented New Hampshire's second congressional district from 1901–13.

could write its songs. We composers of America take the other view. We are very anxious as to who makes the laws of this land. We are in a very bad way. I think when the old copyright law was made, the various perforated rolls and phonograph records were not known, and there was no provision made to protect us in that direction. Since then, the talking machines have come out, and the claim is made that the record of sound is not a notation.

There are three ways for the composer to make a living by his music: By sight or by sound or by touch. The notation of my compositions or the compositions of any other composer for the blind must be entirely different from the ordinary, because it must be read by the sense of touch. The notation that is made for a combination of instruments is brought out by sound. The claim that is made about these records is that they can not be read by any notation—simply that no method has been found to read them up to the present time, but there will be. Just as the man who wanted to scan the heavens discovered a telescope to do it. No doubt there will be found a way to read these records.

We are entirely in favor of this bill. The provisions satisfy us, and we want to be protected in every possible form in our property. When these perforated-roll companies and these phonograph companies take my property and put it on their records they take something that I am interested in and give me no interest in it. When they make money out of my pieces I want a share of it.

Mr. Sulzer.[39] They are protected in their inventions?

Mr. Sousa. Yes, sir.

Mr. Sulzer. And why should you not be protected in yours?

Mr. Sousa. That is my claim. They have to buy the brass that they make their funnels out of, and they have to buy the wood that they make the box out of, and the material for the disk; and that disk as it stands, without the composition of an American composer on it, is not worth a penny. Put the composition of an American composer on it and it is worth $1.50. What makes the difference? The stuff that we write.

---

39   William Sulzer, a Democrat, represented two different New York congressional districts from 1895–1912. He later became notorious when, in his first year as the governor of New York (1913), he was successfully impeached for a range of ethical infractions and removed from office.

Mr. Bonynge.[40] What is the protection by the terms of this bill that is given you?

Mr. Sousa. That in any production of our music by any of these mechanical instruments they must make a contract with us or with our publishers; that they must pay us money for the use of our compositions.

The publishers of this country make contracts with the composers, and agree to give them a sum outright or a royalty on sales for each and every copy that they publish and sell.

The companies making records for talking machines take one copy of a copyrighted piece of music and produce by their method a thousand or more disks, cylinders, or perforated rolls. If they would buy one copy from my publishers and owners of my copyright and sell that one copy, I would have no objection; but they take the copyrighted copy and make what they claim is a noncopyrighted copy, sell it, and do not give the owner of the copyright a penny of royalty for its use: and they could not do this if the composer had not written it and the publisher had not published it, and I want to be paid for the use they make of my property.

Mr. Webb.[41] Does this affect records already made?

Mr. Currier. No; it does not affect existing copyrights.

Mr. Sousa. No. That is a sop— I am willing to let it stand for the sake of the future, but I think it is wrong. That is a sop to them, the talking-machine companies, and hereafter they will make money after this law passes on the pieces that I made before the law went into effect.

Mr. Chaney. So that we will get "El Capitan" from the phonographs in various places?

Mr. Sousa. Yes, sir; and I'll get nothing for it; and I am the man that made "El Capitan." [Laughter.]

I speak in the interest of the publishers and the composers, and some of them asked me to come here because I could talk from the heart, and I do. I am sure of what I say. There may be some interests opposed to the bill for selfish reasons, but these interests know the bill simply gives us rights we are entitled to.

---

40   Rorbert W. Bonynge, a Republican, represented Colorado's first congressional district from 1904–09.
41   Edwin Y. Webb, a Democrat, represented North Carolina's ninth congressional district from 1903–19 before becoming a federal judge.

As to the artists, Mr. Millet said that he got $8.75 for one of his pictures. You can take any catalogue of records of any talking machine company in this country and you will find from 20 to 100 of my compositions on it. I have yet to receive the first penny for the use of them.

There is another point to consider. These talking machines are going to ruin the artistic development of music in this country. When I was a boy— I was born in this town—in front of every house in the summer evenings you would find young people together singing the songs of the day or the old songs. To-day you hear these infernal machines going night and day. [Laughter.] We will not have a vocal cord left. [Laughter.] The vocal cords will be eliminated by a process of evolution, as was the tail of man when he came from the ape. The vocal cords will go because no one will have a chance to sing, the phonograph supplying a mechanical imitation of the voice, accompaniment, and effort.

On this river, when I was a young man, we went out boating and the music of young voices filled the air.

Last summer and the summer before I was in one of the biggest yacht harbors of the world, and I did not hear a voice the whole summer. Every yacht had a gramophone, a phonograph, an æolian, or something of the kind. They were playing Sousa marches, and that was all right, as to the artistic side of it [laughter], but they were not paying for them, and, furthermore, they were not helping the technical development of music. Go to the men that manufacture the instruments that are nearest the people—the banjo, the guitar, and the mandolin—and every one of them will tell you that the sale of those instruments has fallen off greatly. You can not develop music without these instruments, the country singing school, and the country brass band. Music develops from the people, the "folk songs," and if you do not make the people executants, you make them depend on the machines.

Mr. Currier. Since the time you speak of, when they used to be singing in the streets—

Mr. Sousa. Well, Mr. Currier, I am 50 years old—

Mr. Currier. I was just going to ask you: Since that time, the law has been passed to protect the authors of musical compositions, which would prohibit that. Is not that so?

Mr. Sousa. No, sir; you could always do it.

Mr. Currier. Any public performance is prohibited, is it not, by that law?

Mr. Sousa. You would not call that a public performance.

Mr. Currier. But any public performance is prohibited by the law of 1897?

Mr. Sousa. Not that I know of at all. I have never known that it was unlawful to get together and sing.

Mr. Currier. It probably has not been enforced to that extent.

Mr. McGavin.[42] You think it ought to be against the law for some people to attempt to do it, do you not, Mr. Sousa? [Laughter.]

Mr. Sousa. Yes.

Mr. Currier. It is possible that that has deterred the young people from singing.

Mr. Sousa. Would you not consider it a greater crime to turn on a phonograph—

Mr. Currier. I do not consider singing a crime.

Mr. Sousa. If you would make it a misdemeanor, do you not think it much worse to have a lot of these machines going than to have a lot of fresh young voices singing?

Mr. Currier. I think a great many people in this country get a great deal of comfort out of the phonograph.

Mr. Sousa. But they get much more out of the human voice, and I will tell you why: The phonograph companies know that. They pay [*Italian opera singer Enrico*] Caruso $3,000 to make a record in their machine, because they get the human voice. And they pay a cornet player $4 to blow one of his blasts into it. [Laughter.] That is the difference. The people, the homes, want the human voice. First comes the country singing school, and next comes the country brass band. Let us do something to help them. You can do it by making these people pay me for everything that I compose. [Laughter.]

[*Editor's note: At this point Victor Herbert made his statement and was questioned, largely concurring with Sousa. Horace Pettit then testified on behalf of the Victor Talking Machine Company and others followed. Sousa was asked a few questions along the way, as transcribed below.*]

---

42 Charles McGavin, a Republican, represented Illinois's eighth congressional district from 1905–09.

Senator Smoot.[43] I would like to ask Mr. Sousa a question. I was very much interested in your statement, Mr. Sousa, pertaining to talking machines taking the place of the human voice, and I will ask you this question: If you were protected in your productions and received a royalty from the talking machines, would that lessen the use of the talking machines any and strengthen the use of the voice and the brass band and the home choir, and so on?

Mr. Sousa. I do not think so, but I think it will reduce two wrongs to one.

Senator Smoot. Then, it is simply a question of your receiving the royalty that you think you are entitled to?

Mr. Sousa. Yes, sir.

Senator Smoot. I think there are other causes besides the general use of the talking machine that account for the fact that there is less singing than there used to be. I think we do not live quite as close to nature as we used to, and that that is what used to make us sing.

Mr. Sousa. That is very true. But the more leeway you give the talking machine the greater encroachments they will make. If they are made to pay a royalty on all compositions that they use, perhaps they will not have so many bad ones in their records. [Laughter.]

Senator Smoot. That is what I intended to find out, as to whether it was simply a personal affair.

Mr. Campbell.[44] Is not the real reason that if it protects you and other composers, there is an incentive to you to compose?

Mr. Sousa. Oh, yes; I can compose better if I get a thousand dollars than I can for six hundred. [Laughter.]

Mr. Campbell. That is the real reason.

[Sousa did not make any statements on Thursday, June 7, but on Friday, June 8 he made occasional interjections. These include a remark on the differences in "notation" between a piano roll and sheet music, his experience with international copyright, and a few testy comments in response to the presentation of an unauthorized recording of one of his

---

43   Senator Reed Smoot, a Republican, represented Utah from 1903-33. A prominent Mormon, Smoot became (after a good deal of controversy) the first member of Congress affiliated with the Church of Jesus Christ of Latter-day Saints.

44   William Wildman Campbell, a Republican, represented Ohio's fifth congressional district from 1905-07.

marches as an exhibit. He also stated that he had never been approached by the recording companies to negotiate a contract, an assertion that led to a heated exchange when S. T. Cameron, a representative from the American Gramophone Company, testified to the contrary.]

Mr. Webb. I was going to ask, how do you get Mr. Sousa's pieces? Do you pay him for it?

Mr. Cameron. We do not; no, sir.

Mr. Webb. Who does?

Mr. Cameron. The Victor Talking Machine Company has an exclusive contract with Mr. Sousa, and he gets paid for that. He did not tell you that the other day.

Mr. Sousa. That is absolutely untrue.

Mr. Cameron. If it is untrue I am ready to beg the gentleman's pardon. I had that information direct this morning, but I will gladly withdraw it upon Mr. Sousa's word—gladly. I do not want to make any misstatement.

Mr. Sousa. I have never received one penny for my compositions from any kind of talking machine, nor have I ever made a contract with any of those companies.

Mr. Cameron. I did not state that. I stated that Mr. Sousa, with his band, played into the horns of these instruments to make these records and was paid for doing it.

Mr. Sousa. An organization known as "Sousa and his band," employed just as any other body of musicians, in which I have no part myself, plays into the instrument. That goes under arrangements made with the management of that organization to play anybody's compositions that these firms may elect; it may be a noncopyrighted piece or a copyrighted piece, or anything else.

Mr. Cameron. I am very glad Mr. Sousa stated that. He says that he does not play his own music only, but his band stands ready to play any other man's music, copyrighted or not copyrighted, into these machines.

Mr. Sousa. Not myself; no.

Senator Latimer.[45] I want to ask a question of Mr. Sousa, so as to clear the matter up a little further. The statement is that you have a band that plays into these instruments, and you, I understand, have denied that?

---

45 Senator Asbury C. Latimer, a Democrat, represented South Carolina from 1903–08.

Mr. Sousa. No, sir; I do not deny that "Sousa and his band," an organization known as "Sousa and his band," play for talking machines.

Senator Latimer. Do I understand you to say that you have no connection with that band?

Mr. Sousa. I am the director of that band, but I have no personal part in the performance of those pieces. I have never been in the gramophone company's office in my life.

Mr. McGavin. Do you play for anyone else besides the Victor Talking Machine Company?

Mr. Sousa. My manager has a contract with them for so many performances.

Senator Latimer. You have an interest in the band and receive profit from it?

Mr. Sousa. Yes; surely.

Mr. Webb. You allow your name to be used all over the country?

Mr. Sousa. In the performance of these pieces, certainly.

Mr. Cameron. That was my charge.

Mr. Herbert. In regard to the untruth the gentleman has stated—

The Chairman. Do you want to deny any statement that he has made?

Mr. Herbert. Yes. In regard to this, naturally it would be inferred that it was the same case with me. In fact, he mentioned us two together. A band played into these instruments, calling itself "Victor Herbert's band," and I sued the talking machine company. That is what I got out of the company.

Mr. Cameron. The gentleman misunderstood me. I have made no statement in regard to him, and I have no information in regard to him one way or the other.

Mr. Currier. He made no charge against you. Mr. Herbert.

Mr. Herbert. Since our names have been linked all the time, I thought he intended what he said to apply to me also.

Mr. Pettit.[46] I would like to say to Mr. Cameron in regard to his statement about the Victor Company and Mr. Sousa, that whenever we have used Mr. Sousa's music, or rather whenever we used his band on Victor records, we always paid him for it—that is, we pay Mr. Sousa for playing.

---

46   Horace Pettit testified on behalf of the Victor Talking Machine Company.

Senator Latimer. I want to bring out one point in connection with that. In making these records, if I understand, now, Mr. Sousa has a band that represents him, playing these pieces, and you pay for that music when you get it, or do you not?

Mr. Cameron. Whoever employed Mr. Sousa pays for it.

Senator Latimer. Then it is paid for when you get these records?

Mr. Cameron. I do not wish to be misunderstood. We can take and do take one of Sousa's marches and have another band, with which Mr. Sousa is not connected, play, and we make the record; and in that case Mr. Sousa does not get any of the compensation whatever. None of that goes to him.

Mr. Webb. But you do not advertise it as being played by Sousa's band?

Mr. Cameron. Not at all. We advertise it as Sousa's march.

Mr. Webb. You advertise it as a march by Sousa as a composer, but played by somebody else as the executant?

Mr. Cameron. Yes. That is recognized as such a valuable thing to the composer, that John Philip Sousa has been to the office of the American Gramophone Company, in years gone by, with advance scores, and asked them to send them out, to advertise and help John Philip Sousa along. He will not deny it. Moreover, we are flooded to-day with artists that are struggling on the lower rounds of the ladder, that are not as high up as John Philip Sousa was a few years ago, either, begging us to do the same thing for them. I mention that to show you that even John Philip Sousa, before he got where he bestrode the musical world like a colossus, even he recognized the advertising value of the talking machine to a composer. We are not doing him such a great injury.

Mr. Sousa. I would like to say, Mr. Chairman, that the gramophone, these talking machines, are really of very recent date. I believe the gentleman will agree with me when I say that if we go back fifteen years or sixteen years ago, we looked upon them purely as a toy. I remember the first one I saw here in this city where I was born. A gentleman had a man bark into it, and it was a remarkable thing to hear this thing bark—

The Acting Chairman. I would suggest, Mr. Sousa, that you are taking up this gentleman's time. Unless you want to specifically deny something that he has said, or ask a question, it is hardly fair to him.

Mr. Sousa. If I ever did allow the Gramophone Company to do it, it was because I did not think it was as important to them or to me as I do now.

Mr. Cameron. Please do not confuse us with the Gramophone Company. It is a different thing.

Mr. Currier. Do you wish to deny that you are a musical colossus? [Laughter.]

Mr. Sousa. No. I will admit that. [Laughter.]

"The Menace of Mechanical Music"

Source: *Appleton's Magazine* 8, September 1906, 278–84.

In this his most well-known essay, Sousa begins with biting parody before outlining his arguments on mechanical reproduction rights in earnest. Ever the patriot, Sousa clearly relished the chance to be a scholar of Constitutional law even as he defended his intellectual property and financial security.[47]

What might be called a fair reproduction of   Will the infant be put to sleep by the
Jove's prerogative   machinery?

---

47   Further on this essay and the controversies surrounding it see Warfield, "Menace."

Sweeping across the country with the speed of a transient fashion in slang or Panama hats, political war cries or popular novels, comes now the mechanical device to sing for us a song or play for us a piano, in substitute for human skill, intelligence, and soul. Only by harking back to the day of the roller skate or the bicycle craze, when sports of admitted utility ran to extravagance and virtual madness, can we find a parallel to the way in which these ingenious instruments have invaded every community in the land. And if we turn from this comparison in pure mechanics to another which may fairly claim a similar proportion of music in its soul, we may observe the English sparrow, which, introduced and welcomed in all innocence, lost no time in multiplying itself to the dignity of a pest, to the destruction of numberless native song birds, and the invariable regret of those who did not stop to think in time.[48]

On a matter upon which I feel so deeply, and which I consider so far-reaching, I am quite willing to be reckoned an alarmist, admittedly swayed in part by personal interest, as well as by the impending harm to American musical art. I foresee a marked deterioration in American music and musical taste, an interruption in the musical development of the country, and a host of other injuries to music in its artistic manifestations, by virtue—or rather by vice—of the multiplication of the various music-reproducing machines. When I add to this that I myself and every other popular composer are victims of a serious infringement on our clear moral rights in our own work, I but offer a second reason why the facts and conditions should be made clear to everyone, alike in the interest of musical art and of fair play.

It cannot be denied that the owners and inventors have shown wonderful aggressiveness and ingenuity in developing and exploiting these remarkable devices. Their mechanism has been steadily and marvelously improved, and they have come into very extensive use. And it must be admitted that where families lack time or inclination to acquire musical technic, and to hear

---

48   Sousa references a number of issues in American life at the time in this paragraph. For reference, the "Bicycle Craze" swept the United States in the 1890s with the introduction of the "safety" bicycle, a chain-driven bicycle with two equal-sized wheels. It was followed in the first decade of the 1900s by the "Roller Skating Craze"—a health and recreation fad itself linked to women's fashion and sexuality—which was about to peak when Sousa wrote this essay. The English sparrow was introduced to North America in the 1850s to combat insects, but within a short time were themselves seen as an invasive threat to native songbirds.

public performances, the best of these machines supply a certain amount of satisfaction and pleasure.

But heretofore, the whole course of music, from its first day to this, has been along the line of making it the expression of soul states; in other words, of pouring into it soul. Wagner, representing the climax of this movement, declared again and again, "I will not write even one measure of music that is not thoroughly sincere."[49]

From the days when the mathematical and mechanical were paramount in music, the struggle has been bitter and incessant for the sway of the emotional and the soulful. And now, in this the twentieth century, come these talking and playing machines, and offer again to reduce the expression of music to a mathematical system of megaphones, wheels, cogs, disks, cylinders, and all manner of revolving things, which are as like real art as the marble statue of Eve is like her beautiful, living, breathing daughters.

Away back in the fifteenth and sixteenth centuries rebellion had its start against musical automatics, Palestrina proving in his compositions, that music is life, not mathematics; and Luther showing, in his sublime hymns for congregational use and in his adaptations of secular melody for the church, that music could be made the pouring out of the souls of the many in one grand, eternal song. From the days of these pioneers, all great workers in the musical vineyard have given their best powers to the development of fruit, ever finer and more luscious, and in the doing have brought their art near and nearer to the emotional life of man.

The nightingale's song is delightful because the nightingale herself gives it forth. The boy with a penny whistle and glass of water may give an excellent imitation, but let him persist, he is sent to bed as a nuisance. Thunder inspires awe in its connection with nature, but two lusty bass drummers can drive you mad by what might be called a fair reproduction of Jove's prerogative. I doubt if a dramatist could be inspired to write a tragedy by witnessing the mournful development and dénouement of "Punch and Judy"; or an actress improve her delineation of heroic character by hearing the sobs of a Parisian

---

49   This does not seem to be a direct quote from Wagner's writings, but it may be a reference to his essay "Wibelingen or Wibelungen" which addresses the sincerity and truthfulness of "the folk" in their expressive capabilities.

doll. Was Garner led to study language and manners of the orang-outang and his kin by watching the antics of a monkey-on-a- stick?

It is the living, breathing example alone that is valuable to the student and can set into motion his creative and performing abilities. The ingenuity of a phonograph's mechanism may incite the inventive genius to its improvement, but I could not imagine that a performance by it would ever inspire embryotic Mendelssohns, Beethovens, Mozarts, and Wagners to the acquirement of technical skill, or to the grasp of human possibilities in the art.

Elson, in his "History of American Music," says: "The true beginnings of American music—seeds that finally grew into a harvest of native composition—must be sought in a field almost as unpromising as that of the Indian music itself—the rigid, narrow, and often commonplace psalm-singing of New England."[50]

Step by step through the centuries, working in an atmosphere almost wholly monopolized by commercial pursuit, America has advanced art to such a degree that to-day she is the Mecca toward which journey the artists of all nations. Musical enterprises are given financial support here as nowhere else in the universe, while our appreciation of music is bounded only by our geographical limits.

This wide love for the art springs from the singing school, secular or sacred; from the village band, and from the study of those instruments that are nearest the people. There are more pianos, violins, guitars, mandolins, and banjos among the working classes of America than in all the rest of the world, and the presence of these instruments in the homes has given employment to enormous numbers of teachers who have patiently taught the children and inculcated a love for music throughout the various communities.

Right here is the menace in machine-made music! The first rift in the lute has appeared. The cheaper of these instruments of the home are no longer being purchased as formerly, and all because the automatic music devices are usurping their places.

And what is the result? The child becomes indifferent to practice, for when music can be heard in the homes without the labor of study and close

---

50   Elson, *American Music*, 1.

application, and without the slow process of acquiring a technic, it will be simply a question of time when the amateur disappears entirely, and with him a host of vocal and instrumental teachers, who will be without field or calling.

Great Britain is experiencing this decline in domestic music and the English press is discussing it seriously in its editorials. A recent writer in the London *Spectator* dwells at considerable length upon the prevailing condition, and points to the novel as a sign of the times. The present-day fashionable writer of society fiction, he declares, does not find it necessary to reënforce his heroine with vocal accomplishment, "as in the good old days." He ascribes the passing of home performance, both vocal and instrumental, to the newborn love of athletics among the maids of Albion, together with the introduction of the phonograph as a mechanical substitute for amateur performances.

He believes that the exclamation of the little boy who rushed into his mother's room with the appeal: "O mamma, come into the drawing-room; there is a man in there playing the piano with his hands," is far less extravagant than many similar excursions into the domain of humorous and human prophecy. He states from observation, that music has been steadily declining in Great Britain as a factor in domestic life, and that the introduction of machine-made music into the household is largely helping to assist in the change.

While a craze for athletics may have something to do with the indifference of the amateur performer in Great Britain, I do not believe it is much of a factor in this country. It is quite true that American girls have followed the athletic trend of the nation for a long while; at the same time they have made much headway in music, thanks to studious application. But let the mechanical music-maker be generally introduced into the homes; hour for hour these same girls will listen to the machine's performance, and, sure as can be, lose finally all interest in technical study.

Under such conditions the tide of amateurism cannot but recede, until there will be left only the mechanical device and the professional executant. Singing will no longer be a fine accomplishment; vocal exercises, so important a factor in the curriculum of physical culture, will be out of vogue!

Then what of the national throat? Will it not weaken? What of the national chest? Will it not shrink?

When a mother can turn on the phonograph with the same ease that she applies to the electric light, will she croon her baby to slumber with sweet lullabies, or will the infant be put to sleep by machinery?

Children are naturally imitative, and if, in their infancy, they hear only phonographs, will they not sing, if they sing at all, in imitation and finally become simply human phonographs—without soul or expression? Congregational singing will suffer also, which, though crude at times, at least improves the respiration of many a weary sinner and softens the voices of those who live amid tumult and noise.

The host of mechanical reproducing machines, in their mad desire to supply music for all occasions, are offering to supplant the illustrator in the class room, the dance orchestra, the home and public singers and players, and so on. Evidently they believe no field too large for their incursions, no claim too extravagant. But the further they can justify those claims, the more noxious the whole system becomes.

Just so far as a spirit of emulation once inspired proud parent or aspiring daughter to send for the music teacher when the neighbor child across the way began to take lessons, the emulation is turning to the purchase of a rival piano player in each house, and the hope of developing the local musical personality is eliminated.

The country dance orchestra of violin, guitar, and melodeon had to rest at times, and the resultant interruption afforded the opportunity for general sociability and rest among the entire company. Now a tireless mechanism can keep everlastingly at it, and much of what made the dance a wholesome recreation is eliminated.

The country band, with its energetic renditions, its loyal support by local merchants, its benefit concerts, band wagon, gay uniforms, state tournaments, and the attendant pride and gayety, is apparently doomed to vanish in the general assault on personality in music.

There was a time when the pine woods of the north were sacred to summer simplicity, when around the camp fire at night the stories were told and the songs were sung with a charm all their own. But even now the invasion of the north has begun, and the ingenious purveyor of canned music is urging the sportsman, on his way to the silent places with gun and rod, tent and canoe, to take with him some disks, cranks, and cogs to sing to him as he sits by the firelight, a thought as unhappy and incongruous as canned salmon by a trout brook.

In the prospective scheme of mechanical music, we shall see man and maiden in a light canoe under the summer moon upon an Adirondack lake with a gramophone caroling love songs from amidships. The Spanish cavalier must abandon his guitar and serenade his beloved with a phonograph under his arm.

Shall we not expect that when the nation once more sounds its call to arms and the gallant regiment marches forth, there will be no majestic drum major, no serried ranks of sonorous trombones, no glittering array of brass, no rolling of drums? In their stead will be a huge phonograph, mounted on a 100 H. P. automobile, grinding out "The Girl I left Behind Me," "Dixie," and "The Stars and Stripes Forever."

How the soldiers' bosoms will swell at the thought that they are being led into the strife by a machine! And when in camp at night, they are gathered about the cheery fire, it will not be:

> Give us a song, the soldier cried.

It will not be:

> They sang of love, and not of fame,
> Forgot was Britain's glory;
> Each heart recalled a different name,
> But all sang "Annie Laurie."[51]

But it will be:

Whir–whir–whir–Song by the Bungtown Quartet: "Your Name is Dennis."

Shades of Alexander, of Washington, of Napoleon, of Wellington, of Grant, and of the other immortal heroes! Never again will the soldier hear the defiant call of the bugle to battle, and the historic lines must be changed to:

"Gentlemen of the French guards, turn on your phonographs first."

And the future d'Auteroches will reply:

"Sir, we never turn on our phonographs first; please to turn yours first."[52]

---

51   Bayard Taylor, "The Song of the Camp" (1856), opening line and verse 5.

52   This refers to an incident during the Battle of Fontenoy (May 11, 1745) related by Voltaire and others. In an act of chivalry the leader of the English troops called out "Gentlemen of the French Guards, fire!" The Comte d'Auteroches, lieutenant of the French Grenadiers replied "Fire yourselves, gentlemen—the French Guards never fire first!" The side that actually fired first varies from source to source.

It is at the fireside that we look for virtue and patriotism; for songs that stir the blood and fire the zeal; for songs of home, of mother, and of love, that touch the heart and brighten the eye. Music teaches all that is beautiful in this world. Let us not hamper it with a machine that tells the story day by day, without variation, without soul, barren of the joy, the passion, the ardor that is the inheritance of man alone.

And now a word on a detail of personal interest which has a right to be heard because it voices a claim for fair play, far-reaching in its effects beyond the personal profit of one or many individuals. I venture to say that it will come as an entire surprise to almost every reader to learn that the composers of the music now produced so widely by the mechanical players of every sort draw no profit from it whatever. Composers are entirely unprotected by the copyright laws of the United States as at present written on the statute books and interpreted by the courts. The composer of the most popular waltz or march of the year must see it seized, reproduced at will on wax cylinder, brass disk, or strip of perforated paper, multiplied indefinitely, and sold at large profit all over the country, without a penny of remuneration to himself for the use of this original product of his brain.

It is this fact that is the immediate occasion of the present article, for the whole subject has become acute by reason of certain proposed legislation in Congress at Washington. The two phases of the subject— fair play to music and fair play to musicians—are so naturally connected that I have not hesitated to cover the legal and the artistic sides of the question in a single discussion.

A new copyright bill was introduced in Congress at the last session, a joint committee met on June 6th, to hear arguments on the bill as presented, and the following paragraph was cause for lively discussion on the part of the various talking-machine interests and composers represented:

Paragraph (G) of Section I, which provides "that the copyright secured by this Act shall include the sole and exclusive right to make, sell, distribute, or let for hire any device, contrivance, or appliance especially adapted in any manner whatsoever to reproduce to the ear the whole or any material part of any work published and copyrighted after this Act shall have gone into effect, or by means of any such device or appliance publicly to reproduce to the ear the whole or any material part of such work."

I was among those present, and became particularly keen on the efforts of opposing interests to impress upon the committee by specious argument and fallacious interpretation that the composer of music had no rights under the Constitution that they were bound to respect; and that remedial legislation was wholly out of the question until the Constitution had first been amended.

One gentleman went the length of declaring that he would never have worked out his reproducing apparatus, had he not felt confident that the Constitution gave him the right to appropriate the brightest efforts of the American composer, and he voiced the belief that any act giving the composer ownership in his own property would be most unconstitutional.

Asked if he claimed the right to take one of my compositions and use it in connection with his mechanical device without compensation to myself, his unselfish reply was: "Under the Constitution and all the laws of the land, I say Yes, decidedly!"

Asked if he was not protected in his patents, his answer was promptly in the affirmative, but he seemed wholly unable to grasp the proposition that a composer should ask for similar protection on his creative work.

Asked finally if he desired the Constitution amended, he replied magnanimously: "No, sir, I want the Constitution to stand as it is."

Of course it must not be overlooked that in the United States Circuit Court of Appeals a case has just been decided adversely to the composer's rights in the profits accruing from the use of his compositions on the talking and playing machines, but this case awaits final adjudication, on appeal, in the United States Supreme Court. Judges Lacombe, Coxe, and Townsend rendered a decision as follows:

"We are of the opinion that a perforated paper roll, such as is manufactured by defendant, is not a copy of complainant's staff notation, for the following reasons:

"It is not a copy in fact; it is not designed to be read or actually used in reading music as the original staff notation is; and the claim that it may be read, which is practically disproved by the great preponderance of evidence, even if true, would establish merely a theory or possibility of use, as distinguished from an actual use. The argument that because the roll is a notation or record of the music, it is, therefore, a copy, would apply to the disk of the phonograph or the barrel of the organ, which, it must be admitted, are not copies of the sheet music. The perforations in the rolls are not a varied form of symbols substituted for the symbols used by the author. They are mere adjuncts of a valve mechanism in a machine. In fact, the machine, or musical playing device, is the thing which appropriates the author's property and publishes it by producing the musical sounds, thus conveying the author's composition to the public."

May I ask, does this machine appropriate the author's composition without human assistance? Is the machine a free agent? Does it go about to seek whom it may devour? And if, as quoted above, the machine "publishes it," is not the owner of the machine responsible for its acts?

Is copyright simply represented by a sheet of music? Is there no more to it than the silent notation? The little black spots on the five lines and spaces, the measured bars, are merely the record of birth and existence of a musical thought. These marks are something beyond the mere shape, the color, the length of the pages. They are only one form of recording the coming into the world of a newly fashioned work, which, by the right of authorship, inherent and constitutional, belongs to him who conceived it. They are no more the living theme which they record than the description of a beautiful woman is the woman herself.

Should the day come that the courts will give me the absolute power of controlling my compositions, which I feel is now mine under the Constitution, then I am not so sure that my name will appear as often as at present in the catalogues of the talking and playing machines.

Evidently Judge Abinger, of the English bar, believes in the doctrine of substance, for he says:

"The most unlettered in music can distinguish one song from another; and the mere adaptation of the air, either by changing it to a dance, or by transferring it from one instrument to another, does not, even to common apprehension, alter the original subject. The ear tells you that it is the same. The original air requires the aid of a genius for its construction; but a mere mechanic in music can make the adaptation or accompaniment. Substantially the piracy is where the appropriated music, though adapted to a different purpose from that of the original, may still be recognized by the ear."

Again the English court says:

"The composition of a new air or melody is entitled to protection; and the appropriation of the whole, or of any substantial part of it, without the license of the author, is a piracy, and the adaptation of it, either by changing it to a dance, or by transferring it from one instrument to another, if the ear detects the same air, in the same arrangement, will not relieve it from the penalty."

The section of the Constitution on which my whole legal contention is based provides:

"The Congress shall have power to secure for limited time to authors and inventors the exclusive right to their respective writings and discoveries."[53]

And my claim is, that the words "exclusive" and "writings," particularly the latter, are so broad in their meaning that they cover every point raised by existing copyright laws, even to the unauthorized use of musical compositions by mechanical-reproducing apparatuses, and all this because these two words deal, not alone with the letter, but with the spirit as well.

But let the ambiguities in the text of law be what they may; let there be of legal quips and quirks as many as you please, for the life of me I am puzzled to know why the powerful corporations controlling these playing and talking machines are so totally blind to the moral and ethical questions involved. Could anything be more blamable, as a matter of principle, than to take an artist's composition, reproduce it a thousandfold on their machines, and deny him all participation in the large financial returns, by hiding back of the diaphanous pretense that in the guise of a disk or roll, his composition is not his property?

Do they not realize that if the accredited composers, who have come into vogue by reason of merit and labor, are refused a just reward for their efforts, a condition is almost sure to arise where all incentive to further creative work is lacking, and compositions will no longer flow from their pens; or where they will be compelled to refrain from publishing their compositions at all, and control them in manuscript? What, then, of the playing and talking machines?

---

53   Article I, Section 8 (Clause 8) of the United States Constitution reads: "The Congress shall have Power... To promote the Progress of Science and useful Arts, by securing for limited Times to Authors and Inventors the exclusive Right to their respective Writings and Discoveries."

"The Year in Music"

Source: *Town Topics* (New York City), December 6, 1906, 45–6, in *SPB* 21:2, 45.[54]

A farcical conclusion to his more serious essays on the "menace" of recorded music, this essay describes a dystopian future for musical life in America. When he mentions that the publishers of Gounod's Faust *could not afford to attend the performance at half-price, he is getting at the heart of the copyright and royalties problems about which he had testified before Congress earlier that year.*

The year in music has been rich in promise and prodigal in fulfilment. The time is pregnant with harmonic happenings, and reincarnated art is nestling in the lap of Melpomene.[55] During the season no less than 23,023 new talking-machine conservatories have been established throughout our broad country, and—to paraphrase slightly—"the time of the pumping of pedals is here, and the voice of the phonograph is heard in our land."

The advantages of the new conservatories are manifold. The inability to tell a barcarole from a boiler explosion, a rallentando from a railroad smash-up, is no barrier to matriculation or graduation. Thirty seconds constitute a semester, and sixty, a full course. Diplomas are awarded when the students are able to decipher the titles of the compositions on disk, roll or cylinder. The claim of the school is: fixed routine of mechanical ingenuity triumphs over the idiosyncrasies of mere man, and automatic action proves the uselessness of eyes and hands and soul.

'Tis well!

Fiddles and flutes, cornets and contraltos are to be no more, and the chaste solicitation of the shy bassoon will be heard but by memory's ear. The boundless domain of human endeavor gives way to the Harlem flat of a wax cylinder. The soul-laden song of the daughters of man is supplanted by the whirling disk of the gramophone. The phonograph's horn is the trumpet of Fame, and Melody's life is a cog and a wheel. Judging by the progress made by the champions of self-playing instruments, it will be but a short time

---

54   This essay was also reprinted in the *Musical Courier* (New York City), December 19, 1906, in *SPB* 21:2, 191.

55   Melpomene is the ancient Greek muse of singing and of tragedy.

when every man, woman and child of our ninety-odd million will own a talking-machine, and life in America will be one grand, sweet song.

The first important musical function of the year was the great concert given on January the second, by the New York Phonograph Symphony Orchestra, under the auspices of Mrs. W. Wing Sweeps and the ladies of the Dust-pan Social Coterie. At the hour of the performance the main hall of the Penny Vaudeville Phonograph Galleries was crowded to suffocation. As Professor Punk, conductor of the famous body of young and ambitious phonographs, made his appearance, he was received with vociferous applause, and, rapping for attention, he admonished the audience in a few well-chosen words not to forget to drop the usual penny in the slot; the guests carefully adjusted the hearing tubes in their respective auditory meatuses and waited for the orchestra to begin the performance. Professor Punk rapped attention for the second time, there was a jingle of countless pennies, and the body of talking-machines was launched into the intricacies of Beethoven's immortal Ninth. A look of ecstatic joy suffused the face of each listener; the immortal Ninth, played as Beethoven himself would have played it—on the phonograph—was ringing in their ears.[56] It was grand, it was marvelous, it was awe-inspiring!

Mr. Sweeps held the watch and timed the entire field, the run being made in 4.10; the allegro non troppo was done in 52 seconds, the molto vivace in 1 minute 8⅛ seconds, the adagio molto e cantabile reached the three-quarter post in 1 minute 26 seconds, and a glorious rush down the homestretch was made in 43⅜ seconds, thus establishing a new record for the Beethoven stable of symphonies. Strong men wept and proud beauties, oblivious of Mrs. Grundy, hugged Professor Punk and the better-looking of the phonographs.[57] It was an evening long to be remembered in the art life of the metropolis.

The mastodonic affair of February 13, when Haydn's mighty work, "The Creation," was given by the Choral Organgrinders' Society and the

---

56   Beethoven's Ninth (or even just the "Ode to Joy") does not seem to have been recorded by 1906, but Victor did have its own house orchestra (perhaps Sousa's "New York Phonograph Symphony Orchestra"), which began making recordings in 1903.

57   1906 saw the unveiling of the Victrola, Victor Talking Machine's enormously popular phonograph, perhaps the "better-looking of the phonograph" to which he refers. Further on the Victrola see Holms, *Music Technology*, 327.

Phonograph Orchestra combined, made lovers of oratorio sit up and take notice. Nothing like it was ever heard before. Although the pure Italian school of organgrinding seems almost too emotional for the stately numbers of the great school of sacred music, still there was a leaven and a recompense in the beautiful work of the four solo self-playing pianos—Style N. G., price one twenty-five. The great chorus, "The Heavens Are Telling the Glory of the Phonograph," which was encored seven times, was given this up-to-date alteration in the line by the celebrated author of "Everybody His Own Poet."

It has been a banner year in prodigies. From every section of the country have come reports of discoveries of musical geniuses that have taxed the credulity of the most trusting. Early in the season a most sensational story emanated from Frog Hollow, Kansas; it appears that a newly-married man, without any previous knowledge of music or the comforts of home, played the Lohengrin Wedding March on the pianola with one foot, while he kicked the stuffing out of his mother-in-law with the other. This wonderful feat was for a time accepted *cum grano salis*, but a published diagram showing the position of the pianola and the mother-in-law dispelled all doubts. The memory of this most artistic achievement still lingers as an example of the possibilities of the pianola at the feet of the earnest student.

The leading metropolitan journals of February 23 contained intensely interesting despatches from Squash Run, Arizona, anent an astounding exhibition by a child of seven. This little Algernon Augustus, the offspring of Mr. and Mrs. John de Smith, well-known social leaders of that city, had evinced an intuitive knowledge of harmonic structure and melodic grace that mystified alike the savant, the scientist and the dilettante. Until February 22, the child had never heard or seen a phonograph. On that eventful day he accompanied his mother to the talking-machine recital, given by Miss S. Sudds, of Rattlesnake Gulch, where the little tot fairly drank in the performance of the contributing artists. After the plaudits for the efforts of Miss Sudds subsided, Baby Algernon was strangely silent; a far-away look appeared in his bright blue eyes and he rose and walked toward the phonograph, as if in a dream. Everyone present realized that there was something doing. Dressed in his little knickers of white, his blond curls forming a halo around his head, little Algernon Augustus slowly mounted a chair and stood breast-high before the instrument. The morning-glory shape and variegated coloring of the search-light horn appealed to the love of nature in him; with a resistless impulse he "hollered" into it as if it were a rain-barrel, then waited. Suddenly his eyes spied the crank, quickly he turned it, once—twice—three times, then with his chubby little hand, he moved the lever, and forth gushed a limpid stream of melody, printed on the disk as the "Intermezzo from Cavalleria Rusticana" by Pietro Mascagni. The stillness of death pervaded the room; nothing was heard save the sounds called into being by little Algernon Augustus. At the conclusion of the composition there was one mighty burst of applause, the child was smothered with kisses and everyone present realized that a new and transcendental star had appeared in the musical firmament.

In making an investigation into the ancestry of little Algernon Augustus, it was discovered that his great-great-grandfather had occupied the most responsible position of organ-grinder-in-chief to the first Akoond of Swat.[58] At the same time it came to light that Algernon's mother, three months before the birth of this wonderful child, had accidently swallowed a toy music-box, which had been wound up to run for an indefinite period. It is therefore not difficult to understand that the power of the little genius to bring out the soulful and the temperamental qualities of the phonograph was the result of combined hereditary and prenatal influences. It is the intention of Mr. and Mrs. de Smith to allow little Algernon Augustus to be heard in concert at a later date, assisted by agents of the various talking-machine companies.

The very oldest theatre-goer in New York cannot recall a scene of greater brilliancy and enthusiasm than was witnessed at the closing performance of the Opera. The grand Palace of Automatic Music contained the most fashionable gathering of the Winter. The audience and the performance were the finest of a season that stands alone in the annals of the lyric drama. No single event, since Melody meandered down the corridors of Time, can trot in the same class. The magnet that drew beautiful women and gallant men to the home of the Automatic Opera was the all-star phonograph cast in Gounod's "Faust," a gem performance of a gem work.

---

58   Akoond of Swat refers both to a Persian dignitary—Akhund Abdul Ghaffur (1793-1878)—and a nonsense poem by Edward Lear (1812-1888).

The Cast

Marguerite. . . . . .Mme. Columbia Cylinder

Siebel. . . . . .Mlle. Victor Disk

Martha . . . . Mlle. Zeno Phone

Faust . . . . Sig. La Voce del Suo Padrone[59]

Mephistopheles. . . . . Duplex two horn Phonograph

Valentine. . . . . M. Graphophone

Mme. Columbia Cylinder's performance of Marguerite was poetical in the extreme and brought tears to the eyes of every automatic player in the audience.

She sang without a scratch.

In the scene where the fair heroine first meets her betrayer, *Faust*, a slight mistake happened: the human musical director, with all the faults of omission and commission common to his species, adjusted the wrong cylinder for *Marguerite*, and in reply to *Faust's* well-known pleading, "High-born and lovely maid," instead of "No, my lord, not a lady am I," came in rasping tones "If you ain't got no money, you needn't come 'round."[60] A few of the less musical in the audience suppressed a titter with difficulty, but were quickly shamed into silence by a warning hiss from the students and music-lovers present.

At the meeting of *Valentine* and *Mephistopheles*, after the former smashed *Mephistopheles's* guitar, a most appropriate bit of dramatic effect was produced by a ten-inch disk's playing "Throw him down, McCluskey," and in the prison scene there was a beautiful domestic touch added to the evening, for at the closing measures, in response to repeated demands on the part of her audience, *Marguerite* and *Faust* sang with beautifully blended voices "Baby Mine."[61]

To quote the words of the eminent critic of the *Phonograph Operagoer*, the performance was the finest rendition of "Faust" ever given in New York. The

59   This character references a Victor advertising slogan and 1895 painting by Francis Barraud where a dog looks questioningly into the horn of an Edison Bell phonograph thinking he is hearing "His Master's Voice."

60   Arthur Collins wrote the popular song "If You Ain't Got No Money, You Needn't Come 'Round" in 1899. It had been recorded prior to 1906.

61   These are both references to popular songs. J. W. Kelly wrote "Throw Him Down, McCluskey" in 1890 and Charles Mackay wrote "Baby Mine" in 1874.

critic continues: "However, we should like to inform the musical conductor that when *Valentine* was carried off dead at the end of the fourth act, we do not consider it in good taste to allow a chorus cylinder to say, 'Rattle his bones, over the stones, he is only a pauper whom nobody owns.' We are willing to admit that the line has a certain musical value, is euphonious and very direct in its meaning, but if it was necessary to add to that which Gounod had already written and the phonograph had improved upon, it would have been more in sympathy with the audience assembled if a song such as 'Climbing Up the Golden Stairs,' or 'Is There Room Among the Angels?' had been used as the climax of the scene.[62]

"*Mephistopheles's* work was unusually fine and places him in the very first rank of phonographs. It is true that his crank slipped once or twice and that a careless stage-hand dropped a brick on his diaphragm, which slightly interfered with his lower notes, but even that detracted but little from the unusual excellence of his performance. Certainly, after his song, 'The Calf of Gold,' which was rendered with force, power and temperament, nothing could have been more realistic and appropriate than his encore, 'The Cows Are in the Corn,' which was given with bucolic power and bovine playfulness.[63] *Siebel* was forced to omit the solo, 'In the Language of Love,' owing to her sounding-box being warped. New York's climate is so treacherous.

"It was due to the generosity of the managers of the performance that the owners and publishers of Gounod's work were offered seats at half-price, but not having the half-price, they were unable to attend."

With a passing notice and a few remarks about the minor affairs of the year, it may be necessary to mention the Conried Opera Company, consisting of men and women, which gave some performances at the Metropolitan Opera House during the season.[64] While these representations were not entirely devoid of melodic and harmonic traits, they were sadly lacking in that unchanging perfection so noticeable in the work of the artists of the Palace

---

62 F. Heiser wrote the minstrel song "Climbing up de Golden Stairs" in 1884. The reference to "Is There Room Among the Angels?" may be to H. Theodore Driessen's song of 1872, though other songs and hymns with similar titles or lyrics are possible.

63 E. H. Harding wrote the popular song "The Cows Are in the Corn" in 1878.

64 Heinrich Conried managed the Metropolitan Opera from 1903–1908. 1903 was the same year Enrico Caruso made his debut.

of Automatic Music. There were also some performances given with what are fast becoming archaic instruments, such as the violin, flute, clarionet, trombone, etc., in combination, by organizations styling themselves the Boston Symphony Orchestra and the New York Philharmonic and others not necessary to mention. When it is considered that a whole man is necessary to manipulate each separate one of these nearly-obsolete instruments, the waste of space and energy seems appalling. These primitive orchestras may have satisfied the audiences of unmechanical days, but they show only too palpably the limitations of hand-made music as opposed to the perfection of the automatic machine.

1908–1917

Opinions and Pastimes

"How I Earned My Musical Education"

Source: *The Etude* 26, November 1908, 695–96.

> *Subtitled "A Collection of Short Articles by Representative Musicians and Teachers upon a Subject of Particular Interest to Many Students," the editor of* The Etude *included essays by Homer Norris, William C. Carl, E. E. Truette, Perlee V. Jervis, Emil Liebling, and Sousa (in that order). Sousa's submission is by far the shortest of the group, and his answer takes a markedly different angle than the others by focusing on the fallacy of "earning" an education rather than speaking autobiographically. Only the penultimate paragraph of the essay was reprinted in his collection of anecdotes* Through the Year with Sousa; *his thoughts on persistence (and "music school girls") were omitted.*

The struggle for existence after I left the parental roof and the school room was terrific. Looking back and down the Road of Life I can see the whitened homes of many of my companions who perished in the fight for place and power. Why did they fail and I succeed? From the earliest period of my professional life I had confidence in my ability to win out. A momentary reverse increased my persistency; a lack of appreciation increased my combativeness.

In reply to your query "How I earned my Musical Education," I beg to state I did not earn it. That is, my father put up for it.

It sounds wonderfully romantic and mysterious when we read of one of our profession coming into this cold, cold world with nothing on but a big yell and even lacking a golden spoon in his toothless mouth. It brings large and luminous saline tears to my sad optics when I read of the weary days and sleepless nights spent by the average musical genius in his salad days.

How I shudder when I read of one of the starters in my profession fired by a wild ambition, but minus the wherewithal, paying for his tuition by sawing wood, carrying water, digging sewers, in fact, working at any of the numerous dollar a day jobs, and then reading how finally, he, with indomitable will and dauntless courage[,] emerged from the subway of doubt and despair into the bright sunlight of full-fledged harmonist, contrapuntist, composer, theorist, violinist, pianist, organist, and yellow clarinetist.

No, Mr. Editor, between two most earnest and capable teachers, two most loving and doting parents, splendid boy companions, a rose garden of American beauties of music school girls, I cannot see where my struggle came in. Golly, but I'd like to go back and do it all over again.

"How I Built the Sousa Band"

Source: *Life* (Australia), September 1, 1911, 265–66, in *SPB* 34, 99.

The Sousa Band spent virtually all of 1911 circumnavigating the globe on a world tour. After stops in Ireland and England the band proceeded to South Africa and from there to Australia, Hawaii, and the Western United States. The international press covered the tour, and a number of the interviews and essays Sousa wrote during the trip provide insights because they were addressed to audiences that had never heard or seen him before.[65]

(Music as written by Sousa has been well known in these Southern lands for many years, and during the past few weeks Australia has had the opportunity of becoming acquainted with Music as interpreted by Sousa— in other words, with Sousa and his Band. In every city where a series of concerts has been given, considerable interest has been aroused, not merely in the programmes as arranged in sequence, but in the composition of the band itself. Mr. Sousa, who is a fairly prolific writer, was asked to explain something of his ideals and methods to the readers of "Life," and replied with the following article.)

The company of musicians which have been advertised throughout Australia under the term "Sousa and his Band," represents just about as near

---

65   Further on the 1910–11 world tour see Warfield, "Essence of Uncle Sam," 359–78.

my ideal combination of performers as I hope to see brought together, both as regards numbers and quality. The term I have just used probably suits the bill-board best, but it does not cover what I have aimed to build up—namely, a band-orchestra. It is, in reality, a fifth orchestral body, essentially modern in the best mechanical equipment, which, without arrogating the sphere of privilege of any instrumental combination hitherto known, has made a wider and often a more artistic scope for sweet, discoursive, descriptive, inspiriting, or inspiring music in all its varied forms.

I learned very early in life that if musicians depended upon musicians for their support there would be no musicians. It is necessary to heed the wishes of the masses if one hopes to succeed. The dramatic world shows the leaning of the masses in the fact that there must be a proportion of at least fifty to one, when Romance and Comedy are opposed to Tragedy. The fact is that the Drama has depended, almost since its inception, upon the will of the people, as opposed to the hothouse form of subsidised Art, artificially heated, antiseptically watered and aesthetically cultivated by long, lily-white academic hands.

In the early days of the Sousa Band the question was often asked why, with my training as a violinist and leader of string bands, I did not organise a symphony orchestra rather than a wind combination. It is, perhaps, an exemplification of the old adage that man proposes and the Almighty does the rest. Up to my twenty-fifth year it never occurred to me that I would ever be associated with a military band. My training and profession from my eleventh year had been entirely in string orchestral work, and up to my seventeenth year I was either a violinist in a large orchestra, or leading a small string band with violin or baton. About my twenty-fifth year I attracted the attention of the Government authorities at Washington, and was tendered the conductorship of the United States Marine Band, the National Band of America. I considered the offer one of great honour, especially to a man as young as myself, and immediately accepted it.

The Marine Band is formed on the lines of the vast majority of the German and English military institutions, for it was a "double-handed" band. That is, one day it played as a string orchestra, the next as a brass and reed combination; and like all outfits of that character, whose duties are a part of a function, it was vague in its instrumentation and elastic as to numbers. Duplication of the commoner instruments was oftener found than characteristic tone-colouring, and the desideratum seemed principally to confine the thematic material to three leading instruments—the clarionet, the cornet, and the euphonium, in their reed band work.

There was at first no great opportunity to depart from the traditional instrumentation of the military band. After a while, the marches which I composed and used became fairly widely known in the States, and as a composer of marches there was a demand on the part of the American public to hear the band I conducted. Therefore, President Harrison permitted me to make two tourneys [sic] of the United States with the Band, and it was during the second one that a group of capitalists of New York and Chicago made me a most flattering offer to resign the Government position, and organise a band or orchestra on lines of my own selection. That led to the formation of what is known to-day as "Sousa and His Band." These people guaranteed my salary for five years, and gave me carte blanche in organising the band.

I had before me four distinct bodies, comprising the instrumental combinations, to select from. First, the purely brass band, of which there are several excellent examples, notably the Black Dykes, the Besses o' the Barn, the Halifax Brass Band and a few others in Great Britain, France, Canada, and the United States. Secondly, the so-called military band, differing in its composition in every country, and negative as to its positive instrumentation, the best examples of which are found amongst the famous military bands of England, France and Germany. Third, the Beer Hall or Casino string band, large or small, according to its environment. Amongst the best known are the Strauss, the Ziehrer, the Komzak of Vienna, the Parlow of Germany, the Casino of Monte Carlo and the Bial of America. And fourth, the symphony orchestra, containing the essentials for a perfect performance of the classic writers such as Beethoven, Mozart, Bach, etc. The field lay before me, and the roads were very clearly defined, to that extent that I realised that each of these musical bodies was hemmed in by hidebound tradition. Any attempt to go outside the province of the brass band would rob it of its charm as a brass choir. Any effort to alter the simple instrumentation of the military band would weaken it in its most important duty—that is, as a musical body intended for the open air primarily. To change the character of the Casino orchestra and mix its potpourri of marches, waltzes and genre performances with symphonies, toccatos [sic] and the highest form of musical composition would weaken it in its sphere of continuous sunshine, and with a symphony orchestra to descend from its lofty pedestal as the exponent of the Tragic Muse and the highest form of academic Art, would be entirely out of place. I therefore decided to form a fresh combination in which I would be untrammelled by tradition and in a position to cater for the million rather than the few, and the outcome, after considerable experimenting, is the combination I have the honour to conduct.

In building up the organisation, I looked first for balance of tone, and second for multiplicity of quartets, third for virtuosity in execution, and fourth for the absolutely eclectic in programme. I realised in the beginning that those composers known as the classicists would not lend themselves at all times to my scheme of orchestration. Therefore, very little is heard at my concerts of Beethoven, Haydn or Mozart. They belong to the primitive, simple, uncomplex instrumentation of the symphony orchestra of their day, with the strings as the predominating feature, and should never be played by any combination except the one for which they were originally intended and orchestrated. A Shakespearian scholar would be outraged if absolute changes in the master's lines were made in these times; yet we have some of the big symphony conductors and arrangers who are making changes to-day in the scores of those masters of bygone days. Probably these men making these ill-advised alterations in the scores of the masters do it because they think the present age requires progress, but that progress in complexity of orchestration and harmonic device is being supplied by the big writers of to-day, such as Wagner, Richard Strauss, Elgar, D'vorak, Tschaikowsky and others, and it is in compositions of this class that the combinations of instruments such as constitute my organisation find fullest scope and are most effective.

The tone colouring of those composers is so lavish, and goes so deeply into the instrumental body, that unless you have perfect balance the full effect and intention of the composer is lost. And my own claim is that my organisation stands unique in its composition as a sound complement, being world-reaching rather than class-confined in the scope of its programmes. It is not incongruous to me to see a comedy scene immediately follow a tragic scene in Shakespeare, or any other of the master dramatists, nor laughter follow tears in the romantic drama, nor a cloud obscure the sun on a summer's day. Therefore, as I have Nature and the best examples of men as my champions, I have no hesitation in combining in my programme clever comedy with symphonic tragedy, rhythmic march or waltz with sentimental tone-pictures. Now the historian asks for the results, and are my methods justifiable? I say most emphatically, yes! For twenty years I have toured America and the countries of Europe, and now, in the ripeness of experience and reputation, we are making this all-world tour, the Australasian part of which is rapidly drawing to a close.

"No Nationalism in Music"

Source: *San Francisco Chronicle*, October 3, 1911, in *SPB* 36:1, 100.[66]

> *This is, to be sure, one of Sousa's more eyebrow-raising writings, and given the editorial response printed shortly afterwards in the source directly below, it was controversial even at the time. He had just returned from South Africa and Australia, but his experience compiling the* National, Patriotic, and Typical Airs of All Lands *(1890) seems to have made a more lasting impression on him than any music he had encountered first-hand on tour. If his final paragraph is any indication, the 1890 book skewed his views on nationalism in music away from folk or traditional music in favor of officially recognized music in the form of national anthems.*

I do not believe there is any such thing as nationalism in music. Music is a universal thing, and what is usually termed nationalism in music is really but environic [sic] suggestion. Supposing Wagner had been born in New York. Is there any reason to suppose that he would not have written just the same music as he did? And he would have had as many imitators in America as he has had in Germany, and his music would have come to be regarded as a thing native to the American soil, just as it is in Germany. But

---

66   Bierley (*Works*, 206) together with this *San Francisco Chronicle* version list this essay as a reprint of a September 2, 1911 letter to the editor of the *Westminster Gazette*. It seems likely that the original is not contained within the *Sousa Press Books*, and as Bireley seems to have gotten his information from this later printing, it has been included in lieu of the missing British printing. A broadly similar version of this letter—presented as an interview—appeared a few years earlier in *The Etude* (27 [1909], 574) with a credit to the *New York Herald*.

this is a wrong idea: music is not a growth of the soil. The fact is, when a great musical genius bursts upon the world he always has scores of imitators, who take up the master's ideas and do less with them than he did; but they spread and popularize these ideas, and they come to be regarded as something native to the soil of the master's birth, which, of course, they are not. They are simply the ideas of one musical genius.

I remember when I was playing the violin in Washington[,] John Strauss [sic] paid a visit to America, and there was a tremendous amount of enthusiasm over the waltze [sic] king.[67]

His waltzes were called Viennese, not at all because they were typical of Vienna, but simply because he came from that city. Now mark what happened. Strauss had a number of followers and imitators in America, and when he left a waltz was published called "The Strauss Autograph." It achieved a great vogue, and what was termed the Viennese style was recognized in it and warmly praised.

But, as a matter of fact, it was not Strauss who wrote the "Autograph," but a young American named [Alfred E.] Warren, who had picked up the style and spirit of the music of the Viennese school, and his work was accepted as typical of it, but it might just as well have been accepted as typical of America.

Again, look at the negro melodies of the Southern States. They certainly are regarded as native to the soil and the national product of the South; but are they? The foremost composer of these melodies, and the man who originated that particular style of composition, was a Northerner, by name Stephen Foster, who lived in the North. He wrote for negro minstrel performances in New York, and wrote of the South, for the south in all countries is the land of romance, and the rare charm with which he invested his music came to be regarded as typical of the South; but you see it was not really so.

There is, by the way, a striking peculiarity about the national airs—the great countries have short and the lesser countries long ones. England's

---

67   Johann Strauss, Jr. visited the United States in 1872, conducting at the World Peace Jubilee in Boston at the invitation (and expense) of P. S. Gilmore. The culminating moment was his leading a massive (estimates range from 17,000–20,000 musicians and singers) ensemble in a performance of the *Blue Danube* waltz.

national anthem has fourteen measures; America's contains twenty-four; the Russian hymn sixteen. Siam, on the other hand, has a national hymn which contains seventy-six measures, while San Marino has the longest national hymn in the world.—P. Sousa [sic] in *Westminster Gazette*.

Editorial Response to "No Nationalism in Music"

Source: *The Musical Times and Singing Circular*, October 1, 1911, 646.[68]

> *Sousa's suggestion that nationalism in music was nothing but "environic suggestion" was certainly an unusual position to take in the early decades of the twentieth century, let alone for someone so overtly patriotic. The letter prompted at least one critical response, as seen below. It seems unlikely that Sousa would have known about this specific item: it does not appear to be in the* Sousa Press Books, *and he never responded to it in print (which was his habit when publically criticized). This response is unsigned, though it is noteworthy that only a few pages later in the issue there is a lengthy article on a recently completed "Summer School of Folk-Song and Dance" held at Stratford-upon-Avon directed by Cecil Sharp.*

We are not aware if Mr. P. Sousa, who wrote an article on 'National music' in a recent number of the *Westminster Gazette*, is the well-known march-king. At any rate it is curious to find a writer whose name is identical with that of so intensely national a composer arguing that nationalism does not exist in music. He commences:

["]I do not believe there is any such thing as nationalism in music. Music is a universal thing, and what is usually termed nationalism in music is really but environic suggestion. Supposing Wagner had been born in New York, is there any reason to suppose that he would not have written just the same music as he did?["]

Supposing Mr. John Philip Sousa had been born in Naples, or Buda Pesth, or Pekin [sic], is there any reason to suppose that he would not have written the same marches and cake-walks? There is. The writer, if the last-quoted sentence is printed correctly, apparently considers that Wagner's inborn Germanism would be strong enough to resist all opposing

---

68   See the entry above for Sousa's original and a discussion of the dating of that essay.

influences—even 'environic suggestion.' In demolishing nationalism he seems to be establishing it more firmly than ever. Of course there is much force in 'environic suggestion,' but since the various compartments of environment happen in general to coincide with the various nations of the world, 'nationalism' is the better, and accepted, word. Mr. P. Sousa would presumably describe the American twang, French excitability, and Scottish canniness, not as national, but as environic. His instance of an American composer who so successfully imitated a Johann Strauss waltz as to delude the public tells us, as we knew already, that a pronounced type of light music can be successfully imitated, but it adds little to a discussion on nationality. The next phase of the article, which is highly kaleidoscopic, deals with Stephen Foster, a New York composer who originated a type of melody that came to be regarded as native to the soil of South America [i.e., the American South]. This does not interest us, unless it is intended as an argument that there are no negro or any other folk-melodies native to the soil!

"Sousa's Views on Woman"

Source: *Berkeley Independent*, October 4, 1911, in *SPB* 36:1, 124.

> *Growing in popularity throughout Sousa's career, the Women's Suffrage movement did not reach a climax until widespread protests in 1917 led Woodrow Wilson to take actions that would eventually lead to ratification of the Nineteenth Amendment in 1920. In this article Sousa presents his progressive attitudes on the subject, especially when pressed on the topic in person. While the modern reader might question his exact notions given the final sentence, the final paragraph as a whole has an undeniable power. The absence of a march promoting suffrage cannot be taken as indifference on Sousa's part: he consistently avoided composing on commission or suggestion (see his essay on inspiration from 1924, on page 170.*[69]

John Philip Sousa, the march king, has declared himself a champion of equal suffrage in no uncertain tones. Mrs. Wm. Keith, president of the

---

[69] It is also noteworthy that Sousa employed female vocal soloists regularly for his tours. Further see Kreitner, "A Splendid Group."

Berkeley Political Equality society, recently wrote to the famous composer asking him to compose a march for the suffrage movement. On his arrival in San Francisco, the band leader wrote Mrs. Keith the following letter:

"Your letter reached me in Honolulu on my arrival, and awakened a great interest in me, but for some reason I could not find an inspiration while sailing on the azure main to write a march worthy of such a magnificent subject as—woman. As women have controlled me ever since I was a baby and I haven't got the worst of it, I can't understand why they shouldn't control the rest of the world. It occurred to me that the proper composer to write militant music for the women's movement should be a woman, and there are a number of excellent women composers in the world, among them Mme. Chaminade, Mrs. H. H. Beach and Edith Smith.[70] I should say a composition from the pens of one of these women composers would excite a greater interest than one written by me, a mere man."

In a later conversation with Mrs. Keith in the St. Francis hotel, Sousa reiterated his approval of the system of political equality for women. He said:

"When a man who holds no property has a vote, how can we deny the ballot to a woman who owns property and pays taxes? How can a man not believe in equal suffrage, when he has a mother or wife or daughters? This is a serious subject and should not be taken flippantly. Women rule in America—the land of the free—and they always should."

"Here's Sousa's First Self-Written Interview"

Source: *Los Angeles Times*, October 16, 1911, pt. II/4, in *SPB* 36:1, 104.

The title is likely misleading in that many of Sousa's interviews were formulaic to the point where they were self-written in spirit if not fact. At least we know

---

70   Cécile Chaminade, a French pianist and composer, toured the United States in 1908 and became the first female composer awarded the Légion d'Honneur (1913). Her popularity in the United States led to the creation of numerous "Chaminade Clubs"—gatherings of amateur female musicians for Schubertiad-style performances. Amy Beach was the most famous female American composer-pianist of the era. Her *Gaelic Symphony* (1896) was the first such work written by a woman to be published in the United States. Edith Smith, really Ethel Smyth (1858-1944), championed the women's suffrage movement in England through her music. Her "The March of the Women" premiered under her own baton with the London Symphony Orchestra and the Crystal Palace Choir in 1911; it quickly became the musical rallying cry for the cause, much as Sousa hoped.

that he penned this one in its entirety. The subheading is tantalizing enough, and although the essay was relegated to the newspaper's last page it provides crucial insights into Sousa's business practices and entrepreneurial mindset.

Famous Bandmaster Tells in Own Graphic Way of the Vagaries of Concert Receipts and Round-the-World Experiences—Tales from South Africa to Texas—The Booby Prize Goes to Bakersfield.

Coming down from San Bernardino yesterday morning, John Philip Sousa dictated the story below to his secretary, who transcribed his shorthand, exactly as given herewith, on an Alexandria Hotel typewriter an hour later. Mr. Sousa gave this interview in response to a story-request from The Times Pink Sheet. Though he has written magazine articles, is the author of one or two librettos and several well-known novels, and has given innumerable newspaper chats all over the world, this is, as Mr. Sousa says, the "first newspaper interview which I wrote myself." After correcting the sheets of his own story, Mr. Sousa followed his band to Long Beach, where he gave an afternoon concert to an immense audience. He is just concluding a tour of the world, and will spend the week in Los Angeles.

"The vagaries of receipts for concerts are most interesting, and as I have probably given more concerts than any man alive or dead, perhaps some figures would be interesting to the public.

"First of all, I must explain that in my career I have given concerts under four different conditions: The first where we play with theatrical or hall managers, in which each of us take a certain percentage of the receipts and each have certain expenses relating to the giving of the concert. The second, where the attraction assumes the entire responsibility, paying rent, advertising, etc., and taking the entire receipts. The third, where our attraction has been guaranteed a fixed sum and the local manager or society assumes all the risk and takes all the receipts. The fourth is the common form of employing a band for an exposition, park or summer resort, where the band's reputation is used as a drawing-card for a number of other attractions. Of all these forms of concert giving, the first has always appealed to me as the best, and strange as it may appear, the guarantee is the least attractive, for the reason that if the house is very big the financial backer pockets a lot of money and praises the concert, whereas if the house is small he pays his losses grumblingly and openly damns the organization. Therefore, I prefer to take my chance, and be a partner in the greater gains or greater losses.

The greatest single week's receipts taken in a single city by my organization was over $24,000 in London.[71] The greatest two nights' receipts in any one place was on the occasion of my first visit to England, where we opened at Albert Hall and played Friday and Saturday evenings to $10,000, while the sale of programmes amounted to $500 more. The largest single "gross business" was in the old Convention Hall in Kansas City, where a single concert drew $5960.[72]

On the other side of the picture, the smallest sum my band ever blew a note for was in Bakersfield. Total, gross, $64.[73]

The biggest week I ever had, embracing different towns and as a result entirely different audiences, was a six-day period covering Richmond, Va., Washington, Baltimore, York, Pa., Philadelphia, New York and Boston. Our receipts here totaled $25,500.[74]

As for audiences: in open-air concerts I have had audiences at Willow Grove estimated at considerably more than 100,000 people, and also enormous gatherings at the World's Fairs in Chicago, St. Louis, Paris, Buffalo and other big international affairs. But at Glasgow, on the last

---

71 Note that the original source omits quotation marks at the opening of each paragraph from this point until the closing sentence. Sousa presumably refers to November and December of 1901 here, when the band spent fourteen days in London playing two concerts a day. The tour started in October with the Albert Hall concerts mentioned in the next sentence. Further see Beirley, *Incredible Band*, 160.

72 The band played in the "old" Kansas City Convention Hall only once: for its opening ceremony on February 22, 1899. The building burned down in April 1900 and was replaced (hence Sousa's reference to "old"). Ironically shouts for "Pryor" to play a solo (misheard as "fire") led to a brief stampede in the audience, which was calmed by the playing of "Dixie." The band played at the "new" hall on a number of subsequent tours. Further see Beirley, *Incredible Band*, 137–38.

73 The band first played in Bakersfield for a matinee concert on February 26, 1896, the likeliest date given that, in spite of nearly annual tours through California, they did not again play in that city until 1904. Sousa then returned more consistently, with visits in 1909, 1911 (on October 11, just five days prior to the publication of this interview), and 1921. Further see Bierley, *Incredible Band*, 150, 165, 172, and 184.

74 Bierley (*Incredible Band*) does not corroborate such a six-day span in the Sousa Band's itineraries prior to 1912, leaving the exact cities and dates open to question. In three cases the band visited six of the seven cities within a two-week timespan. Over nine days, November 17–25, 1897, the band played in all the locales except Richmond, in the order listed by Sousa. Again over nine days, March 24–April 1, 1900, the band played in all the locales except Boston, also in the order listed by Sousa. Over thirteen days, January 10–22, 1906, the band played in all the locales except Philadelphia, roughly in reverse order compared to Sousa's list (the closest they came to Philadelphia on that occasion was Reading and Lancaster on the way to York).

evening of my engagement in 1901, I drew by actual turn-stile count, more than 153,000 people.

Isn't that going some for a concert audience?

Among the things amusing though profitless that have occurred to me one of my choicest recollections is of Owosso, Mich.[75]

We were billed for a matinee in the town, and when we arrived the treasurer of the band came back to me, with the none-too-pleasant remark: "Pretty rotten advance sale here. Only $84."

"Never mind," I replied. "Maybe they'll buy at the window."

Before I get into the plot of the thing I must add that we were next door to the city fire department. In fact a part of it was above us.

The concert was announced for 2:15 and the doors were to open at 1:45.

About 1:40 I strolled up to the "opryhouse" and found the whole front a congested mass of people. True to rural traditions, they were there, but were intending to pay as they passed in. About sixty seconds before the ancient Cerberus opened the gate the fire-bell rang; immediately the Sousa Band became a nonentity. The intending audience and the already-paid audience alike clattered down the street, and we played to just $84 in money, but by no means to $84 worth of people.

The greatest "jump" in receipts that I ever experienced happened this year in South Africa. Our initial city was Cape Town. We opened to $600. The next day we played to $3400.

Cape Town possesses—apparently—the characteristics of our dearly beloved Missouri.

The biggest "tumble" in receipts was also in South Africa, at Johannesburg. We opened to large houses, and on the fourth evening our intake was $4000. The management refused an offer of $5000 cash for Sunday night whereupon a storm came in full South African fury and the box office gathered less than $500.

---

75   The Sousa Band played at Salisbury's Opera House in Owosso—a town in central Michigan with a population of only 6,564 in the 1890 census—on October 5, 1892, midway through their first-ever tour. Bierley (*Incredible Band*) lists no other visits until after 1911.

A misdirected sympathy for our efforts happened once in Texas. We were in the State during a terrible blizzard.[76] The theaters mostly were very cold, and the audiences, under those conditions, far from promising. We got into a small town for the matinee and there was $128 in the house while most of the audience sat wrapped like Indians in blankets—some even shrouded in quilts. My men played in their overcoats.

We began the concert. At the end of the first number—absolutely not one hand. Then followed the second number, with no applause, and then a third, fourth and fifth. Not a selection received the slightest recollection from the chilled collection of statues in front. The band retired from the stage during the intermission.

I was waited upon by the Mayor of the town, the editor of the village newspaper and the manager of the hall. The Mayor explained, hesitantly, that he thought it must be very hard on our men to play under such conditions, and that the audience, with unusually delicate feeling, had refrained from applauding so that they would not be cruelly urged to further efforts.

"But," said the Mayor, "we do want to hear 'Dixie' and 'The Stars and Stripes Forever.' Will you play them for us?"

"Play them!" I exclaimed, "Of course I'll play them, but I must have some sign that you would like to hear them. I am willing at all times to respond to an encore, but I must get some encouragement from the audience. I will play those numbers, but as encores, as I have the music of my regular programme laid out. Don't trouble yourselves to any great extent, however; merely have some man drop his foot off a chair after the next selection, and that will be sign enough for me."

"We will see to it, sir, that you have some sort of demonstration after the next number," said the editor, backing out respectfully.

The next number happened to be a long, heavy "Parsifal" excerpt.

After a second of silence at its close the uproar commenced. Feet, hands, canes, umbrellas, voices and furniture joined in the uproar. Several boys took

---

76   Bierley (*Incredible Band*) lists February 1899, February 1902, and February 1906 as the only wintertime visits to Texas prior to this interview. Of these a matinee concert in Marshall, Texas (a small town between Dallas and Shreveport) on February 10, 1899 is most likely the event in question. A massive blizzard broke many all-time low temperature records from the Gulf Coast all the way to the Northeast from February 10–14. Dallas recorded a low of -8°F and a small town across the border in Northwestern Louisiana reached -16°F. Further see Kocin, et al., "Great Arctic Outbreak."

a chair in each hand and pounded the floor until the plaster threatened to fall. I not only played "Dixie" and "The Stars and Stripes Forever," but a medley of plantation songs, two current ragtime hits and no less than four of my marches before they would let my men rest. I was in a profuse sweat at the last and most of my band's overcoats were lying over the feet of the men.

"That editor, mayor and manager must have done missionary work with a vandal's vengeance."

"Some Suggestions to Young Men"

Source: *The Violinist* 14, no. 3, December 1912, 16.

> *Included in Gertrude Bowes Peabody's "Hints to Pupils" column, Sousa here deals equally with instruments and personnel decisions, recommending that aspiring musicians choose their instruments strategically to better their chances of success. That he avoids recommending the violin must have been disheartening to Peabody's readership!*

"To the young man with talent I would advise that he study and learn to excel as a player of the saxophone, oboe, bassoon, bass and also clarinet, tuba and French horns if he desires to command a good salary in the musical profession," said Mr. Sousa the other day.

According to Mr. Sousa, a peculiar condition exists in musical circles today because of the number who are devoting their energies to the violin, cornet and trombone. He sees a way out of the difficulty for the observing ones who follow the wise course of choosing the path that is not overcrowded.

"The young man who has talent is sure of making a good salary if he goes about it in the right way," continued the March King. "Salaries are large in all the first class musical organizations to players of the instruments I first mentioned. The marvelous growth in symphony orchestras and concert bands is resulting in a large demand for good players of the oboe, bassoon, bass and alto clarinet, saxophone, tuba and French horns.

"A first class musical organization requires first class players on all instruments, from the violin to the snare drum. But those who would make satisfactory salaries—unless they be marvelous performers on the more extensively chosen instruments— will do well to take up those I have specified." –John Philip Sousa.

"American Musical Taste"

Source: *Modern Music and Musicians*, part 2, vol. 3 (New York: University Society, 1912), 643–45.

> *Printed within the "music appreciation" section of a music encyclopedia, this essay stands among the most scholarly of Sousa's writings. While his views on Wagner show an idiosyncratic understanding of that composer's views on music, Sousa provides detailed insights into both his own mindset as a bandmaster and composer and into those of the American audiences for which he played. The division between popular music and art music comes into focus here in a way not seen in his earlier writings— perhaps because his essay appears alongside many of the more venerated names in turn-of-the-century classical music in America (Horatio Parker and Henry Krehbiel, for instance) and abroad (C. Hubert H. Parry, for example).*

Cosmopolitan Requirements—Growing Popularity of Good Music—What Makes the High-class Composition Popular—Wagner's Wonderful Hold on the Public—Power of Descriptive Music—Military Marches—A Forecast.

The American demand for music is the most cosmopolitan demand in the world. It represents the composite tastes of more different people than were ever brought together under one flag, and in one country, since the famous tower of Babel took its ominous tumble. The American people hate a rut, and no one knows better than I do that in order to please them they must have an infinite variety. They must have all kinds of music by all kinds of composers. Like our appetite for food, our appetite for music has been cultivated by tasting a little of the products of all nations. We have come to eat and enjoy Irish potatoes, English roast beef, French mushrooms, Italian macaroni, Spanish saffron and Spanish onions, German sausages and cheese, Russian caviar, Chinese ginger and rice, to say nothing of a hundred and one other dishes coming from all parts of the globe. We recognize the genius of the French composer long before Germany takes him up, and Wagner was well known and widely played in the United States before the French came to realize his true greatness. Mme. Liza Lehmann came to America with her dreamy "In a Persian Garden" under her arm.[77]

---

77   A soprano-turned-composer, Liza Lehmann toured the United States in 1910. She composed *In a Persian Garden*, a song cycle for four voices, in 1896.

London couldn't hear the beauty of the thing, but New York did, and Mme. Lehmann's reputation as a composer was established.

I am not a believer in national schools of music. The very idea seems ridiculous in itself. National music is nothing more nor less than international imitation. A striking genius like Wagner arises, and he starts in to compose just as all his contemporaries composed. He writes a work like "Rienzi," which is nothing more nor less than an advanced form of Italian opera of the day. Then he does a little original thinking and realizes that if he wishes to make a bid for real greatness he must work not as an imitator but as a creator. The consequence is that he brings forth a number of genuinely inspired works, and, lo and behold, we are told that a new German school has been founded. It would have been precisely the same if Wagner had been born in Russia or in Tasmania. In no other art is individualism so strong as in music. In Wagner there is really no suggestion of a national school. It is simply Wagner, a musical mountain peak, and that is all. If Wagner had written music suitable only for Germans it would not be as popular in New York, Sydney, Bombay, London or Paris as it is in Bayreuth. Wagner wrote good music, great music, and the world identifies it, irrespective of any school.

Public taste in America is unquestionably improving. All changes of this kind must be gradual. Musical taste is all a matter of becoming accustomed to certain kinds of music. I remember that when I commenced horseback riding in my childhood I noticed that horses were liable to shy at bits of paper flying about the road. Later they were frightened by the bicycles, trolley-cars, and automobiles. Now there are more of these vehicles in the road than ever, but horses are accustomed to them. The horses will doubtless have a new lesson to learn if the flying-machine industry continues to grow as it has started.[78] It is much the same with the public. The people who were ridiculing Wagner forty years ago are now clamoring for his music. The brain of the public grows and becomes more responsive to new impressions every day.

The public lets one know very quickly whether it is interested or not. How do you suppose I tell? If I hear a few people cough during the performance of a new number I rarely ever play that number again. Coughing in an audience is a sign of restlessness and impatience. When they are interested they are

---

78   The Wright Brothers' first successful flight was on December 17, 1903; by the time of this essay their corporation was in active competition with that of Glenn Curtiss for military orders.

quiet, and it is really very astonishing how one can veritably feel the interest of an audience. It is something in the atmosphere and the sensitive artist knows and feels it at once.

The commercial side of America has unquestionably interfered with the development of music in the past, though it has, in another sense, been the means of developing it. People who have interviewed me seemed to be most interested in how much money I have made out of it. It happens that a great number of my compositions have been what can only be described as "hits." They have brought me large returns, but I am willing to make the statement that no composer has ever made less attempt to make money than I have. While writing I never think of the possible financial reward. My sole object is to turn out a good piece of music, a worthy piece, a piece that I can be proud of, no matter whether it is a military march or a more elaborate suite. I have one composition which I think far and away above anything I have ever written. It is called "The Last Days of Pompeii"; I have played it for years in public, but I have always avoided publishing it, as I desire to keep it and work at it until I am sure that it cannot be improved by further work.[79] One reason why the love for music in America has been somewhat more difficult to develop than the love for music in Europe is attributable to the vast number of other amusements which the American people possess and enjoy. In Europe the principal sources of amusement are to be found in the gatherings at local inns or taverns, the occasional picnics or excursions to the country, and visits to the theater, the opera house, and the concert hall. Americans have a host of other amusements which take their time and attention. Baseball, for instance, is one of the leading interests of thousands of men in our large cities.[80]

---

79   Sousa composed *The Last Days of Pompeii*, his first of many concert suites for band, in 1893. The Sousa Band performed it relatively frequently on tour. His statement about publishing it may be less genuine given that it was actually first published in July 1912, the same year as this essay. In his defense, however, the work was nineteen years old by then and Sousa had published many of his other suites shortly after composing them. Further see Bierley, *Works*, 101

80   The first World Series between National and American Leagues was played in 1903, only nine years prior to this essay. Sousa was an avid fan, and the Sousa Band played games of their own against local teams while touring. Arthur W. Bauer, a trombonist in the band in 1902, composed the "Three Strikes Two-Step" in 1902. Sousa composed *The National Game* (1925) at the request of the Major League Baseball's first Commissioner, Kenesaw Landis. Further see Bierley, *Incredible Band*, 51–52, and idem, *Works*, 73.

Sheet music of a two-step by Sousa trombonist A. W. Bauer (pictured bottom left separately) featuring the Sousa Baseball team. Sousa, seated middle. John Philip Sousa Jr. stands at left wearing a "Nassau" jersey.

The automobile, combined with American wealth and prodigality, is another amusement which draws thousands away from the serious pursuit of studies forming the basis of culture.[81] The Sunday newspapers, piling ton upon ton of printed matter upon the tons and tons of magazines, booklets, advertisements, etc., all of which have to be read by an eager public, also take up an enormous amount of time. What the Americans have accomplished in music is truly amazing in face of the countless distractions they meet

---

81 Automobiles had become more affordable only recently; Ford began production of the Model T in 1908.

every day of their lives. There is a big difference between the German, calmly sitting in his Bierhalle sipping his malt and hops and listening to a Beethoven symphony, and the strenuous and commercial American who hears his "Tristan und Isolde" with half his mind set upon the problem of how he is going to squeeze a sea bath, a roller-coaster ride, a moving-picture show, and a course dinner into the next hour.

But we are commencing to stand alone, and when I say "we," I mean the whole American people, and not a few blue-nosed "highbrows" who, after a residence of many years in European countries, have come back to us with a kind of snobbish all-knowing superiority which is, to say the least, aggravating. Until very recently, music has only been part of a function for the American people. They were willing to accept it as one of the many events in a day's outing. Now good concerts of standard works are becoming commercially profitable. People find such delight in hearing good music that they are willing to pay well for it. That is what we can call real musical culture. Moreover, the day of big reputations is passing in a most encouraging manner. The American people are waking up, and they refuse to be deceived. It is impossible for a singer with a reputation gained during the Civil War and a voice that strikes terror to the heart of the most courageous to tour America and hoodwink the people. I do not believe that any musical performer or organization of performers can succeed unless they can exhibit ability which entitles them to public appreciation.

High-class compositions become popular because the real composer is always inspired. I should say that about ninety per cent. of all the musical compositions written are uninspired. What is inspiration? Ah, one could write volumes and volumes in the telling of that and still be just as far away from a definition as at the beginning. No one doubts its existence who has had the kind of musical experience that I have had with the public. The public seems to recognize musical inspiration at once, whether it comes to them through the music of Wagner, Schubert, or Brahms, or through the music of Stephen Foster, or the trite but clever tunes of some unschooled writer of ballads of the day.

The success of a piece is due to the composer, the power beyond the composer (inspiration), and to the public. The higher power which has incited the composer's mind and empowered him to write a musical masterpiece seems to be at work preparing the public to receive that masterpiece as it should be received.

The mere acquisition of the technical knowledge will never make a composer any more than a knowledge of grammar will make an author. What is a string of words without ideas, and what is a string of notes without the spark which distinguishes them from dead, dull, uninteresting ink and paper? Potboilers are rarely ever successful. The man who sits down and says "I need the money, therefore I will write a kind of composition which I know the public will like, and make money with it," is almost invariably a failure. The composer must believe in his work and have faith in himself, whether he be writing a three-act grand opera or a popular valse. Above all things, he must forget the idea of gain. Gain and music don't go together. I remember the case of a composer of considerable renown who brought one of his lighter compositions to me and asked me to put it upon my programme. As a favor to him I consented, although I did not like the piece. Then he said, "Of course, I don't want my own name to be connected with this, you know. You must play it under an assumed name." Then I told him that if he was ashamed of it I was even more so, and we had better not play it at all.

One of the most notable instances of the popularity of good music is seen in the case of Wagner's works. Wagner, the composer who was first heralded as the writer of marvelously complex and intricate works which could only be understood by the advanced musician, is now demanded by popular audiences. I rarely play a programme without a Wagner number, and my band has in its repertoire practically everything which Wagner has written. This means that the public demands not only the beautiful melodies like the "Evening Star," "Preislied," "Bridal March from Lohengrin," "The Spinning Song," etc., but also is delighted to hear the complicated music of the "Kaisermarsch," "Tristan und Isolde," and "Parsifal." The reason for this is that Wagner was one of the most inspired of all composers and was the greatest composer of dramatic music. In fact, if I were to send a missionary orchestra to a people who knew nothing of music for the purpose of making converts, I should have the orchestra commence upon them with Wagner's "Ride of the Valkyrs."

The people are fond of dramatic music because they are fond of the pictorial in music. They have read the plots of the operas and like to associate the stories with the music. They love color, movement, and lights. We are all very primitive in this respect. Of course, when it comes right down to the truth of the matter, descriptive music must depend very largely upon literal conceptions which the hearers have previously formed. There is mighty little difference between the musical representation of a storm and of a boiler explosion, but if I tell you it is a storm and not a boiler explosion you immediately picture a storm, hear the thunder, and see the lightning flash. This is one of the reasons why operatic and descriptive music is so popular.

Some composers carry descriptive music to an absurd extreme. You can't depict a man taking off his shoes, and the representation of a domestic quarrel is often more ridiculous than descriptive. It must be admitted, however, that there is an appropriateness which must govern all descriptive music. Although, as I have said, I do not believe in national schools, but rather in individualism in musical composition, it is, nevertheless, a fact that the music of certain peoples has racial characteristics. The Scotch, for instance, are influenced in their music by their national instrument, the bagpipes. Mendelssohn knew this, and in his "Scotch" symphony he shows the study of the characteristics of the bagpipes throughout the entire piece. Only once does he make a slip and omit this characteristic. Donizetti, however, in his Scotch opera "Lucia di Lammermoor" has hardly a suggestion if anything that might be called Scotch in the entire work. The audience must rely upon the plaids and kilts for local color, but in the Mendelssohn work an audience in a concert hall which is at all familiar with Scotch music would detect the unmistakable atmosphere at once.

I have often been asked to account for the success of my own military marches. Of course it is impossible for any one to tell what makes a piece of this kind popular, but I have always felt that a march must have an element of the barbaric in it to make it go. It must be robust, it must stir the blood, it must be filled with Oriental splendor, suggesting the flash of the bayonet, it must make you think of battalions of big-chested men in motion. Europe remembers our marches while America almost forgets them. Some of my first marches are just as popular in Europe to-day as when they were first written. In writing a march I always try to make it sound so that any one in the audience would say after hearing it, "That is the way I would have wanted it to sound if I had written it." No matter how refined and cultured we may be, we all have an element of the savage, the man of the wilds and the steppes in us. We like the clashing of cymbals, the roar of the drums, the intoxicating rhythms, and the blare of the brass that carries us off our feet whether we will or not. All this I try to put into my marches. Sometimes I wait for months before I get the right melodic inspiration. Then the musical idea comes and I can't wait until I have it worked out.

Once a young lady asked me: "Why is it that I like military marches better than any other kind of music?" I told her that it was because of the barbarian, the savage, the Oriental in her. She seemed shocked at this and said: "How can you detect anything of the savage in me?" I called her attention to the feathers in her hat, the skins of wild animals with which she trimmed her dress, and the little ornamental tassels on her slippers. She was quite willing to admit that we are not so very far from the forest and the desert after all.

There will always be cheap and trite music because there will always be a certain class of people who will have to evolve from no music whatever to music that is worth while through music which requires very little taste or intelligence to understand. The problem is to get them interested in good music by first gaining their attention through music of less esthetic value. I have no sympathy with those who would build a Chinese wall around the good music and keep all those out who honestly confess that they don't understand it. Because a man cannot understand Strauss or Debussy is no reason why he should be musically excommunicated. The people themselves readily determine what they like and what they dislike. There has been a great deal printed about Strauss and about Debussy, consequently there has been a kind of a fad for their music, but I notice that the compositions of Puccini among the later composers elicit more real applause than those of any other writer, and I am quite willing to predict that twenty years from now they will be equally popular.[82] Musical fashions cannot be determined by printer's ink. The public in the end will demand the kind of music it likes best, and not what critics and writers say ought to be most popular.

---

82 Puccini's popularity in the United States intensified when the Metropolitan Opera successfully commissioned and premiered *La fanciulla del West* in 1910. This marked the organization's first world premiere.

"Ready! Pull! Dead!"

Source: *National Sunday Magazine* (*New York Sun*), June 14, 1914, 9.

> *This essay ties together a number of themes seen in Sousa's writings of the previous few years, including baseball and women's rights. He also reveals some recent reading and promotes his own exercise regime: trapshooting. Sousa had acted as a public advocate for trapshooting for many years by 1914. He was a founding member and the first president of the American Trapshooting Association (later renamed the Amateur Trapshooting Association). A second essay on trapshooting (broadly similar in content and style to this one) appeared in the same month's issue of* Country Life in America.[83]

Sousa posing with one of the shotguns he used for trapshooting.

The vernacular of sports is most mystifying to the uninitiated. As a game grows in popularity there is created a jargon, a cant, and a slang peculiarly its own. Baseball furnishes the most familiar example in this respect, and [once] an old lady watching a game of tennis deplored the fact that those who accumulated "Love" the most, were the grouchiest. Had she known that "Love" means nothing, and nothing is so exasperating as nothing, she would have understood.

Trap-shooting is the youngest of all the great sports; but it is increasing in popular esteem by jumps and bounds. It is estimated that there are

---

83   "My Hobby—Trapshooting," *Country Life in America*, vol. 26, no. 6 (June 1914), 54–55, 80.

over two hundred thousand men and women who face the Trap during the season. Gun Clubs exist in all cities and towns in the country. Like Baseball, Golf, Tennis and other pastimes, Trap-shooting has risen to the dignity of a language of its own. When you hear a group of men and women discussing "Bulk" and "Dense," "Full choke," "Drop," "Comb," "Pull," "Regulation birds," know ye, they are Trap-shooters. For "Bulk" and "Dense" mean the smokeless powders used by the shooters. "Full choke" explains the special boring of the gun-barrel; "Drop," the inches the heel of the stock is below the sight when the gun is in position at the shoulder. "Comb" is the crest of the stock. "Pull" the power required to release the trigger. "Regulation birds," the speed, height and the angle of the saucer-like targets known as "Blue-rocks," "White-fliers," etc., when thrown from the trap.

The flying target pastime makes many appeals to the lover of sports. It is a wonderful developer of self- reliance. It is your own game, and no one can do it for you. It is not a sport for the vacillating; for it requires great concentration and a happy blending of mental and physical attributes. The exercise in lifting to the shoulder, an eight-pound gun hundreds of times daily is a muscle-building factor and a sure death to insomnia. The recoil of the gun acts as a stimulating massage for tired nerves and muscles.

It has one great advantage over field shooting. There are many to whom it is abhorrent to destroy God's feathery creatures for sport. At the traps you shoot at inanimate clay; and to the most tender hearted, there can be no compunction in smashing the little black discs. All one's mental faculties are quickened, for the bird thrown from unknown angles with varying speed, made illusive by the force of wind currents keeps one keenly alive to new conditions. ["]Shooting where they ain't" successfully, adds to the exhilaration of the game.

As a promoter of correct living it is ever on the job. Local option and Fletcherism are not in it as detergents of one's appetites.[84] A contestant

---

84   "Local option" refers to the ability of cities and counties to restrict or ban the purchase or consumption of alcohol in the years before and after Prohibition. "Fletcherism" is a reference to Horace Fletcher (1849–1919), a healthy eating advocate who, among other things, argued that chewing food 100 times a bite was the best way to avoid obesity and other ailments. His book *Fletcherism: What It Is or How I Became Young at Sixty* was just published in 1913—Sousa turned 60 only a few months after writing this essay.

desiring success must be temperate in all things. A foggy brain or a gorged, overworked stomach, means a sluggish shooter, and a sluggish shooter means a defeated contestant. Spartan abnegation is absolutely necessary to success. I recall some six years since, while attending an important tournament in the Middle West, a young shooter led the field at the close of the first day. He shot with such splendid rhythm and accuracy that he was picked by the experts as the probable winner of the trophy. That night he proceeded to "paint the town." When he appeared at the traps next morning he was bleary-eyed, nervous and sluggish, and at the end of the day he was at the tail-end of the field of over two hundred shooters. I have shot with him many times since, and nothing can persuade him to put another coat of paint on the town. The humiliation of defeat was the greatest temperance lecture possible.

Trap-shooting is a splendid pastime for women. It is a tonic for the nervous system and makes a woman agile and alert. I have shot in many matches with women and have never seen an ungraceful one at the traps. The sport is most suitable to the gentle sex, for woman's quick perception both of eye and brain are splendid factors in the make-up of the shooter. In the beginning, women did not take to the shot gun because it was synonymous with death to the feathery denizens of the air. She who we call Grandmother, Mother, Aunt, Sister, Wife and Daughter love innocent nature too much to destroy it for sport. With the coming of the clay bird women shooters have become nearly as numerous as women golfers and tennis players. In the shooting game she is not segregated; she is not classified as a woman, but as a shooter. She meets all men shooters on an equality and there is nothing in which she so delights as beating mere man at his own game. Among the growing number of women trap-shooters, it is significant that two prominent eastern clubs are composed of women members exclusively.

The trap-shooting world embraces all from potentate to peasant, from octogenarian to callow youth, from grizzly warrior to sweet sixteen; and all are happy when they call "Pull" and hear the referee announce "Dead."

"A Horse, a Dog, a Gun and a Girl"

Source: *The American Shooter* 1, no. 16, August 15, 1916, 3, in *SPB* 44:1, 3.

At first glance this is just another of Sousa's writings on leisure and lifestyle. He here expands his ideas away from trapshooting and baseball to include other activities he embraced in his "golden" years. As the essay continues, however, Sousa's spirituality and its American roots in the Jeffersonian and Transcendentalist traditions becomes apparent. He maintained a rigorous touring schedule through 1931 in spite of it all.

The atavistic intuition or instinct is strong in all of us, but I believe the call of the woods—of the fields, of man's two most loyal friends, the horse and the dog—is stronger in the city-bred man than he who spends his life in the country.

Some years since, the then Vice-President Fairbanks gave a dinner in Washington in honor of the late James Whitcomb Riley, the beloved Hoosier poet.[85] I had the pleasure of being among the invited, and the poet's post-prandial speech was one of the most fascinating I have ever heard. He was a keen observer of men and a lover of nature; his heart bubbled with affection for all. He spoke of the yearning for the country by the men hemmed in by the exigencies of city life; how, when prosperity came, the city man would add a suburban home and when possessed of riches he would build far into the country a home, and when he was independent of the city's demands he would don the farmer's habiliments and guide the plow through the fields, proud of his achievement and at peace with all mankind, for he is back with Mother Nature.

My happiest days have been spent away from the city, with the horse, the dog and gun as my companions. I was once asked what my hope of a heaven is, and I said: "A place of horses, dogs, guns and girls, with music on tap"; and, of course, trees and flowers and birds to add to the general joy.

I remember once, while traveling on horseback in the heart of the Shenandoah, stopping at an old plantation for the night. The farm was in a beautiful valley, and at least 40 miles from a railroad. The planter's little

---

85   Charles Warren Fairbanks (1852–1918) served as a senator from Indiana until his election as vice president under Theodore Roosevelt from 1905–1909. Poet James Whitcomb Riley had just died on July 22, 1916, perhaps stimulating Sousa's memory.

daughter, a veritable Virginia beauty of 15 or 16 summers, was very much interested in our horses. They were beautiful in their pride and conformation, and probably the first bitted horses with corset-fitting hunting saddles the little maid had ever seen. After supper we sat in the parlor, and the little Miss started the Victrola. The first piece was one of my compositions, and before the evening was over there were at least 15 of my pieces played.

The next morning, as we mounted our horses about to resume the journey, the little girl bade us good- by. She said: "When I hear your music and see your beautiful horses, I hope my heaven will be horses and you."

The ideal way to make a horseback trip is, apart from your saddle horses, to have a surrey containing change of clothing, raincoats, food, etc. If the weather is warm, one should travel early in the morning and late in the afternoon. In a long journey, nurse your horse, and whenever there is a steep incline, dismount and lead your horse. Thirty-five or forty miles a day is sufficient distance to go, allowing the horse to change his gait from walking to trotting and cantering.

The horse should be treated with every kind of consideration, encouraging him with soothing words, using neither whip nor spur; see that he is housed, watered and fed before you bother about yourself. Make him your companion—not your slave. At the end of the day's journey a few lumps of sugar, an apple or a carrot always make him happy.

Select dirt roads whenever possible. With views of clover-clad fields, of mighty trees, of shaded lanes, of waving corn and pearling brook, life is one glad song, and when you reach a town where there is a trapshooting tournament, get out your gun and smash the elusive clay birds to your heart's content.

And then, if there is a pretty girl to talk to, or a setter to pat, do so, and go on your way rejoicing. Therefore, with a horse and a dog and a gun and a girl this mundane sphere becomes really a cousin- germane to the Paradise beyond.

I have spent many, many pleasant hours on the back of my favorite mount, and found that it was just the proper training for my season at the traps—for I attend all possible tournaments during my vacation. Would that my vacation were longer.

"If I Had to Begin All Over Again"

Source: *The Etude* 34, December 1916, 847, in *SPB* 44:1, 58.

Another of the publisher's efforts to collect the thoughts of leading musical figures, The Etude *in this case only enticed a lackluster group of singers (David Bispham, and Johanna Gadski) and composers (Paul Corder, Henry Holden Huss, and Giuseppe Ferrata). Sousa's response was shorter and more evasive than the other writers, avoiding speculation as was his custom in cases where he was asked "what ifs" about his upbringing and early career.*

In answer to your "Won't you send us a few lines or as much as you choose to send, telling what you might do if you found yourself obliged to start all over again" I beg to respectfully submit that I would become a pupil at the age of somewhere between seven and ten at the Esputa Academy of Music, Washington, D.C., [and] at my fourteenth year I would take private instructions in harmony, orchestration and violin from George Felix Benkert of Washington, D. C.[86] As soon as I was able to play professionally and orchestrate professionally and compose professionally I would hawk my wares in the highways and by-ways of musical commerce; and, if I was offered a position to conduct a theatrical orchestra I would accept it; and if I was offered a position as first violin in a symphonic orchestra I would accept it; and if I was offered a commission to write a musical comedy I would accept it; and if I was offered the position of Conductor of the United States Marine Band I would accept it, and if I was offered a large salary and a percentage to organize a band of my own I would accept it;[87] and if my compositions caught the fancy of the world I would be very happy; and if I wrote the operas of *El Capitan, Bride Elect, The Charlatan, Free Lance,* etc. I would be very happy; and if I wrote *Washington Post, High School Cadets, The Stars and Stripes,* etc., I would be very happy. In fact, if I had to go over it again I'd be most happy to follow the same path I have followed since babyhood.

---

86   Further on John Esputa see Warfield, "John Esputa."
87   Sousa mentions a "large salary and a percentage" because he managed the Sousa Band in partnership with David Blakely. Further see Brown, "David Blakely" and Cipolla, "Business Papers."

"Differences of Opinion as to Correct Metronomic Tempo Indications"

Source: *The Metronome* 33, no. 4, April 1917, 19, in *SPB* 45, 27.

> *Gustav Saenger wrote this article in an effort to better understand the problem of seemingly erroneous tempo markings in Suppé's* Pique Dame Overture. *The opening of Saenger's article notes that the written metronome markings in the Carl Fischer printing of the overture (♩=84 for the first section, ♩=144 for the second, ♩=80 for the third, ♩=126 for the fourth, and ♩=160 for the fifth) was "retained from the original edition," but that "every movement is taken considerably quicker nowadays than called for by the original tempo marks."[88] Included as part of his research are letters and interviews on the topic from a number of band directors, most notably Sousa, Vincent F. Safranek, and Patrick Conway, whose responses are included below for comparison.*

Auditorium Hotel, Chicago, January 30, 1917

To the Editor of *The Metronome:*

My Dear Sir:—I am sending with this the violin part of "Pique Dame" with the metronome marks as I usually play it. Metronome marks are perhaps of suggestive good, but not positive. Some composers mark their composition, allowing of great latitude in the tempi. You will note that in the five movements of the overture, the tempo of the first I placed at ♩=100; the second at 144; the third at 84; the fourth at 138, and the fifth at 176. Of course, much depends on just how fast one's blood circulates in nearly all matters of tempi. I remember the occasion when I heard Theodore Thomas' Orchestra for the first time. I was a student in Washington, and was accompanied by a bespeckled old German professor, who found fault with all Mr. Thomas' tempos on the ground that they were much too fast. They suited me, and have ever since. Conductors, if they have orchestras of great individual excellence in the players, are apt to show off both in making adagios slower, and allegros faster than the ordinary orchestra. Of course, you

---

88   While the Carl Fischer version was undoubtedly the one used by all the American bandmasters Saenger contacted, an earlier 1860s German printing actually differs regarding the second section, marked at ♩=138 rather than 144. Other editions and arrangements also include the 138 marking.

remember the story ascribed to either Wagner, Verdi, Rossini, or any other popular composer, who was asked by a conductor not possessing authority or personality, to signify the tempi of a composition of his (one of the various composers). Reply was: "If you do not feel the tempo, I cannot give it to you."

Very sincerely,
John Philip Sousa

In response to an inquiry regarding correct metronome markings for this overtures, Mr. Safranek responded in part as follows:

To the Editor of *The Metronome*:

Dear Sir:—In reference to metronome markings for the "Pique Dame" overture, will say the following: Using the violin part as arranged by Charles J. Roberts: quarter notes always opening the movement at 104 until [rehearsal] 4 when the tempo is slightly increased in order to connect with the next movement, as the end of the first movement from 4 on and the next movement are musically related. Second movement *Allegro con fuoco* at 152 until [reh.] 13, when the time slows up just a trifle to 144. The next movement, *Andantino con moto* at 56 or 58, the difference being very slight. The next movement, *Allegro*, at the printed marking (126) until *Più mosso*, which I increase to 176 until toward the end, which is slightly quicker.[89] These tempi I have found most desirable for the best effect of this overture, and have played it that way for probably twenty years.

Very truly yours,
V. F. Safranek

Mr. P. Conway, the popular bandmaster of Conway's Band, when interviewed by a representative of *The Metronome* regarding this matter, expressed himself as follows:

"In regard to the tempo of 'Pique Dame' overture, will say that I don't think leaders pay much attention to metronome marks and most of them

---

89   Suppé did not give a metronome marking for the end of the overture, marking only "Presto." Safranek's "Più mosso" and his tempo comparison as "quicker" refers to the indications in the Roberts edition he was using.

play an overture like 'Pique Dame' as they feel it, but to make sure, I tried it with a metronome and have always heard all of the movements except the *Andante con moto* played a little faster than the metronome marks.

"I think the tendency is to play things faster nowadays and the tempo marks may be correct and just as the composer intended the movements to be played. But my opinion is that it is usually played in faster tempo than marked."

In Mr. Conway's opinion the metronome markings for the various movements (always quarters) should be: the opening *Moderato* at 108; *Allegro con fuoco* at 168; *Andantino con moto* at 72; the next *Allegro* at 152 and the last *Più mosso* at 170.

"The Symphony Orchestra and the Concert Band"

Source: *The Etude* 35, May 1917, 299–300.[90]

> *The editor's header for this essay is true insofar as it is one of the bandmaster's clearest writings on music history, the place of the concert band in that larger context, and his own status (most notably as a pioneering quasi-Haydn figure for bands as an ensemble). He here clarifies his longstanding beliefs and practices even as his wit appears at its sharpest.*

Mr. Sousa's Article is one of the Most Original and Distinctive *The Etude* has ever been Privileged to Present

It is Filled with Unusual Interest for all Music Lovers

At the very dawn of history, vocal and instrumental combinations existed, for do we not read in [1] Chronicles [13:8]:

"*And David and all Israel played before God with all their might, and with singing, and with harps, and with psalteries, and with timbrels, and with cymbals, and with trumpets;*"

Again, is it not recorded in Daniel [3:14–16]:

"*Nebuchadnezzar spake and said to them, 'is it true, O Shadrach, Meshach and Abed-nego? Do not ye serve my gods nor worship the golden image that I have set up?*

---

90   Although the editor of *The Etude* included the header "written expressly for *The Etude*," Sousa eventually reprinted the essay in the Sousa Band's 1920 souvenir program (SPB 55, 24a9–a10).

"Now if ye be ready that at what time ye hear the sound of the cornet, flute, harp, sackbut, psaltery, and dulcimer, and all kinds of music, ye fall down and worship the image which I have made; well: but if ye worship not, ye shall be cast the same hour into the midst of a burning, fiery furnace; and who is that God that shall deliver you out of my hands?'

"Shadrach, Meshach, and Abed-nego, answered and said to the King, 'O Nebuchadnezzar, we are not careful to answer thee in this matter'."

Evidently, Nebuchadnezzar and his band were not very popular.

Poor old Neb had as much trouble securing an audience as some of the moderns.

"Be sure and do not miss my concert to-night," says the Nebuchadnezzar of to-day.

"Sorry, but I can't," says the Shadrach of these times, edging away, "I have a previous engagement to take a nap in a boiler factory."

Hugo Riemann, Sir Charles Villiers Stanford, and Cecil Forsyth, those indefatigable delvers into the mystical mines of musical antiquity agree that everything in music, up or down to 900 A. D. should be considered ancient. They record the use of voices and instruments giving melody only, or, at most octaves in singing and playing. Of course, the rhythmic instruments of percussion were used to mark the time and accentuate the melodies.

If, as some claim, music is a man-created invention, its improvements in the innumerable years that preceded the makers of modern harmony were slight indeed.

It is self-evident that man, in the ancient days, had brain, eyes, voice and hands, even as he has to- day, but polyphonic music did not exist until the breath of God warmed into music a soul, and cold mathematics gave way to creative genius, inventive skill and inspiration.

The Messiahs of Music
The Messiahs who brought the glad tidings—Palestrina, Bach, Beethoven, Wagner and a multitude of divinely-endowed musicians, have led the world out of the wilderness of crudity into the dazzling realm of the present—a present rich in the treasures of the masters who have arrived, rich in the promise of those to come.

The precursor of the present in relation to the combination known as the Symphony Orchestra dates from the Eighteenth Century.

Joseph Haydn has long been known as the "Father of Instrumental Music." Many of his symphonies remain in the repertoire of the famous orchestras of the world and are played with never-ending delight to the auditor, the performer and the conductor, each succeeding year.

Although it is a far cry from the combination of strings, wood-wind and brass of "Papa Haydn's" orchestra to the instrumental tools employed by Richard Strauss—to the composer of "The Surprise," "The Farewell," "The Clock" and other immortal works, should be given the honor of establishing the classic orchestra.

The group of the "Father of Instrumental Music" (1766) consisted of six violins, one cello, one bass, one flute, two oboes, two bassoons and two horns. The earliest of the Haydn symphonies were given to the world by these instruments. The "Alpine Symphony" of Richard Strauss (1914) calls for two flutes, two piccolos, two oboes (doubled), one English horn, one heckelphone, one E-flat clarinet (doubled), two B[- flat] clarinets, one C clarinet (doubled), one bass clarinet, three bassoons, one contra-bassoon, sixteen horns, four tenor-tubas in B[-flat] and F, six trumpets, six trombones, two bass-tubas, two harps, organ, celeste, timpani, eighteen first violins, sixteen second violins, twelve violas, ten cellos, eight double basses, small drum, bass drum and a host of "effect" instruments, which we, in America, call "the traps." Besides the above instruments, Strauss, in a previous composition, employed saxophones.

The Modern Symphony Orchestra

It will be noticed that between 1766 and 1914 composers have added a multitude of wood-wind, brass and percussion instruments to the primitive symphonic combination. With the single exception of the harp, there has been no effort made to permanently incorporate into the string band any other stringed instrument. While the guitar, the lute, the mandolin, the banjo, the zither and the viola-d'amour have been used in orchestral combinations, they have only been employed for some effect believed necessary by the composer. In fact, "the symphony orchestra," to quote W. S. Rockstro, "has become a large wind band plus strings, instead of a string band plus wind."[91]

---

91   This quotation comes from Rockstro's (1823–1895) entry on "Orchestration" in Grove, *Dictionary*, vol. 3, 511 (volume published in 1907). Sousa's views on the evolution of the orchestra's makeup as seen in the preceding paragraphs seem to rely on the same source.

Why?

The most aesthetic of the pure families of instruments is beyond question the violin group. In sentiment, mystery, glamor, register, unanimity of tonal facility and perfection in dexterity it more than equals all other families. But, aside from its delicate nuances and diffident dynamics, it reduces itself to the skeleton of the symphonic structure, because, like bread served with each course, it loses its novelty; and, if violins are used alone, beyond a certain time limit, they suggest an Adamless Eden, which, however beautiful, does not appeal to Eve. Instruments can be likened to man. Man is a social animal; orchestral instruments crave company.

Of the separate instrumental groups, apart from the violin, the vocal, while in compass, lightness or mobility, is not the equal of the violin family, it possesses a power for pathos, passion and soul-gripping quality not possible by any other group. The wood-wind has a slightly greater register than the violin. In marbleized chastity, crystallized coquetry, humorous murmurs and voicing animated nature, it is in a class by itself. The last orchestral family, the brass, in gamut is less than any save the vocal, but has the power to thunder forth the barbaric splendor of sound or intone the holiness of the Cathedral.

The Orchestral Pallet

Therefore, composers have found a greater diversity of tone color in a multitude of wind instruments, cylinder or conical, single-reed, double-reed, direct vibration by blowing into an aperture, or cup-shaped mouthpiece, taking the vibrations from the trumpet muscles of the human lip and various sizes of tubes, than in the string family alone. All these wind instruments have added to the pallet of the orchestrator and have permitted him to use his creative power in blending the various colors. In this connection, it is not amiss to point out that that giant of the music drama, Richard Wagner, in nearly every instance, enunciates the "leit-motifs" of his operas through the agency of wood-wind or brass.

The Band at the Beginning—the Band of To-day

The so-called Thurmer (Watchman) bands of the Middle Ages seem to be the progenitors of the present-day concert band. They were made up of fifes, oboes, zinken, trombones and drums. Trumpets were not at first used, because they were for royal ears alone; not for the common herd. As time passed numerous wind instruments were added to this group; some of the originals became obsolete and others were improved upon, until to-day, 1917, the wind band consists of four flutes, two piccolos, two oboes, one English horn, two bassoons, one contra-bassoon, or sarrusophone, two alto saxophones, two tenor saxophones, one baritone saxophone, twenty B[-flat] clarinets, one alto clarinet, one bass clarinet, four cornets, two trumpets, two fleugel horns or added cornets, four horns, four trombones, two euphoniums, six basses (double B[- flat]), one harp, one timpani, one small drum and one bass drum. (This is the instrumentation of Sousa's Band.)

The tendency of the modern composer to place, on the shoulders of the wood-wind corps and the brass choir of the orchestra, the most dramatic effects of the symphonic body has much to do with the development of the wind band, although there is no question that the inventive genius of Boehm, Klose, Wieprecht and Sax have been important factors. With the improvements in mechanism, looking to purity of intonation and facility of execution, observant musicians and capable conductors saw the coming of a new constellation in the musical firmament—a constellation of star players on wood-wind, brass and percussion instruments.

Pioneer Instrument Makers
The pioneers were Wieprecht and Parlow in Germany, Paulus and Sellenik in France, the Godfreys and George Miller in England, Bender in Belgium, Dunkler in Holland, and, last but not least, Patrick Sarsfield Gilmore in America. Gilmore organized a corps of musicians superior to any wind-band players of his day, many of them coming from the leading orchestras of the world and possessing a virtuoso's ability on their respective instruments. He engaged his musicians regardless of expense and paid them salaries commensurate with their talents. Conductors and players alike should tenderly cherish the memory of Patrick Sarsfield Gilmore for what he did in the interest of instrumental performers.

The only distinction that can be made in the name of progressive art between the modern string band and the modern wind-band is[:] which at the moment presents the most perfect massing of sounds and tonal colors[?][92] An

---

92   This sentence has a comma before the italicized portion and ends with a period, but Sousa's words seem to require a colon and a question mark.

incessant playing of all groups combined, or the serving of music pabulum in solid blocks of string, wood-wind or brass becomes wearisome. Recitals by a single vocalist or instrumental performer are made attractive through the personality and pedagogy of the performer rather than through the entertainment itself. When personality is missing, auricular fatigue prevails sooner or later.

In placing the string band and the wind-band on the same plane, I see, in my mind's eye, the lover of Haydn, of Mozart, of Beethoven and the violin family standing aghast at the thought and asking why wind instruments should attempt the immortal symphonies of these beloved masters; and well may they stand aghast and question. These compositions were created for one purpose only, to be played by the instruments the masters intended for them, and never by any other combination.[93] The efforts on the part of some misguided conductors and orchestrators to "improve" on the original, and the equally self-elective task of some wind-band arranger to transcribe Mozart, Beethoven and Haydn to the wind instrument combination are greatly to be deplored. The earlier symphonies are the musical flowers, plants and trees grown in the shadowy lane of the past, and it is not necessary to put up barbed-wire fences and telegraph poles to modernize these masterpieces. Either play them as they were, or let them alone entirely.

The New and the Old

I recall attending a concert in London in the early 90's conducted by the great Hans Richter. The program was, with the exception of a symphony of Haydn, entirely Wagner. The orchestra for the Wagner excerpts numbered fully one hundred men. When the time came to play the Haydn symphony all the musicians left the stage save eight first violins, six second violins, six violas, four cellos, four basses, two flutes, two oboes, two clarinets, two bassoons, two horns, two trumpets and one timpani, leaving less than one-half of the musical force on the stage. The effect, after the highly dramatic and overwhelming Wagner numbers, was charming in its simplicity. It was like looking at an exquisite miniature after viewing a canvas of a mighty battle scene.

---

93   This statement may seem contradictory to Sousa's actual practice, but while he often transcribed and arranged classical works for his band, he generally avoided arranging symphonies. Medleys or "reminiscences" provided an adequate alternative in some cases. For clarification see his statement at in the final paragraph of the next section.

On the other hand, there is much modern music that is better adapted to a wind combination than to a string, although for obvious reasons originally scored for an orchestra. If in such cases the interpretation is equal to the composition, the balance of a wind combination is more satisfying.

The Aim of the Composer

The all-pervading aim of the composer is to produce color, dynamics, nuances, the story-telling quality, and the greatest number of mixed and unmixed quartettes, and the combination and composition that vivifies that result is the most desired one. To presume that the clarinet, the cornet and the trombone should be simply used to blare forth marches and ragtime tunes, or that the violin family should devote its days to scraping waltzes, two-steps and fox trots is equally ludicrous. The string band and the wind-band are among the brightest constellations in the melodic heavens. The former may be likened to the feminine, the latter to the masculine, for like maid and man, they can breathe into life the soulful, the religious, the sentimental, the heroic and the sublime. The mission of each is to uplift humanity; the doctrine, "God's Sunshine is for All;" the motto, "Beauty, Love and Harmony Must Prevail."

"The Xylophone" by Joe Green

Source: *The New York Musician and Knocker*, November 1917, in *SPB* 46, 145.

> *Although less famous and much shorter-lived than his younger brother George Hamilton Green (1893–1970), who marketed himself as "the greatest xylophonist in the world," it was Joe Green (1892–1939) who joined the Sousa band for four seasons beginning in 1915. He would later play timpani for the NBC Symphony and host a radio show for General Motors.*[94] *This essay presents an opportunity to see the Sousa Band from the perspective of a "typical" member.*

(Editor's Note—Mr. Joe Green and his brother, George Hamilton Green, are admittedly the greatest xylophone players before the public. They are sons of Bandmaster Geo. Green, of Omaha, Neb., and after having been very

---

94   Further on the Green brothers see Lewis, "Much More than Ragtime."

successful in their careers throughout the Central West came to New York, where their playing has caused the most favorable comment and attracted international attention.)

It was my intention at the beginning to be a drummer and tympanist and the xylophone was only a side issue and used as a part of the ordinary drummer's outfit. It is necessary that the successful drummer play the xylophone and bells and most of them do, but it was many years before I considered specializing on them.

For four or five years I played drums, bells and tympani around Omaha. Really held no very important places [sic] and had no decided ideas about getting on in the world. Played at the Empress Theater among others and through conversations with different traveling musicians and seeing that I could do about the same things they were able to, decided to change my location. This was more the traveling fever than any studied intention to improve my position.

My first venture was to Chicago where I led the usual "jobbing" drummer's life playing among other places at the Gaiety Theatre and at the LaSalle Hotel. In Chicago I came in contact with better musicians than I had met before and in a way my ambitions were fired. I decided to really learn how to play. After close inquiry I found that Mr. Zettelman of the Chicago Symphony was considered the finest tympanist and went to him for lessons.[95] He was all that had been said about him. I consider him the greatest tympanist today and am proud of the fact that he was my teacher.

After concluding my studies with Zettelman I accepted a position as tympanist with Kryl's band where I gained considerable experience which has since proved very valuable to me.[96]

My next engagement was in the "Dutch Room" at the National Hotel, Minneapolis, and from there to the Hotel Muehlebache at Kansas City, Mo.

---

95 Joseph Zettelman was the timpanist for the Chicago Symphony Orchestra from 1891–1930. In 1921 and 1930 he wrote method books for the instrument published by Chicago's Ludwig Drums, for which he was a spokesman. Jazz drummer Vic Berton, another of Zettelman's pupils, also played in the Sousa Band.

96 Cornetist and bandmaster Bohumir Kryl (1875–1961) left the Sousa Band in 1898 apparently in a dispute over making unauthorized copies of the band's music for himself. He went on to make a number of significant early recordings of cornet solos.

Up to this time my work had not included xylophone playing except as I stated before, as a side issue. But at the Muehlebache the leader favored this instrument and it was soon made a feature of every concert. During my engagement there I practiced the xylophone seriously and felt that I was making good on it. My brother had come to New York and I also aspired to the larger places. So, packing my various accessories, I took the plunge.

It took some time for me to secure work in the city. I found there were many other drummers and xylophonists who were also very fine performers and it is not an easy matter for any one to "break in" in the large city. Finally, however, I was engaged for the Fritzi Scheff review, being featured at the Palace Royal, and from there soon transferred to Rector's. The season was opening for Sousa's Band and I was engaged for that. The following is one of our last programs at the Willow Grove engagement.

Concert, Willow Grove, Sept. 4, 1917:

Overture—Coronation . . . . Kela-Bela [Béla Kéler]
Xylophone Solo—Raymond . . . . Thomas
Mr. Joseph Green.
Fantasia—Eugene Oneguine. . . . . Tschaikowsky
Baritone Solo—My Dreams . . . . Tosti
Mr. Percy Hemus.
Serenade—My Lubly Queen. . . . . Middleton
March—The Gladiator . . . . Sousa

Am now making records at the Columbia Phonograph with the Jazzarimba Band and have accepted a place in the orchestra at the Century Theatre for the winter.[97]

Being familiar with the piano keyboard is almost a necessity for the xylophonist if he intends to make that instrument his specialty. He should practice carefully and diligently on all the scales, broken chords, arpeggios and especially on double notes. This last, double notes, is where the average player is weak. He can play a melody, but when it comes to playing the second part with it he misses badly.

97   The Yerkes' Jazzarimba Orchestra, directed by Harry A. Yerkes, made dozens of recordings from 1917 to 1923.

The xylophone is a great asset to the drummer and every one should have one. The instrument records well on the phonograph although the extreme high notes do not come out as well as the lower ones.

The marimba with its lower register makes a very fine accompanying instrument but the xylophone is really best for the soloist.

Editor's Note—Mr. Herbert L. Clarke, the eminent cornetist of Sousa's Band, has stated that he considers Mr. Green a wonderful soloist and an extraordinarily fine musician. Coming from such an authority, there could be no higher praise for a young and ambitious man.[98]

---

98   Actually Clarke, who played in in the Sousa Band's Chicago debut in 1893 and finally joined the ensemble full-time in 1898, had just resigned his post as cornetist and assistant director in September 1917.

1917-1918

Sousa at War

"Mrs. Sousa Aiding the Soldiers"

Source: *Musical Courier* (New York City), November 8, 1917, in *SPB* 47, 69.

The United States had only been at war for six months—actually the first troops arrived in Europe only in late June—when Mrs. Sousa (Jane van Middlesworth Bellis) lent her influence to aid the soldiers. The couple met during an 1879 production of Gilbert and Sullivan's H. M. S. Pinafore *and married on December 30 of the same year. Mrs. Sousa only rarely penned a public essay and she received virtually no attention from interviewers.*

To the *Musical Courier:*

I am trying to collect some music and musical instruments for the boys "Over Seas." The Commission on Training Camp Activities will handle the matter. Lee Hanmer, the gentleman connected with it, is very grateful for any co-operation in the matter, especially for the contribution of musical instruments. Banjos, mandolins, guitars, ukuleles, cornets, clarinets, flutes, accordions, mouth organs, violins—in fact, anything can be used in the billets and for drilling. That is, the music contributed will be used for drilling. It is to keep the boys from being homesick and getting into mischief.

Anything any of us can do in the present tragic, abnormal condition of the world seems too little, whatever it may be. I feel sure that the *Musical Courier* will publish a notice to the effect that music or musical instruments may be sent to the office of Lieutenant John Philip Sousa, 1 West Thirty-fourth street, New York City.[99]

---

99   This twelve-story hi-rise was constructed from 1903–06 and still stands. The Empire State Building would be built across the street in 1930–31.

[Editor's note:] There is no need to emphasize the point Mrs. Sousa makes or to urge all individuals and families who are in possession of musical instruments they do not actually need to contribute them for Mrs. Sousa's useful and patriotic purpose.

"Muck Should Get Out of U.S., Thinks Sousa"

Source: *Detroit Journal*, November 19, 1917, in *SPB* 47, 96.

> *World War I strained professional relationships in the American musical world, where Germans had always been overrepresented. The conflict reached a peak when Karl Muck (1859–1940), conductor of the Boston Symphony Orchestra, refused to open his wartime concerts with the national anthem. Although Swiss by birth (and thus theoretically neutral), by the end of 1917 he was removed from his position as conductor. Shortly thereafter he was arrested and placed into an internment camp for the remainder of the war. Even his notoriety as a conductor of Wagner, including at Bayreuth, could not save him from Sousa's patriotic outrage. Years after the war he was still referred to as the "terrible Dr. Muck."*[100]

"If Dr. Karl Muck doesn't like his orchestra to play the Star Spangled Banner, or any other American anthem, he had better get back to Germany, where he belongs."

Thus did Lieut. John Philip Sousa criticize the leader of the Boston Symphony orchestra.

Continuing, Lieut. Sousa declared:

"Germans have no business in America in times such as these. I am sure, had I been in Germany when war was declared by the United States, that I would not have remained there. My duty would have been to my country. I could not have stayed away from it. I cannot understand why Dr. Muck, if he is so loyal to the kaiser, does not get out of our borders.

"He cannot raise the question that a patriotic number has no place on a symphony orchestra's program. For years they have been playing 'Heil Dir Im Siegerkranz,' into which is written the Prussian national anthem. Symphony orchestras have, for ten years, been making Tschaikowsky's

---

100	See for instance Rosenfeld, "Bruckner (1921)" in *Musical Chronicle*, 197.

'Overture of 1812' one of their principal numbers, and in this there are snatches of 'La Marseillaise.' There are any number of other instances, so Dr. Muck could not be in need of a precedent.

"He should understand, also, that patriotism comes first—art afterwards.

"This one thing is absolutely certain—

"Were Dr. Muck an American taking this stand in Germany he would be looked after mighty quick!

"Back in 1900, when my band made its first tour of the world, we were playing in a hall in Berlin and one of our numbers included the quick firing of a revolver, twice in succession. I did not know, at the time, that there was a law in Germany against discharging firearms in a hall. We played this selection the first night, and early the following day I received notice from the police that I would not be permitted to repeat the pistol shots.

"So, you see, even in time of peace Germany would not permit a violation of its code of laws, in so small a thing as this, and in spite of the additional fact that my band was heralded, by Germans, as the greatest in the world.

"Dr. Muck is not alone in this criticism. Other German artists who may be in this country should accept our demands, or get out. We have no place for them. No time for them."

"Parents of Patriotism are Mother and Music"

Source: *Chicago Examiner*, March 7, 1918, in *SPB* 45:3, 94.

Now well into World War I, Sousa draws upon his earlier research into national anthems to point out the continuing relevance of music in times of war. He also repurposed material from his April 27, 1905 editorial on British copyright law (see page 45). The essay's subtitle says it all: "All Powerful in Bringing Out the Loyalty of Man in All Lands; Constitute the Undefiled Soul of the Nation."

More than two hundred years ago Andrew Fletcher of Saltoun, a philosopher and a keen observer of men and their ways, said: "I knew a very wise man who believed if a man were permitted to make all the ballads he would not care who should make the laws of a nation." A short half-year ago a law was passed by Congress, signed by the President, talked about by fully three-fourths of the population of our country, and is known as the Adamson law, supposedly of vast import to a large body of our citizens.[101] That law has already been declared invalid by one of our courts. Over a hundred years ago a song was written by Francis Scott Key and called "The Star Spangled Banner." It is sung and played today with as much fervor and patriotism as ever during its long life. No court has declared this song either invalid or unconstitutional.

Fletcher's wise man was indeed wise.

✦ ✦ ✦

When the heart of this nation throbs with patriotism it does so to the rhythm of "The Star Spangled Banner," "Hail Columbia," "Columbia, the Gem of the Ocean," "Dixie," "Yankee Doodle" and "The Stars and Stripes Forever."

Music and song have ever been the handmaids of loyalty and love. They reassure, they comfort, they sway the multitude, and buckle on the armor of victory.

The first popular song recorded is the one sung by Moses and the children of Israel, in exultation after the destruction of Pharaoh's hosts. Words alone were not adequate to celebrate such an event, so the children of Israel raised their voices in mighty unison, and, carried away by the greatness of the occasion, sang, played upon the timbrels, and danced in graceful abandon, led by the beautiful Miriam of Biblical history. That happened in the days of Moses.

Let us come down to the days of McKinley. The land, Cuba. The year, 1898. Just as the children of Israel lifted their voices in those ancient days we did in 1898.[102] The unison, the abandon, the joy were the same, only the music was different. Moses and his people sang, "The horse and his rider hath He thrown into the sea—the Lord is a man of war." Uncle Sam

---

101 The 1916 Adamson Act instituted labor protections for interstate railroad workers in an effort to avert a national strike. It was the first time Congress regulated working hours for employees of private corporations. While a lower court struck it down as unconstitutional (as noted by Sousa), in 1917 the Supreme Court upheld the law's constitutionality.

102 The text reads "1983" at this end of the sentence. Presumably it is a misreading of 1898 from the previous sentence.

and his people sang, "There'll be a hot time in the old town to-night."[103] After all, human nature is pretty much the same, looking up or down the avenues of time.

✦ ✦ ✦

Twice blest is the hero whose deeds awaken the muse of the poet or the musician. Henry of Navarre will ever remain the White Plumed Knight through Macaulay's poem.[104] Many warriors of equal courage and daring will be dimly remembered only through the prosaic utterances of bald history, because no poet has sung of them.

"Little Phil's" niche in the temple of fame is made more luminous by Buchanan Reid's thrilling "Sheridan's Ride," ever bringing to mind that the great general started "twenty miles away." However great Sherman's generalship was to us in the civil war, the thrill to the boys in blue comes when they hear "Marching Through Georgia."

The heroes of the world remain perennial when they are recorded in song and story. The deeds of "Charley Is My Darling," "The Tales of Hoffman," the romance of "Tannhauser," and the story of "Thais" will never die while the music describing them lives.[105]

The love of a people for a melody I would liken unto the love of a mother for her babe.

✦ ✦ ✦

A thrilling episode of the power of music is shown when Jessie Brown tells the besieged garrison at Lucknow that she hears the pipers coming:

> There Jessie Brown stood listening
> Till a sudden gladness broke

---

103 This 1896 song by Theodore August Metz was particularly popular among American troops stationed in Cuba. For an account roughly contemporary with Sousa's essay see Browne, *Our National Ballads*, 208.

104 Thomas Babington Macaulay (1800–1859), a British politician and literary figure, wrote Ivry, A *Song of the Huguenots* in 1824.

105 These references are to, in order, a traditional Scottish song and operas by Jacques Offenbach, Richard Wagner, and Jules Massenet.

All over her face; and she caught my hand
And drew me near as she spoke:

But Jessie said, "The slogan's done;
But winna ye hear it noo,
The Campbells are comin', it's no dream
Our succors hae broken through."

It was the pipes of the Highlanders,
And now they played "Auld Lang Syne."
It came to our men like the voice of God,
And they shouted along the line.

And they wept and shook one another's hands,
And the women sobbed in a crowd;
And every one knelt down where he stood
And we all thanked God aloud.

And the piper's ribbons and tartans streamed,
Marching round and round our line,
And our cheerful hearts were broken with tears
As the pipes played "Auld Lang Syne."[106]

And "Auld Lang Syne" is as dear to the ears of the world to-day as when Jessie Brown and the besieged garrison heard it [during] those terrible East Indian times.

When "Dixie" is played or sung in the South the very atmosphere seems surcharged with enthusiasm. The transformation from tropical tranquility to that mighty yell that surges as a Niagara of human sound is familiar to any one who has heard that infectious tune in the land of cotton.

✦ ✦ ✦

Music, in all lands, is a greater power to bring out the patriotic in man than any other force, except the influence of motherhood. We know, and

---

106 This is an excerpt from Robert Lowell's 1858 poem "The Relief of Lucknow." Sousa's version of the text, printed here as given, includes slight differences when compared to the original.

all highly civilized people know, that at times we criticize our laws, call our government weak, speak about a climate as detestable, utter tirades against the shortcomings of our fellow citizens, invoke the wrath of God on our political opponents, gaze with jealous eyes upon our competitive professional brethren, and become pessimistic of everything in the land of our birth. But suddenly there is a criticism or an attack made on us by others, and we fly to the defense of our country.

Why? Because—

We draw sustenance and patriotism from the breasts of our mothers and from the inspiration of our music. These are the two great things that present no "ifs" or "buts," and they constitute the pure, undefiled soul of the nation.

◆ ◆ ◆

J. A. Kappey, in his compilation of songs of Eastern Europe, says: "When Swiss mercenary soldiers were serving in the Netherlands and in France, accidental hearing of one of the strains, the 'Ranz De Vaches,' led to frequent desertions, in consequence of which the penalty of death was decreed upon any one who sang or performed the 'Kuhreihen' within hearing of the Swiss troops."[107]

I feel this point so strongly that I can never conceive of a man being "naturalized" or "nationalized." Undoubtedly, of those that are "naturalized," their sense of honor brings them to obey the laws of their adopted country, for which at times they have willingly given their lives, but even with this votive offering, I fully believe that the vitalization of the birthland, born of the mother, and the music of the fatherland remain with them for all time.

There is an incident told in Bayard Taylor's exquisite poem, "The Song of the Camp," that shows the single-heartedness of man when music is in his soul. It is a story of the day before the bombardment of Sebastopol, when the soldiers of the British Empire, whether from the Severn, the Clyde, or the banks of Shannon, sang one song, a song universal to the English speaking people:

---

107 Kappey and Kappey, *Songs of Eastern Europe*, 150. Given its contents include national anthems from much of Eastern Europe, Sousa presumably came across this book while researching his *National, Patriotic, and Typical Airs of All Lands* (1890).

—Each heart recalled a different name,
But all sang "Annie Laurie."

✦ ✦ ✦

While propinquity has much to do with bringing two hearts in unison, there is no doubt that many and many a happy marriage has started with the singing of the folk songs of a land.

The genius of the American people is tinged with the sunshine idea of a God, a good-natured, smiling God, a God who says in His goodness: "The basic principle in your republic is that the individual is the institution, your flag the sign and symbol of your land. As the individual is the all-powerful, he himself must determine where he belongs in the scheme of your national life. In Europe society at large determines on three classes, strongly defined—the aristocratic, the middle, and the lower—but as you in America have elected to make man the institution, you can have but two classes, the polite and the vulgar."

The polite are never ashamed of the elemental, therefore they cherish the songs of the church and the songs of the fireside. And just as long as they get together and sing "Abide In Me," "Rock of Ages," "Lead, Kindly Light," "Beulah Land," "Home, Sweet Home," "Suwanee River," "Annie Lisle," and "The Mocking Bird," just so long will the American heart be attuned to love of home, love of country, and love of God.

"'Don't Propose Until I Compose,' Sousa Warning"

Source: *New York Herald*, May 30, 1918, in *SPB* 49, 13.

Again the bandmaster presents himself as a patriot fighting on the musical front of the Great War. Sousa completed his Wedding March *shortly after this interview and Arthur Pryor conducted the Sousa Band in a recording for Victor in December, by which time the war was over. Sousa still conducted occasional works by Mendelssohn and Wagner in 1917, however there is a marked absence of the two composers' works on concerts from 1918 until about 1922.*[108]

---

108 See Bierley, *Incredible Band*, 380–81 and 420–21.

Projects New American Wedding March to Replace Two of German Origin.

Although Mendelssohn's Wedding March and the strains of "Lohengrin" may constitute an agreeable sound at Prussian weddings they will in the very near future be considered something less than music when the blushing brides and startled bridegrooms of America romp altarward. Something had to be done in the matter and yesterday Lieutenant John Philip Sousa made it known that just as rapidly as he can compose it America will have a wedding march made in America and ideally calculated for American moments of happiness.

Returning from a trip to the Great Lakes, Ill., station of the Naval Reserve Force to which he is attached, Lieutenant Sousa said the first thought which had come to him of the need of an American wedding march developed with an article in the *Herald* of Tuesday.

"And, as the *Herald* said, something must be done about that matter at once," said Lieutenant Sousa. "It cannot be done in a day, for it must be a good march, but I propose to devote myself to the task immediately, and very soon American brides and grooms who are patient in the matter will have a march which will be distinctly American. My only word to the young men and women of America is that from a musical standpoint it is their duty to hesitate until proper music can be prepared for their great experience. In other words, don't propose until I compose."

Mrs. Oliver Cromwell Field, who is active in the American Defense Society and is president of the American Relief Legion, was to a great extent responsible for the agitation for American wedding music for America. The Relief Legion made the suggestion which led to the *Herald* article of Tuesday on the subject. As a result of the enrolling of the famous American bandmaster in the project, a meeting will be arranged for Friday at which Lieutenant Sousa will be present to receive the suggestions and thanks of the legion.

"Sousa's Ridiculous Assignment"

Source: *The Oklahoman*, early June 1918, in *SPB* 49, 64.[109]

> *News of Sousa's intention to write new wedding music to replace the traditional works of Mendelssohn and Wagner traveled fast. As this editorial indicates, the idea was met with skepticism. The march he wrote failed to replace the others' works in the end. The way in which the author isolates Sousa from "classical" composers provides an interesting perspective of his reputation within an increasingly fragmented musical world.*

The report that John Philip Sousa is at work upon a wedding march which will mark the step of bridal couples hereafter instead of the familiar strains of Wagner and Mendelssohn must be attributed to the June temperature. There are many mansions in the House of the Muse, to be sure, and Mr. Sousa's plate is on one of the doors, but it is a different house from that occupied by either Mendelssohn or Wagner. The assignment is about as apposite as would be that of Bud Fisher to do a Mona Lisa or a soulful novice in clay modeling to restore the dimpled elbow of Venus' lost arm.[110]

It is possible, perhaps probable, that, were they living today, both Mendelssohn and Wagner would be corrupted by the virus of junkerism that has perverted practically all Germany; but such hypothetical judgment is gratuitous and unkind.[111] Wagner was every whit as much a radical in politics as he was in music and knew long years of penury and exile for joining in the revolt of the German people against the tyranny of their kings. There has been no Goethe in the militaristic, materialistic Germany, but it is worth remembering that that singer of democracy was Mendelssohn's closest personal friend, and from that friendship we may infer that the musician like the poet was a believer in freedom.

It may be well enough to taboo German composers by way of accentuating our loathing of the monstrosity that is now Germany, but we need not make ourselves ridiculous and stupidly Prussian by ordering Sousa

---

109 The *SPB* clipping gives a date of May 30 for this essay, but the first sentence of the article indicates it was written in June.

110 Cartoonist Bud Fisher's (1885–1954) *Mutt and Jeff* strip was a staple of newspaper sports sections.

111 "Junkerism" was a term of contempt referring to the East Prussian nobility that dominated German politics during World War I.

to do something "just as good" as Mendelssohn or Wagner. The haunting melodies of Mendelssohn and the eloquent, virile beauty of Wagner will entrance and inspire the world long after William Hohenzollern is forgotten and long after the evanescent triviality of our own John Philip Sousa has pinky-panked back into the silence.

"Leave German Music to Germans"

Source: *Musical Leader* (Chicago), October 10, 1918, 350, in *SPB* 49, 143.

> An article by Mrs. William Jay opposing the performance of German music during wartime published in the August issue of the Musical Leader prompted the editor to seek out more opinions on the issue. Bombastic statements by vaudevillian performer Joe Weber, operatic soprano Frances Alda, Italian bandmaster Giuseppe Creatore, and composer Edward Schaaf, among others, not only agreed that the ban was necessary, but argued that prominent German musicians should be barred from performing (as happened earlier with Karl Muck). Sousa's response echoes those sentiments.

"The old adage, 'Love and Art have no frontiers' must be held in abeyance at this time. The mental attitude of the German has compelled the rest of the world to modify its views on all that pertains to honor, chivalry and fair play. The world outside of Germany is brought face to face with the ugly fact that the German estimate of the rest of the globe is based on the belief that he himself is a superman; that no one has any rights that he need respect. The war has shown that from his view, all he does is right and what the rest of the world does is wrong. Argument has no weight against such an attitude—action only counts.

"To tell a German that you play German music for art's sake would probably meet with his approval, but owing to his peculiar style of reasoning he would add that you also play it because it is the only music fit to play; as you know this is false reasoning you have but one recourse; leave German music to the Germans.

"In this western world of ours it is an undisputed fact that we have not one German tradition; we dress our women as the French suggest; our laws are based on those of the English; our ideas of chivalry are Spanish; our standard of honor is British. If we speak of the greatest writer we speak of Shakespeare; if we wish to link a poet of our own land with that of another, we couple a Tennyson with a Longfellow; of a humorist, a Thackeray with a Twain; when we enumerate our states we find some named for the Spanish; some for the French; some for the English; some for the Indian, but not one remotely named for the German. It would seem that the God of Nations has watched over our beauty with a kindly vigil.

["]At the present time the bluest blood, the brightest brains and the best brawn of our land is in martial array against the German, and our boys in blue and our boys in khaki are rushing into battle and victory to the tunes of our land. Therefore, it is the duty of every American to suppress anything and everything that in any way brings comfort, profit or satisfaction to the Hun. He has forfeited every consideration from a fair-playing world and the only way to get it through the hide of his vanity, obtuseness and stolidness is to bludgeon him physically, mentally, morally, financially, and perpetually."

1919–1928

The Roaring Twenties

"Appreciations of Rachmaninoff from Famous Musicians in America"

Source: *The Etude* 37, October 1919, 617–18.

> *It is unclear exactly what prompted* The Etude *to solicit opinions on Sergei Rachmaninoff, but most likely it was his flight from the Russian Revolution. He reached the United States in November 1918, where he would live until his death in 1943. Leopold Stokowski, Josef Stransky, Percy Grainger, and others contributed alongside Sousa to this outpouring of appreciation.*

Perhaps there are no people with greater imagination than the American. Being the most youthful of nations, we are like children absorbing the thrills of a fairy story. We probably show a keener interest in the affairs of the world than the older nations. Therefore, we place anyone who has accomplished great things on our mental throne, and bow with admiration. As a people, we are devoid of envy, and are jealous only of our honor. Let any man give the world something worth while and we take him to our hearts. It is so with Rachmaninoff. With a name but a myth to us in his early days, we took him and placed him in the garden of those we admire. The "C♯ Prelude" has been known for years wherever music is heard in our land. Years ago I played it under the simple title of "Prelude in C♯ Minor" in every town from the Atlantic to the Pacific, from the St. Lawrence to the Gulf Stream. A little later a friend told me he had heard it in Europe as "The Bells of Moscow." A man told me that it was used as the entr'acte music in the Russian play "Crime and Punishment," and I again changed the name and placed it on

my program under its new cognomen, and it sounded just as effective.[112] In
any attempt to name the great men in musical art, Rachmaninoff must be
seriously considered. A long and happy life to him!

"All's Well with the Musical World"

Source: 1921 Sousa Band Tour Program, in *SPB* 51:1, n.p.[113]

> *The rise of ragtime and jazz did not pass unnoticed by Sousa or his bandsmen.
> Where xylophonist Joe Green (see page 126) played in a jazz band while not
> touring, others spoke out against it. Ragtime quickly found its way into band
> programs, but jazz was more controversial. As the 1920s progressed Sousa
> would become increasingly outspoken about the value of jazz, typically stating
> in interviews that when well played it was good music, but that it was usually
> played poorly. Herbert L. Clarke was more blunt, at least in private, calling "jaz
> [sic] music... the nearest Hell, or the Devil, in music."[114] By 1924 Sousa's views
> softened considerably (see page 170).*

A number of well meaning but highly apprehensive people are much
exercised over the popularity of the so-called Jazz music; they fear the Soul of
Art may be contaminated by the tentacles of Syncopation, and the Structure
of Harmony by the extravagance of Counterpoint, but, Lord alive, they have
naught to fear. A glance down the avenues of the past shows the whitened
bones of a myriad of musical ephemera. Stepping high, with head erect,
ever onward and onward, march the works of Beethoven, Mozart, Wagner,
Schumann and the rest of the normals.

At no time in the musical history of our land has music received greater
recognition. The steady increase in the number of symphonic bodies, the
size and excellence of the orchestras of our leading moving picture houses,

---

112 Rachmaninoff's Prelude in C-sharp minor, op. 3 no. 2, was an early (1892) and extremely popular
composition for solo piano. Many spurious names were eventually attached to it, so Sousa's
confusion is understandable.

113 The souvenir tour programs preserved in the *SPB* include a number of essays previously published
by Sousa with a citation of the original source, in this case the December 10, 1920 issue of *Wurlitzer
Magazine*. The *SPB* do not always include the original publications (as is the case for this essay).
Bierley (*Works*) seems also to have obtained his bibliographic information from these later reprints.

114 Clarke, letter to Elden E. Benge, January 13, 1921. The letter is housed in the Sousa Archives at the
University of Illinois and is accessible via their website.

the higher ability of the orchestras in the finer vaudeville theatres, the more complete instrumentations of our bands all show that music in our country is on a healthy and progressive basis. The enormous popularity of mechanical musical players attest the universal acclaim for the concord of sweet sounds, and among the offerings of the musical players are found the names of many great composers.

My own experience during the past year has been the most successful of my career and has shown that interest was equal in all parts of the country. Lastly but not least is the attention paid to music in our Universities—in some of which they have a course in band and orchestral training.

More and more amateurs are studying music solely for the pleasure derived, and instrument makers are reckoning with the output of instruments to be used in a purely amateur way. To the well wisher the present shows a great uplift in the progress of the Art in America.

"Success in Music and How to Win It."

Source: 1921 Sousa Band Tour Program, in *SPB* 59:2, n.p.[115]

This essay might be the most representative of Sousa's attitudes towards his career as a composer, conductor, and impresario. His humility on the podium stands in contrast with the famous tyrannical orchestral conductors that were his contemporaries. His listing of The Stars and Stripes Forever *alongside the classical masterworks strives to situate his compositions in the larger world of art music—a concern shown throughout his career.*

Assuming one has adaptability, talent or genius for music in its various ramifications, that is, as a player, a composer, conductor or combination of any of these, the chance of success is very great if to it is added sincerity and loftiness of purpose.

It is a worthy ambition to hitch your wagon to a star, but if you do not know how to drive, it avails naught.

---

115 This essay was apparently printed at least three separate times. Bierley (*Works*, 200) lists this as a 1926 publication, overlooking the 1921 tour program version presented here. The 1921 source notes that the essay was printed in *The C. G. Conn, Ltd., Magazine* at some earlier point in time. The two 1926 printings noted by Bierley were in another Conn publication and in the October issue of the *Selmer Bulletin*.

It is highly desirable to want to aspire to leadership, but it is more important that one is worthy of leadership.

He who serves his art and his fellow-man conscientiously and intelligently, becomes a leader. He who aims at dictatorship, finds himself without anyone to dictate to.

I should say a great detriment to success is envy, and whenever the musician has it, he stands weakened before his profession and his auditor. It is always proper to admire, applaud and acknowledge greatness in others, and if you are worthy, you will very soon find that the world acknowledges that in you.

One should remember that the first consideration in a career is respect for the public. The public is always hunting for cleverness, but the public does not want you to say, "I am clever, you are not, bow to my superiority!"

It is well to remember that the composite brain of the public is greater than yours, however brilliant you are—or think you are.

It is well to remember that to be successful one must play, direct or compose up to the public. It is the greatest nonsense to imagine that success depends on playing down to the public.

A careful scrutiny of the public's likings will show that what is best in the player's repertoire or the composer's creations are the universal favorites. The most successful of symphonies, operas, suites, overtures, ballads, waltzes, marches and what-not, show the evidence of inspiration, and that which shows slovenly workmanship dies a-borning or very shortly afterwards. The world in its cleverness makes standards, so the most inspired symphony is the successful one, and the most inspired jig is the one most sought for.

It is not a difficult matter to designate the perennial favorites and the addition of the inspired works year after year. One remembers the Eroica, the Pathetique, The Creation, The Messiah, Thanhauser, Lohengrin, Faust, Traumerie, The Spring Song, The Melody in F, The Blue Danube, The Lost Chord, The Stars and Stripes Forever, etc., but who remembers the ephemeral hit of yesteryear?[116]

---

116   The composers and proper titles of these works are as follows: Beethoven's *Symphony no. 3* "Eroica," and *Piano Sonata in C minor*, op. 13, "Pathétique," Haydn's *The Creation*, Handel's *Messiah*, Wagner's *Tannhäuser* and *Lohengrin*, Gounod's *Faust*, Schumann's "Träumerei" from *Kinderszenen*, op. 15 no. 7 (note that Richard Strauss's *Träumerie am Kamin* was composed only in 1924 and never played

Embracing an opportunity is most important in one's career. To cite an instance, I was the Musical Director of a musical show at a liberal salary, when I was offered the leadership of the United States Marine Band.

The Government salary was but a third of what I was receiving at the moment. I accepted the Governmental offer, because I felt there was an opportunity by hard work and attention to the duties of the position to attract attention beyond the hoop of my horizon at that time.

I worked harder during the twelve years I was in the service than I had ever before, and again opportunity knocked at my door. I left the Government service and my career since is well-known history. In each instance, I was advised not to make a change, purely for financial reasons. It is a matter of record that my judgement was sound.

I believe it is fatal to success to consider at the beginning the financial gain, either for the player or the composer. As soon as an artistic recognition has been acknowledged, financial recognition follows as the day the night. Therefore, be true to yourself, to your fellow-man, and to your art, and unless you are extremely unfortunate, your life will be a life of gladness.

"Music, an Ideal Christmas Present"

Source: *The Etude* 39, December 1921, 777.

> *The title of this interview is somewhat misleading as to actual content: the premise of buying music lessons for Christmas provided Sousa with an opening to address music as a career and a means of income. In some ways little has changed from Sousa's time.*

"The idea of making music a Christmas present has no element of originality in it at this date. For years music has been making such strides in America, and the army of people who love music has been growing so rapidly, that at Christmas time the department stores display everything from a grand piano to a mouth organ as possible Christmas presents, just as they used to display bookcases, clocks, shaving mugs and the endless procession of slippers for pater familias.

---

by the Sousa Band while Schumann's work was a staple on the 1921 tour), Mendelssohn, *Songs without Words* op. 62 no. 6, "Frühlingslied," Rubinstein's "Mélodie" in F major, op. 3 no. 1, Johann Strauss's *An der schönen blauen Donau,* op. 314, and Sullivan's "The Lost Chord.'

"But it is not this kind of a Christmas present I am thinking of now. I know a musician, whose name is very familiar to the readers of *The Etude*, who recently told me that his start in music was due at the very first to a present of a term of music lessons, made to him one Christmas time by his beloved grandmother. If I remember correctly, he said that the cost was twelve dollars. From this start came the training which has enabled this man to train scores of other musicians, inspire and help thousands, and serve with the rest of us in endeavoring to raise musical standards in our country. Twelve dollars! Rather an unusual cornerstone for a very large structure!

"There are just now thousands of parents, uncles and aunts wondering what kind of a present to select for Mary or John. In all probability they will invest in many things which are not only dispensable, but which may be detrimental. Who knows that a gift of a term for a year in music may not mean the selection of a career for the young man or woman! Music in these days is by no means a calling to belittle.

The Emancipation of the Professions

"We have witnessed during the last fifty years what might be termed the emancipation of the professions. By this I mean the commercial emancipation. The lawyer was the first to establish his status, largely because he fought for it. The doctor, who a hundred years ago was content to bleed his patients, give them some nostrum and a little hot water, has now developed his science to an amazing degree, and commands enormous fees for his services. Notice that in these two professions, as in all others, the remuneration has depended upon what the professional man has to give, and what the public has most demanded.

"Music is possibly the last of the professions to develop a commercial value. Only a hundred years ago in the days of Beethoven and Schubert, in Europe its commercial value was *nil*, or nearly that. The musician was expected to pour out his wealth in the most bounteous manner and receive a pittance. Now the whole situation has changed because of the enormous demand for music of all kinds, resulting in great progress in the art [and] in the welfare of the musician, to say nothing of the development of one of the largest industries in America.

"Whether it is beneficial for the art or not the musician now receives excellent remuneration for his services.

"There never seems to be any suspicion that huge fees will injure the status of the scientist, the jurist or the doctor, but because musicians were paid such beggarly fees for so long, the exploiters of art seem to fear that they will become tainted if they are not cheated of their just deserts.

"When I was little more than a boy I played the violin in a theatre. Music at that time was looked upon as a highly precarious occupation. The musician was expected to give his services. If he did not he was queer or discourteous. There was a man in Washington at that time who had suddenly grown wealthy through the simple expedient of furnishing shoes for the government during the civil war, and substituting paper for leather in the soles. The people despised him as a profiteer always ready to trick the public or any of his friends when the opportunity presented itself. Once he arranged a party at his house and invited me, underlining the words, '*please bring your violin.*' I realized that such a man wanted me for my ability to play and was unwilling to pay for it. Accordingly I wrote to him: 'I am very sorry that I cannot come, but I shall be glad to send the violin if you wish it.['] The only way to bring such a man as that to a proper understanding of music is to make him pay and pay well for it. As long as he got it for nothing he had little respect for the musical profession. He would never have asked his butcher to come around for the evening and bring around a pound of steak.

"A few years ago there was an altogether false conception of art, a kind of affected squeamishness about money, which held back much musical progress in America. Recognise music as a profession on a rank with every other profession and deserving adequate remuneration at all times and the art side will take care of itself. There never was a time when music stood so high in public estimation, and all musicians are benefiting by it. Melzer, the critic, wrote on the first night of my operetta *The Bride Elect*: 'To think that a man in this day writing a comic opera can make $100,000 from it while Bizet could have died of want a few weeks after the production of his *Carmen*.' All of this preamble is to convince *The Etude* reader of one thing: The so-called and greatly deplored commercial value of music in this day is really an element in convincing the greater majority of the public that the profession is 'worth while.' As long as it was looked upon as a fashionable pastime for young ladies, it was impossible to get the average American father to regard it seriously as a profession for his son.

Turn to Music

"It is for this reason that many parents and friends who desire to make a Christmas present turn to music lessons, musical instruments, talking machine records, books, tickets for concerts, sheet music and so forth. Unlike many presents that lose their value in a few weeks, music often lasts a lifetime. Very little in the way of musical education is wasted. Even though the student has not the slightest thought of music as a profession, unless he is hopeless stupid, he will acquire a mental training and an artistic taste that will stay with him all the rest of his days and add unlimited happiness to his life. How can one possibly make a more delightful present than one of this sort?

"'But,' persists the very material father, 'I don't want to bother with music as a present for my boy. I want something practical.' He probably does not realize that the very cigar which he is puffing was made in a factory in Cuba in which the workers insist upon being supplied with music while they work. For years there have been trained singers employed in some industries to perform during the working hours. Practical fathers should know that there is nothing like music for speeding up the worker. The singing worker is happy and always has been. In the Fiji Islands I remember the natives who were employed to load coal.[117] Singing was as much a part of their working equipment as their brawny muscles. Without song it would unquestionably have taken a much longer time to load the ship. What does practical father think of that? Music in industry is a kind of human lubrication preventing sociological friction.

"Of course there is a great deal of nonsense about the place that music occupies in the scheme of affairs. I have never thought it was the greatest thing in the world, it would be stupid to make such a statement. It seems to me that the most important man of this or any other time is the scientist, he is the pioneer of the age. It is to him that our progress is due—particularly to the inventive chemists, the Edisons, the Kelvins, the Roentgens, and the

---

117   This references the 1911 world tour, when the ship the band traveled on between New Zealand and Hawaii would have stopped at Fiji to refuel.

Marconis. No one makes a bigger contribution to the times than the inventive chemist. He is the wizard of the centuries, every flavor, every perfume, every substance can come out of his laboratory; from synthetic rubber or artificial eggs to precious jewels or fabulous explosives. Without great constructive minds of this type we would be centuries behind in our development.

The Great Inspiration

"Music is the most important thing in its place but who would be bold enough to say that its place is as important as that of the inventive chemist—unless by stretching a point we may insist that the chemist is himself inspired to higher efforts through music, as are workers in all walks of life.

["]Here again there is a great deal of cant about the moral effects of music,—largely due to that well meaning English clergyman Hugh R. Haweis who in his *Music and Morals* [1871] made many beautiful statements hardly borne out by facts. Few people who have not natural inclinations to lead a better life will be reformed through music alone. Some of the toughest characters the world has produced from Nero down to the present day have made a hobby of music. Some of the meanest fellows I have ever known (one man in particular had an eye like a decayed eel) have been proficient musicians from the technical standpoint and have apparently been devoted to their work. No, music makes the weeds grow as well as the flowers.

"Can you think of anything which brings more real joy, more genuine delight to more people than music? Thousands and thousands of dollars are spent at Christmas time on confectionary which is soon forgotten, gifts which soon wear out, but music of the best kind lasts for decades and is heard each time with renewed joy. Make this a musical Christmas and it will be a joyous Christmas."[118]

Music is perhaps one of the safest of Christmas presents to make. The number of people who revel in music is astounding. As with all gifts, try to find out what the recipient wants. Possibly it may be an opportunity to

---

118 Because there are closing quotes both here and at the conclusion of the article, yet no opening quotes in the final two paragraphs, it is unclear if the remaining portion of this essay is Sousa's or was written by *The Etude*'s editor. The article's header states this is an "interview," but there is no editorial introduction as would normally be expected. Furthermore the tone changes and it seems unlikely that Sousa would have enthusiastically encouraged the purchase of a recording as a seemly present after discussing music lessons at length.

hear a great symphony orchestra, Paderewski, Galli-Curci or Kreisler; it may be some favorite piece, an album of Beethoven, Mozart, or Chopin, a long wished for book; [or it may be] a talking machine record[,] all of which will bring the Christmas spirit back every week of the year.

Most of all let the giving be done so that the spirit of Merry Christmas will surround it like an aura of Yuletide happiness."

"Dry Law a Tragedy—Sousa"

Source: *Syracuse Journal*, August 3, 1922, in *SPB* 56:2, 136.

> *What might otherwise have been a typical interview promoting that night's concert in Syracuse turned into a more overt political statement on Prohibition. The Constitutional amendment enacting Prohibition took effect on January 16, 1920. Now nearly two years in it remained a divisive issue despite repeal being a decade away. In this case Sousa's ideas on alcohol in society were far more prophetic than his views on jazz.*

Instead of a farce, as the vaudeville comedians have it, prohibition is a tragedy.

So says Lieut. Com. John Philip Sousa, bandmaster, composer, author, horseman and sportsman, who, perhaps, is as great an enemy of drunkenness as the bluest of the blue law advocates.

Lieut. Com. J. P. Sousa, wearing his cheery smile and displaying the personality that has made him beloved by all American music lovers, arrived in Syracuse shortly before noon at the head of his band, which plays at the Jefferson Street State Armory to-night.

In the course of an interview with The Journal, he said:

Prohibition a Tragedy.

"Prohibition spells tragedy rather than farce, for it is bringing a new class of drinkers, men and women who use only the hard stuff. I believe that I am in a position to judge fairly the fruits of the Eighteenth Amendment. During my 12 years in Washington and my 30 years with the band, I have been entertained at least as much as any other person in the United States.

"I have studied the persons I have met at the dinner table during that period. Before prohibition, I am frank to say that only about one woman out of ten would take a cocktail at dinner. If there were 20 persons present at the affair, I am sure that not more than a third would take a glass of light wine. Whiskey was practically unknown.

"It was, in truth, exceptional to see a woman drink. To-day, the woman who does not drink is rather the exception.

Drink to Defy Law.

"Let me say that I do not consider that they drink because of love of liquor. It is rather a defiance of a badly constructed law.

"When you say that I can go to church and take a glass of wine at communion and be law abiding, but that the minute I take a drink outside the church, I am a criminal and a law breaker, you do not appeal to my reason.

"Before the Eighteenth Amendment was added to the Constitution, there were not more than 500,000 drunkards in America. This element comprised about one-half of one per cent. of our population. The lawmakers should have written a statute to control them, not the rest of us.

"The bootlegger, one of the strongest advocates of prohibition, is gaining the dignity of numbers. Soon he will be sufficiently strong to prevent any change in the law.

"The saloon, to be sure, should have been eliminated. But as it now is, the saloon is only half closed. Personally, I know little of the saloon; in the past 40 years, I have passed through the doors of a saloon but three times.

Would License Drinkers.

"Certainly, we want a Nation of clear-headed people, but I believe that better measures could have been written than the Eighteenth Amendment. I suggest that dispensaries be licensed by the state, with Federal inspection mandatory. Let every man who drinks be licensed. Make him show his license every time he buys a drink. And make drunkenness punishable by forfeiture of the holder's license. That, I feel, would be a certain cure."

What does Sousa think of jazz?

Just this:

"It's dying, and so far as my band is concerned, it's dead. Only the dancers now seem to demand it."

"Sousa in Reply" and "In Reply to Sousa"

Source: *Boston Herald*, October 1922, in *SPB* 58:1, n.p.

> *Sousa's frank discussion of Prohibition (here referred to informally as the "Volstead law"), both in the* Syracuse Journal *interview above and elsewhere, engaged him in a larger public debate. Warren F. Spalding, the secretary of the Massachusetts Prison Association, countered Sousa's argument in specific. He argued here and elsewhere that in the absence of alcohol the general prison population was on the decline relative to its pre-war numbers. Sousa also took issue with the* Boston Herald's *characterization of his position and wrote in with a follow-up of his own.*

To the Editor of *The Herald*:

In The Herald of the 7th appears an editorial, "Spalding vs. Sousa," which quotes from statistics of Mr. Warren F. Spalding of the Massachusetts Prison Association on drunkenness of women and intended to controvert the substance of an interview I gave a metropolitan newspaper some time since. In it I stated: "Before prohibition enforcement at a dinner party it was the exception to find a woman drinking 'hard stuff' and at present it was the exception not to find her doing so; and I believed that it was not on account of love of liquor but rather a defiance of a badly constructed law."

Mr. Spalding shows that the arrest for drunkenness among women during wet times and up to and including the dry years, while slightly fluctuating, has now fallen 67 per cent. under former years, and indicates the danger of basing general deductions upon the observation of a single individual. All of which is sound reasoning if there were no "ifs" stuck in somewhere. Mr. Spalding's statistics have to do with women who drink to excess, are arrested and sent to prison, but Mr. Spalding's statistics have nothing to do with women who now drink moderately, who are not drunkards, and who never figure in prison statistics. In my article I spoke of drinking, not drunkenness, I spoke of defiance, not debauchery.

The saloon, drunkenness and their train of evils do not get the sympathy or support of thinking America. Nor do sumptuary laws. Just there is where the 18th amendment and the Volstead act are weakest. The normal man can understand the regulation of the alcoholic evil, but he resents being whipped into submission and [having to] accept a law that is useless as far as he is concerned. Submission is not obedience.

A grand opportunity was lost by the sponsors of the 18th amendment to make the United States in reality the most temperate of nations. Had they framed an act making it difficult to obtain liquor legally and impossible to obtain it illegally the control of alcohol as an abusive agent would have been absolute.

John Philip Sousa
Duluth, Minn., Oct. 13

To the Editor of *The Herald,*

Mr. Sousa's letter in relation to the Volstead law is interesting in its revelation that the difference between us is due mainly to our viewpoints, and to the background and perspective of our pictures. He sees a few women who, before the days of prohibition, rarely drank "hard stuff" at dinner parties, but now do drink it at such parties in a spirit of defiance and spite. He spoke of drinking, not of drunkenness; of defiance, not debauchery. He spoke of "women who drink moderately, who are not drunkards, and do not figure in prison statistics."

I spoke of women who drank to excess, who were arrested for being intoxicated in public. He wants to arouse public interest in the women who are beginning to drink "hard stuff" out of spite. So do I, but I want, also, to retain that interest in the graduated drinkers. He sees no relation between the two classes. Remembering that every drunkard was at one time a moderate drinker, I see the point of contact between them. (I do not mean that every moderate drinker will become a drunkard, but that every drunkard was once a moderate drinker.)

I have the advantage of Mr. Sousa in this—that I have been a careful observer, in a large way, of the effect of drink upon and among women for 40 years and more; he, for a comparatively few years, among a small group of personal friends.

In 1882 almost 5000 Massachusetts women were arrested for drunkenness, more than 3000 were imprisoned for that offence, and at the end of the year 353 remained in our prisons. If the population had been then what it is now, the arrests would have been 10,000, the commitments 6000 and the number remaining at the end of the year 700.

I have lived to see the number of arrests decrease from 6000 to 2634 in 1922, and the number of commitments decrease from 3000 to 168, while the number of women remaining in our prisons for drunkenness has fallen from 700 to 62. (A part of the reduction in the number of commitments and in the number remaining at a given time is due to the enlarged use of probation, but the falling off in the number of arrests was not affected by that.)

I am especially and very deeply interested in this because a large proportion of the women arrested for drunkenness are mothers. A reduction of drunkenness among them means the great improvement of their homes, for their children, and a great reduction in the number of feeble-minded children born. For a large percentage of the feeble-minded are born by intemperate women.

This reduction in drunkenness among women is not due wholly to prohibition. The Catholic Total Abstinence Society, and the Women's Christian Temperance Union are entitled to great credit. A large number of other organizations have done the same work. Temperance instruction in the public schools has been effective. All of these agencies have taught the wisdom of total abstinence.

In earlier days, temperance societies were organized by men and women who saw no harm in moderate drinking but much harm in drunkenness. They merely pledged themselves not to drink to excess. No such society has been formed in the past 50 years. Perhaps Mr. Sousa will start one; although they all died a very natural death.

Experience has shown that the only effective ways to abolish drunkenness are, by moral suasion, to persuade men and women to total abstinence, and by removing temptation from the paths of the weak. The Volstead law has done this, and is to be credited with remarkable results.

Massachusetts tried permitting the sale of beer and forbidding the sale of "hard stuff" in the 70's (now proposed as though it were something new) and it was followed by an enormous increase in drunkenness. The Volstead law is the first which ever made any deep impression on drunkenness.

Mr. Sousa is interested in his little group of female friends who are drinking hard liquors in a spirit of defiance and spite. So am I, for serious results will follow. I want him, and others holding the same views, to be equally interested in the great multitude of women who cannot drink moderately. I wish he were as grateful as I am for the almost total disappearance of drunkenness among women, but it does not seem to have aroused a single emotion, because he hasn't come in contact with them in his social circle.

If he can devise any way by which his friends can get the drink they want, and the women who are unable to drink moderately, cannot get what they want, it may be worth considering. But no one has ever framed such a law. It cannot be done.

Warren F. Spalding
Boston, Oct 19.

"Sousa on Prohibition"

Source: *Portland Herald*, ca. October 1922, in *SPB* 58:2, n.p.[119]

> It is unclear if this letter—which was more widely published than those above—was a later reaction to Warren Spalding or to someone else's opinion. Given that it involved a different newspaper and that Sousa's response takes a different angle than seen above, the latter seems more likely.

To Editor of *The Press Herald*:

The gentleman to whom I have sent the enclosed letter criticized me for calling Prohibition a tragedy. The letter is my reply.

John Philip Sousa

My Dear Sir:

The article that you sent me is an extract from an interview I gave some time ago to a reporter on one of the metropolitan papers on the shortcomings of Prohibition.

I fear me that you have not glimpsed the right angle regarding my statement that prohibition is a tragedy.

---

119 A reprint of this letter also appeared in the *Minneapolis Tribune*, preserved a few pages later in *SPB* 58:2.

The attitude of indifference assumed by a large number of our people to the enforcement of the Eighteenth Amendment endangers the sacredness of the Constitution and lessens the reverence for law and order. This is tragedy.

The claim of the advocate of the present law of prohibition to "safeguard the birthright of the coming generation" is capable of criticism, for if alcoholic indulgence in the present generation carries a deterioration to the next, it is believed that disregard for law will bring a deterioration in the citizenship of the coming generation. This is a tragedy.

The bringing in the arena of activity hordes of bootleggers, moonshiners, rum-runners, defiant of law and successful financially through the equally defiant buyer of their unlawful product is tragic.

I believe that in a popular vote for or against prohibition will be found the bootlegger, the moonshiner, the rum-runner, the grower of home brew material, on the side of prohibition. This is tragedy.

Somebody said "that politics makes strange bed fellows;" so does prohibition. This is tragedy.

The hatred for the saloon and drunkenness is not monopolized by the members of the Anti-Saloon League. Millions and millions of worthy and law-loving citizens of the United States despise the saloon and the drunkard but believe that the methods brought into being by the Anti-Saloon League law opened a pandora box of great or greater evils than existed during the lawful indulgence in alcoholic beverage. This is tragedy.

Up-rooting alcoholic evils in the old, the young, the poor and the rich "soaks" does not compensate for transplanting that evil to the educated young, the future mothers and fathers of this land. This is tragedy.

Sincerely,
John Philip Sousa

"John Philip Sousa's Spaghetti Portuguese"

Source: *Evening Sun* (New York), November 1922, in *SPB* 58:2, n.p.

Certainly the oddest (and most disorganized) essay ever to flow from Sousa's pen, it nevertheless indicates his status as a household name. At twenty-minutes boiling time, he clearly liked his pasta soft.

[Sauce]

One quart can of tomatoes. Put in kettle on top of stove, simmer or let boil slowly for one and a half hours. Add pepper, salt, two onions cut in fine slices, four allspice [berries] and four cloves. The cloves and allspice to be added after it starts to boil. To sauce, add three bay leaves one hour before taking off the stove.[120] After two and a half hours add:

[Meatballs]

Two pounds chopped beef; add one onion, chopped fine, two cups bread crumbs, a little parsley, salt and pepper. Make into meat balls about the size of a plum. Put into sauce and boil one and one-half hours slowly. This makes fully three hours' slow boiling for the sauce.[121]

Spaghetti.

Use a package or a pound of spaghetti; not macaroni. Have a large pot of boiling water with about one tablespoonful of salt. Slide the spaghetti into water. Do not break it. Boil exactly 20 minutes. Must be tender—not tough nor doughy.

Serve spaghetti on large platter, pouring tomato sauce over it. Serve potatoes on smaller platter, allowing a small quantity of sauce to remain on them.

Serve grated Parmesan cheese on side. Use a piece of cheese to grate—not bottled cheese.

"No Effort Will Be Made to Stop Sousa Concert by Officials"

Source: *Binghamton Press*, ca. November 11, 1922, in *SPB* 58:2, n.p.

Sousa often aired his grievances in the press, but rarely did those arguments amount to much more than rhetorical fireworks. His two concerts on Sunday, November 12, 1922 in Binghamton, New York, however, technically broke the law. At issue was a local ordinance forbidding monetary transactions related to public activities on Sundays. The press began coverage even before the concert

---

120 This sentence originally appears near the end of the recipe, but for obvious practical purposes it has been moved here.

121 His total "slow boiling" time appears to stand at four hours at this point. Perhaps placing the meatballs into the sauce after only 1.5 hours simmering was what he intended.

and the event quickly became the focal point of a larger power struggle between a group of ministers and prominent citizens.

Police Will, However, Serve Warrant if Any Objecting Citizen Can Secure One After First Concert Begins

—

Cite Football Trial as Precedent

—

"The only procedure that will test the question of permitting the Sousa's band concert in the Binghamton theater Sunday afternoon and night will be the arrest of one of those participating in the concert with a subsequent trial before the city judge on a charge of violating the state law relative to amusements on Sunday," Corporation Counsel Leon C. Rhodes said this morning.

Mr. Rhodes said that Commissioner of Public Safety Norman A. Boyd called his attention to an allegation made yesterday that there was a prospective violation of the Sunday observance law due Sunday, according to advertisements of the Sousa concert, and asked what steps, if any, were required to prevent it.

Corporation Counsel Rhodes replied that there is a section of the penal law which forbids outdoor and indoor amusements on Sunday where an admission fee is charged but in this instance it was his understanding that no admission fee would be charged. The entertainment would be operated on the club plan, similar to that adopted for Sunday football games at the First Ward Stadium.

An effort had been made to test the law in this respect, the charge being made that the club plan for football was an evasion of the Sunday observance law, he said. An arrest had been made, a jury trial held and the jury had acquitted the defendant of violating the Sunday observance law. This upheld the contention that the club plan was legal. Courts have held that an injunction to prevent the violation of any section of the penal law could not be obtained as the penal law in itself carries penalties preventing a violation and it would be possible to arrest any person violating the law summarily.

Therefore the only remedy, he said, would be the arrest of the person charged with a violation of the law and a subsequent jury trial, if it were demanded by the defendant.

Acting on this ruling it is improbable that Commissioner of Public Safety Boyd will take any steps in the matter.

If any citizen desires to swear out a warrant for any person charged with the violation, the warrant will be issued but it cannot be issued in advance as the violation must first be committed, and special provisions are required for the issuance and service of a warrant on Sunday.

"Ministers Oppose Sunday Band Concert; Marches Better Than Sermons, Says Sousa"

Source: *New York Times*, November 13, 1922, in *SPB* 58:1, n.p.

The Binghamton concert went forward as scheduled on Sunday, with the expected results now making headlines in New York City.

Binghamton, N. Y., Nov. 12.—Harold F. Albert, Recreational Director of the Endicott-Johnson Corporation, was arrested this afternoon on complaint of the Binghamton Ministerial Association for staging a concert by John Philip Sousa's band at which an admission was charged, in alleged violation of ordinances governing the observance of Sunday.

Following the arrest George F. Johnson, President of the Endicott-Johnson Corporation, announced that he is prepared to fight the so-called Sunday blue laws to a finish in the courts, and Sousa issued a statement in which he declared there was more inspiration in the marches he has written than in the sermons of some of the ministers who objected to the concert.

"Director Albert under Arrest for Staging Sousa Concert on Sunday; 5,000 Hear 'March King'"

Source: *Binghamton Morning Sun*, November 13, 1922, in *SPB* 58:1, n. p.

Emblazoned in the largest fully capitalized font possible, the controversial concerts took up more than a complete page of the morning edition of Binghamton's newspaper. In addition to the lengthy account here, the page included an interview with Sousa inset front and center and a much tamer concert review in the right column (with the ironic headline "Sousa's Band Attains New Concert

Fame: Never Was Welcome More Cordial or Audience More Attentive Than Yesterday"). Aside from the fracas itself, the general description of the audience and concert environs seen here conforms in large part with the coverage of the Sousa Band's concerts in other small-town venues over the course of many tours.

—

George F. Flays City Ordinance, Promises Fight

—

"I don't feel a bit like a criminal and I don't believe any of you people do," said George F. Johnson last night as he faced the largest audience ever packed into the Binghamton Theater.

And the cheering and applause that greeted this and the few other remarks made by Mr. Johnson left little doubt that the thousands who had gathered to hear Sousa's band at a quarter a head appreciated the opportunity to the fullest, and shared Mr. Johnson's views regarding what he termed "Sunday blue laws."

Mr. Johnson appeared first during the intermission of the afternoon concert and again at night in response to the calling of his name and cheers from the big audience. His remarks were prompted by the arrest at the afternoon performance of Harold F. Albert, director of the E. J. recreational department and the man who, under Mr. Johnson's direction, booked the Sousa concert.

Mr. Albert's arrest was the result of protests from the Binghamton Ministerial Association to the police authorities against the holding of the concert on the ground that it was in violation of city ordinances governing Sunday amusements. These protests took form prior to the concert when [the] first announcement was made that Sousa and his band would appear at the Binghamton Theater on Sunday, and when the matinee concert was in progress police officers walked into the theater, notified Mr. Albert of his arrest and took the names of several theater attaches as witnesses. Mr. Albert and the others were directed to appear in City Court this morning at 9:30 o'clock.

Membership cards admitting the holders to the concerts had been distributed, largely among E. J. workers, during the week. The cards entitled purchasers to membership in the "Broome County Community Music Club," this doing away with the necessity for a sale of tickets on Sunday and satisfying, in the opinion of legal authorities who were consulted, the intent of the law relating to Sunday performances. It did not satisfy the Ministerial Association, however, and the movement culminating in the arrest of Mr. Albert was the result of the protest voiced by its members that the law in its strictest sense was being evaded.

Record Crowds Attend

No concerted move, legal or otherwise, was made, however, to stop the concerts. Record audiences began to gather early, both in the afternoon and in the evening. Long before the hour scheduled for the concert the Binghamton was packed to overflowing. Hundreds of seats were placed on the stage. Extra accommodations were provided in the boxes and every available seat in the vast auditorium and balcony was occupied. Standing room was taxed to the capacity established by the fire marshal and in the lobby hundreds of others, who had no hope of seeing the musicians, stood and listened to the music. In the streets a patient overflow audience waited.

Applause that rocked the theater greeted John Philip Sousa, the "March King," his bandsmen and the other artists who appeared in an exceptionally entertaining program. Each number was the signal for an outburst and when, during the first intermission, Mr. Johnson walked out onto the stage, the enthusiasm reached its height.

He spoke briefly, telling just what had happened and announcing that "the blue laws" will be tried in the courts "tomorrow morning." At night, when the intermission came, there were cries of "We want George F!" This was varied with the shouts of "Three cheers for Mr. Johnson!" and "Speech!" The E. J. prep[sident again appeared, walked smilingly to the center of the stage, where he was forced to stand for a full minute and acknowledge the cheering and applauding of his enthusiastic friends.

"There may have been theater audiences representing greater wealth than is represented in this one," said Mr. Johnson, "but there has never been an audience composed of more good American citizens. I doubt if there was ever an audience more representative of clean and honest citizenship. It is good to see so many honest people gathered here tonight. I know you are honest. There are other audiences in this city tonight and I doubt if all of them are so well entertained.

Wants Ordinance Changed

"I congratulate you upon you privilege of hearing this wonderful organization. Notwithstanding the fact that a city ordinance says it is a crime, I do not feel like a criminal and I don't believe any of you do.

"We are told that we have violated the law. I don't believe that stuff. You don't believe that stuff. (Applause.) I wonder if you don't think we should have a Board of Aldermen who will change such an ordinance. (Cheering.) I believe they will. (Cheering and applause.) We will be in court in the morning. Let them prove us guilty."

During his brief remarks in the afternoon, Mr. Johnson invited those who might have felt that they were "partners in crime," to get their money back at the box office. Not one of the 3,000 present availed himself of this offer.[122]

"Mr. Sousa thought it appropriate to play 'Nearer My God to Thee' before I appeared out here," Mr. Johnson remarked, and this was greeted by laughter and applause.

It was explained on behalf of the management of the Binghamton Theater that yesterday's concerts were given entirely on the responsibility of the E. J. recreational department. "The theater was turned over to Mr. Johnson," said H. M. Addison, the manager.

It is estimated that well over 5,000 people heard yesterday's concerts.

"I intend to plead not guilty," said Mr. Albert last night, "and I will demand a jury trial." Probably there will be little more than the formal arraignment this morning.

"Magnificent to Be Broadminded as Well as Christian—Sousa"

Source: *Binghamton Morning Sun*, November 13, 1922, in *SPB* 58:1, n. p.

This interview, given between the controversial matinee and evening concerts, is the only item presenting Sousa's perspective. That evening he played "Nearer My God to Thee," as noted above, and included The Phantom *by local composer W. D. Sabin as a "sign of solidarity" according to a separate concert review printed*

---

122 The 3,000 figure indicates attendance only at the matinee; the headline's 5,000-plus is a sum total for both the matinee and evening concerts.

on the same front page as this interview. The bandmaster's statements insinuate that he came to town in full knowledge that it would foment a controversy.

"There is inspiration in good music. My band doesn't give married couples attending the concerts a chance to quarrel. We play one number right after the other for two hours with but five minutes intermission," said John Philip Sousa yesterday afternoon when asked for an expression regarding the arrest of Director Harold F. Albert.

"Religion is a wonderful thing. It's great to be a Christian, but it's magnificent to be broad-minded," the March King added.

"As to commercializing the Sabbath," Mr. Sousa continued, "why of course we get paid for entertaining on Sunday. But it's true also that clergymen and church choir singers get paid for their services on Sunday as well as other days.

"I do not make a penny on the two concerts in this city, but my men earn a day's pay, the same as choir singers. It costs $2.00 and $2.50 to hear my band in other cities. Here the price of admission was 25 cents."

Mr. Albert then interjected the statement that the Endicott Johnson Recreation Department will have to pay $800 to meet the cost of bringing the band to this city for two concerts.[123]

"Clergymen who oppose band concerts on Sunday hurt themselves more than anyone else," declared the famous band leader. "Why, I'll bet there are many young fellows in the audience this afternoon and others who will be in the audience tonight, who, if they were not in this theater, would be gambling.

"As to committing a sin on the Sabbath. My parents were devoted Christians. I am a Christian. Although I have composed music in my mind on Sundays, never have I written a musical note on Sunday. I have written more marches than ministers have sermons.

"I came here with my band simply because I thought it would do some good," said Mr. Sousa. "There is not a penny of profit for me in the concerts here. My bandsmen and soloists, of course, have to be considered. My band

---

123 On the various financial arrangements made for concert performances by the band, see Sousa's discussion in his Los Angeles "self-interview" on page **98**.

works six to eight months a year, and the members must earn enough money within that time to last them throughout the entire year."

"The Sunday Issue" and "The Sousa Concert"

Source: *Binghamton Sun*, November 13, 1922, in *SPB* 58:2, n. p.

> *After all the morning headlines, the afternoon edition of the local newspaper printed letters from two attendees who felt that it was wrong to arrest the concert's organizer. The letters provide insights regarding the business side of bringing the Sousa Band into town, financial obligations undertaken by the concert organizers, and the view from the audience's seats.*

The Sunday Issue

To the Editor, *The Morning Sun*:

It was with great indignation I read of the arrest of Harold Albert in this morning's paper on account of the concert given by Sousa's Band yesterday and I wish to enter a vigorous protest against the narrow, unfair and uncharitable methods used by a small minority whose ideas and judgment are not to be commended.

The "grand, kind man" of this section, who seems to keep awake nights trying to think up things which will help and give pleasure and comfort to this community, certainly did not bring this wonderful band here as a profit-making proposition. I understand a substantial sum was lost on the two concerts. The different ministers throughout this section ought to give thanks every Sunday that we have in our midst this modern "Santa Claus," who is not thinking of glory, popularity or political preferment, but how much good he can do in his quiet way. I should think that it would be rather discouraging to our "grand, kind man" to be generally invited to head the list either for the rebuilding or refinancing of so many of our churches and then to be so unjustly criticized by an occurrence of this kind.

Good music is one of the main assets in the church of today, and if the ministers who are decrying the lack of attendance at their respective churches and feeling that the people are hopeless would only take an inventory of themselves and ask "what is the matter of me?" and "why can't I interest the people?" a whole lot of this lack of church attendance would be solved.

During the war there was no restraining influence brought to bear to keep the Catholics from going over, with the probability of being killed, and yet when they got home a certain misguided sect at every chance wants to kill them politically. At that time there was no great outcry against our boys smoking cigarets or even drinking beer and light wine when they were fighting for it. Also at that time there was the cry which went up all over the country, "Get together for we must win the war."

Unfortunately a lot of this "get-together" spirit has been forgotten and we are drifting in an aimless, selfish and discontented fashion in so-called "blocs," "isms," "narrow prejudices" and "destructive criticisms." If this keeps on it will cause the utmost trouble in this country. Let us change about front and under the wise leadership of our "grand, kind man" all put our shoulders to the wheel and show the world at large that the people in the "Valley of Opportunity" can get along in peace and harmony without any bickerings, considerate of one another's feelings, creeds and political beliefs and be supremely grateful for all the blessings that have been given us.

James H. Andrews

The Sousa Concert

To the Editor, *The Morning Sun*:

People who attended the concerts of Sousa's Band on Sunday afternoon and evening all agree that it was one of the finest musical entertainments ever given in Binghamton, and that there was not one objectionable feature to the whole performance. We were not surprised, however, at the announcement that the promoters of the enterprise had been put under arrest by the minions of the Binghamton Sunday blue laws, as called by George F. Johnson, after reading the communication in the press by Rev. James E. Russell, calling upon the Ministerial Association to take measures to suppress it, on the plea of commercializing the Sabbath.

Now the attendance at both these concerts only goes to show that the people of this community are hungry, yes, starving, for good, wholesome music, something that is elevating, inspiring, ennobling, and they get it in Sousa's productions. Not only are the higher emotions of patriotism aroused, but the deeper religious impulses are awakened, and all are put in a happier mood, drawn closer to the great infinite source of good, and to one another.

If these concerts were so bad, why have not the thirty Binghamton clergymen forming the Ministerial Association lodged complaints against the riotous entertainments which have been pulled off at the so-called Clinton Street Stadium all summer? Is it because they were afraid to attack the class of people who attend such places, but have the courage to vent their spleen against the best people of this city and neighborhood?

Did you ever attend church on Sunday morning—or evening either in late years—when they did not pass the plate, and you were invited to contribute for this purpose or that? Nearly all the money paid into the churches of Binghamton (or elsewhere) finds its way into their coffers on Sunday, and every enterprise, entertainment or social which they hold to secure money, is advertised from the pulpit on Sunday. On the other hand the whole expense of Sousa's concerts was collected and paid in on "week days," as well as its advertising and other arrangements. Somewhere we have read that consistency is a jewel and are inclined to believe it. The Rev. Jas. E. R. very deferentially says he has no objection to free Sunday concerts. But they have to be paid for by some one. Mr. Johnson has generously contributed for this purpose on many occasions, and no objections raised, but on an occasion like the one under discussion, where the expense must needs be great and the people are asked to share in the minimum sum of only 25 cents, the Ministerial Association and its backers have occasion to show how narrow-minded, bigoted and illogical they can be. It is just such moves on their part that puts the self-styled orthodox churches in contempt by men and women who believe in a square deal.

Every advancement, every enterprise, every attempt to improve the world we live in, has been opposed by men of this caliber—and deity has always been on the side of the people, or there would have been but few of the privileges we enjoy today. I am not in favor of making Sunday an occasion for anything vile or vicious, but in gatherings which serve a high and noble purpose there is no better use it can be put to. If it is not lawful and consistent to hold concerts that require an expenditure of money to produce them on Sunday, in which those who are benefited are asked to contribute, then it is not right for churches, Epworth Leagues, Y. M. C. A., Bible schools or other similar organizations to collect money to pay expenses on that day. We warn the B. M. A. and its affiliations to go a trifle careful. They may be shown just how little people take stock in their moribund creeds.

Addison J. Ellsworth
Sunday, Nov. 12

"'Good Music Waits an Inspiration', Says Sousa"

Source: Sousa Band Concert Program for New Orleans, Louisiana, February 9–10, 1924, in *SPB* 60:3, 58f–g.[124]

> *Sousa's extensive 1923–24 concert tour took him from coast to coast. The band's souvenir program books typically included a variety of essays and interviews as a form of publicity. His assertion in this self-written interview of only composing on inspiration agrees with what is known of his compositional practice (for instance the Women's Suffrage march he had earlier declined to write, see page 97).*

Music of lasting qualities is essentially the product of inspiration, and cannot be turned out while the publisher waits without the door, in the opinion of Lieutenant Commander John Philip Sousa, the famous bandmaster, who is now on tour for the thirty-first year with the great organization which bears his name.

"We have a great number of writers of music who seem to be able to turn out music to order," says Sousa. "In modern theatrical practice, it is customary for a composer to be commissioned to write a score for a certain star and all the time he must have in mind the limitations of that star. Such music as a rule lacks the note of inspiration necessary for more than a fleeting fame.

---

124 This interview-as-article was also published in a number of local newspapers to promote Sousa's 1924 concert tour. Note that the source, a New Orleans program book, is not a typical Sousa Band souvenir program book in that it was printed specifically for that city's concert by a local organization.

"I have found in my own life that my good work has been the result of inspiration, and it is impossible for me to sit down and bid an idea come. The marches without exception have been the result of inspiration. 'Stars and Stripes Forever', the greatest of them all, at least in point of popularity, was written at sea in an hour or two. I wrote 'The Diplomat' which I consider among my first ten at least, in Mitchell, S. D. I was six months writing 'King Cotton', but the six months were spent in developing an idea, which came in a moment.

"I do not mean to say that music cannot be developed by study. My suites, arrangements and comic operas of course were long in the making, but the central idea came in a moment out of the proverbial clear sky, and then was developed.

"I believe I could write a march in an hour or two, and play it within an hour or two more. There are composers for musical comedy who could be told at 1 o'clock to have a new song number ready at two, and who would come through. But march and song number most likely would be without inspiration, and would be an imposition upon the public. So I never hurry inspiration, and so far I have found inspiration each season to do the new work for my programmes. Many years ago, I decided that if I did not receive inspiration for new work, I would not present made-to-order work which lacked this quality, and I am still firm in my resolve."

"Jazz, in Its Present State, May Develop National Style"

Source: *Philadelphia Record*, ca. July 1924, in SPB 64, 9b.[125]

The band world took up ragtime music around 1905, and various current and former Sousa Band members, including Arthur Pryor, wrote rags for band at that early juncture. Sousa was late to the craze, and biased against jazz in particular, but in this 1924 interview he showed a remarkable ability to evolve with the times—with a little prodding from Leopold Stokowski—and to accept both the permanence of jazz and its status as an art form in its own right. Based on Sousa's mention of the era of the "squealing clarionet," it would seem part of

---

125 The SPB do not include a date for this clipping, but it is included in a section largely dating to July 1924.

his conversion was a result of jazz's changing emphasis from group improvisation (as heard on Louis Armstrong's "Hot Five" and "Hot Seven" recordings) to a big band texture (as epitomized by Duke Ellington's bands). While Armstrong did not make his famous records until 1925, Duke Ellington played regularly in Harlem by 1923 and was recording by 1924.

A few weeks ago I let it be known that I expected to add jazz music to the programs for my band during its forthcoming tour. Immediately my morning pile of mail began to grow, as letters came in from all sections of the country voicing every possible degree of approval and disapproval at my decision. The letters ranged from fervent congratulations that I was about to present a style of music which at present is enjoying a great vogue to letters which suggested that I was lowering whatever standards I had raised in the cause of good music during the 30 years or more that I have been directing my own organization. But all of the letters had a question almost identical and that question was: "Why are you going to play jazz?" And while I have a great number of reasons of varying importance, I think the two salient ones are that people generally enjoy jazz or syncopated music and that jazz in its present state may be the beginning of a typically American musical style and tradition.

All of my life I have had a weakness for things of American origin—for things which have come into being entirely in this country and which could not develop in any other country, and I think this is essentially true of jazz. While many stories are current as to the exact origin of the term jazz and also as to the origin of the tempo which we now recognize as jazz, I think it is beginning to be agreed that jazz was of negro origin—developed and fostered by colored entertainers in our own Southern States.

One of the most remarkable stories that I have heard concerning the origin of jazz and its parent form, ragtime, is told me by Fred Stone, the actor. Mr. Stone's version is that a colored performer, one Ernest Hogan, originated the ragtime song with a composition of which I have seen the original words and which was entitled "The Posmala."[126] There is enough

---

126 Ernest Hogan (1865–1909), a minstrel performer who in 1907 became the first African-American Broadway entertainer, helped popularize ragtime through his song (with accompanying dance) "La Pas Ma La" (1895) and his million-copy song "All Coons Look Alike to Me."

supporting evidence to make this seem probable. Hogan was a New Orleans Negro, perhaps with an admixture of French blood for all his Celtic name, for it must be remembered that colored performers along in the nineties, when jazz or ragtime originated, were likely to take Irish names arbitrarily. It is also to be remembered that at the time a great deal of French and corrupted French was spoken by the colored people in New Orleans. Thus "Posmala" well may be a corruption of the French term "pas a mele," which was literally "a mixed step" and that was exactly what ragtime was and what jazz is, a mixed step in broken time, generally done backward and devoid of the regular rhythm common to all dancing up to that time. Negro entertainers of that day originated a great number of songs. Often they were not set down until years afterward, being handed along from mouth to mouth and, as the present copyright laws had not been framed, the average performer felt himself safer with a cherished song if it was not put on paper. Ben Harney, a white man who had been a coon shouter and who had played in a saloon in Louisville, is generally credited with having brought ragtime or jazz for the first time to the New York stage at the old Weber and Fields Music Hall. It is probable that New York had heard the jazz form considerably earlier. There were great numbers of entertainers going about the country in those days playing in saloons and in saloon music halls and it is entirely probable that such an entertainer had introduced ragtime to New York ahead of Harney.

Then came one of the fortuitous circumstances which is likely to implant any music form upon a people. There is a general theory among musicians that some great national crisis is likely to bring a new music form and along came the Spanish-American War, and "Hot Time," the first of the ragtime songs to become national and internationally known. And after "Hot Time" had become as firmly connected in the popular [mind] to the Spanish-American War as had "John Brown's Body" with the civil war, ragtime was firmly established.[127] It died out, revived, died out again and revived to hold its own until the world war, and then after the composers of the world had sought to write a great and inspiring war song, along came George M. Cohan

127   The small portion of this sentence given in brackets is missing in the *SPB* due to the poor condition of the original clipping. Further on Sousa's own musical interaction with the Spanish-American War, see Hess, "Sousa's *El Capitan*."

with "Over There" and Irving Berlin with "Oh How I Hate to Get Up in the Morning." And both songs, essentially in the same type as our jazz, in my opinion, will endure as long as the world war is remembered.

The modern jazz era, as everyone knows, began after the war; in other words, about half a dozen years ago, and it began with all sorts of bizarre instrumental combinations and effects. We had to go through an era of squealing clarinet and tincan tone poems, before someone conceived the idea of making jazz melodic, and that has been the tendency for the past three or four years. Now the chief exponents of jazz emphasize the melody more than the rhythm, and the principal composers of jazz music seek pleasing harmonic effects rather than startling bursts of sound, which are designed to make the listener say: "My Goodness."

The final influence which committed me to a trial of jazz during my present tour was my friend, Dr. Leopold Stokowski, conductor of the Philadelphia Symphony Orchestra. During a visit to Philadelphia last spring, where I conducted my choral work, "The Last Crusade," Dr. Stokowski told me that European musicians were deeply interested in our jazz, and believed that it might contain the elements of a typically American music of the future. He pointed out that Haydn in his day had used dance tunes in his serious musical works with the result that in his own lifetime his works were regarded as common street music.

"The European musicians really are more interested in jazz than the serious musicians of America," Dr. Stokowski told me, "for they see in it the possibilities of great future developments. We are so accustomed to it that it is like a prophet who is without honor in his own country. One of the reasons that we do not see in it the germ of great future possibilities is that some of it is poor and vulgar, and we forget that some of it, in the opinion of great musicians, has wonderful possibilities. Here in America is enormous vitality and great freedom. We make a fresh start when we do anything in this country, while in Europe and Asia they are always looking to the past. In this music, which to us appears vulgar, there may be great inspiration."

So I came home from Philadelphia and wrote my first jazz fantasy, which I have chosen to name, "Music of the Minute." It is my conception of modern jazz, and is my musical comment upon jazz tunes of the present day. I hope to achieve effects which other directors have not been able to get. Most jazz bands consist of about a dozen pieces. On tour I have about 100 men, and it seems that with a greater number as well as a greater variety of instruments that "Music of the Minute" should have a fresh viewpoint, and that the instrumentation at my command may produce melodic effects which are entirely novel.

The important thing is that I am presenting my jazz without apology and without any belief that I am lowering the musical standard of my organization. I am making what is in many essentials an experiment, but I do not wish it to be considered that I am trying to make jazz the coming form of American music. That I could not do if I would. I am merely offering it for the information of my audiences. And it will be at least two decades—perhaps longer—before anyone in America will know whether jazz is going to be a part of the permanent body of our music or whether it is merely a passing fancy with the American people. Personally, I believe that it will achieve permanence, but that is merely an opinion—an opinion as good as but no better than the opinion of any other man or woman.

"Good Jazz is Good; But It Can Be Horrid—Sousa"

Source: *Madison State Journal* (Wisconsin), April 29, 1928, in *SPB* 73:2, 81a.[128]

This essay appeared in a number of newspapers beginning in April 1928. Although prefaced with a header indicating he wrote it for each newspaper individually (in this case reading "By John Philip Sousa, Special to the State Journal"), it is clear that Sousa wrote the essay partly to promote his newly published autobiography and partly to generate interest in his upcoming "Golden Jubilee" tour in the summer and fall of 1928. Sousa's public acceptance of jazz was years in the past by this point, but continued to be a topic of interest in his later years. As might be expected of a father figure in the twilight of his career, his optimism for the future of American music shines forth in spite of his initial negative reaction.

---

128 Insofar as can be determined, this essay was printed in a number of newspapers in 1928. The *Madison State Journal* version was used as the source because it seems to be the earliest included in the *SPB* and because the copy is well preserved.

New York—Will jazz supplant the stirring marches which the American public loved for so long? Fifty years ago I was dubbed the "March King," and in my half century as a conductor of my own band, I think I have learned a great deal about the real taste of the American public.

"Jazz," like the well-known little girl with the curl, when it is good is very, very good, and when it is bad it is horrid. The greater part of it is very bad. Its popularity is the result of the avowed tastes of those people who care only for music which is strongly rhythmical. I feel that it will endure just as long as people hear it through their feet instead of through their brains!

Appeal to Me

Marches, of course, are well known to have a peculiar appeal for me. They are, in a sense, my musical children. The tempo of the march, like the beat of an African war drum, speaks to a fundamental rhythm in the human organization, and is answered. A march stimulates every center of vitality, wakens the imagination and spurs patriotic impulses which may have been dormant for years.

My own marches, of which I have written 103, have been played all over the world, and I have frequently encountered them under strange and amusing circumstances, many of which I have related in my autobiography, published under the title of "Marching Along."

[Abbreviated anecdotes follow, including being given a "Victrola concert" in South Africa and his "Giovanni Filipo Sousa" encounter in Italy.]

I have the greatest faith in the originality and power of American music. We can afford the best in this country, and once convinced that we desire it, we are going to achieve the best in music.

The rest of the world has had a long start, but the American composer with his heritage of creative genius from a race which has produced 13 out of 20 of the great inventions of the past three centuries, is well qualified to catch up. The American public is essentially music-loving and it loves good music. I have "laid my ear to it, to see if it be in tune," as I have gone "Marching Along" down through many years, and it has never discouraged or disappointed me.

Bibliography

Abel, E. Lawrence. *Confederate Songs.* Jefferson, North Carolina: McFarland, 2004.

Bierley Paul E. *The Incredible Band of John Philip Sousa.* Urbana: University of Illinois Press, 2006.

_____. *John Philip Sousa: American Phenomenon,* Revised edition. Miami: Warner Brothers, 2001.

_____. *The Works of John Philip Sousa.* Columbus, Ohio: Integrity Press, 1984.

Brown, Margaret L. "David Blakely, Manager of Sousa's Band." In *Perspectives on John Philip Sousa,* edited by Jon Newsom, 121–33. Washington, D.C.: Library of Congress, 1983.

Browne, C. A. *The Story of Our National Ballads.* New York: Thomas Y. Crowell, 1919.

Chessum, Tracey. "Songs of Salaried Warriors: Copyright, Intellectual Property, and John Philip Sousa's *The Free Lance.*" In *Working in the Wings: New Perspectives on Theatre History and Labor,* edited by Elizabeth A. Osborne and Christine Woodworth, 197–210. Carbondale: Southern Illinois University Press, 2015.

Cipolla, Frank J. "The Business Papers of David Blakely, Manager of the Gilmore and Sousa Bands." *Journal of Band Research* 13 (Spring 1978): 2–7.

Elson, Louis C. *The History of American Music.* New York: MacMillan, 1904.

Fletcher, Horace. *Fletcherism: What It Is or How I Became Young at Sixty.* New York: Frederick A. Stokes, 1913.

Grove, George. *Dictionary of Music and Musicians.* Second edition. Edited by J. A. Fuller Maitland. New York: MacMillan, 1904–1910.

Hess, Carol A. "John Philip Sousa's *El Capitan*: Political Appropriations and the Spanish-American War." *American Music* 16 (1998): 1–24.

Holms, Thom. *The Routledge Guide to Music Technology.* New York: Routledge, 2006).

Kappey, J. A., and Clara Kappey. *Songs of Eastern Europe: A Collection of 100 Volkslieder of Austria, Bohemia, Hungary, Servia, Turkey, and Other Countries.* London: Boosey, 1880.

Kocin, Paul J., et al. "The Great Arctic Outbreak and East Coast Blizzard of February 1899." *Weather and Forecasting* 3 (December 1988): 305-18.

Kreitner, Mona Bulpitt. "'A Splendid Group of American Girls': The Women Who Sang with the Sousa Band." PhD diss., University of Memphis, 2007.

Lewis, Ryan C. "Much More than Ragtime: The Musical Life of George Hamilton Green (1893-1970)." DMA diss., University of South Carolina, 2009.

Mathews, W. S. B., ed. *A Hundred Years of Music in America*. Philadelphia: Theodore Presser, 1900.

Newsom, Jon, ed. *Perspectives on John Philip Sousa*. Washington, D.C.: Library of Congress, 1983.

Rosenfeld, Paul. *Musical Chronicle 1917-1923*. New York: Harcourt, Brace, 1923.

Smart, James R., "Genesis of a March: The Stars and Stripes Forever." In *Perspectives on John Philip Sousa*, edited by Jon Newsom, 105-119 Washington, D.C.: Library of Congress, 1983.

Sousa, John Philip. *Marching Along*. Boston: Hale, Cushman and Flint, 1928. Reprinted Chicago: GIA, 2015.

———. *National, Patriotic, and Typical Airs of All Lands*. Philadelphia: H. Coleman, 1890.

Stebbins, Genevieve. *The Delsarte System of Expression*. New York: Edgar S. Werner, 1885.

Warfield, Patrick. "The Essence of Uncle Sam: John Philip Sousa's 1911 World Tour." In *Kongreß-bericht Oberwölz/Steiermark 2004*, edited by Bernhard Habla, 359-78. Tutzing: Schneider, 2006.

———. "John Esputa, John Philip Sousa and the Boundaries of a Musical Career." *Nineteenth-Century Music Review* 6, no. 1 (June 2009): 27-46.

———. "John Philip Sousa and 'The Menace of Mechanical Music'." *Journal of the Society for American Music* 3 (2009): 431-63.

———. "Making the Band: The Formation of John Philip Sousa's Ensemble." *American Music* 24 (2006): 30-66.

———. *Making the March King*. Urbana: University of Illinois Press, 2013.

Index

Akoond of Swat, 84, 84n
Albert, Harold F., 161, 162, 165
Alda, Frances, 141
Alexander the Great, 76
American Gramophone Company,
    67–70
American Relief Legion, 139
American Trapshooting Association,
    112
Andrews, James H., 166–67
Anthony, Susan B., 24
Armstrong, Louis, 171
ASCAP (American Society of
    Composers, Authors and
    Publishers), 45
Auber, Daniel, 10, 25
Australia, 90, 94

Bach, Johann Sebastian, 11, 92, 121
Bartlett, Homer Newton, 60
Bauer, Arthur W., 106n, 107
Beach, Amy, 98n
Beck, J. G. S., 2, 2n
Beethoven, Ludwig van, 12, 14, 25,
    73, 82, 82n, 92, 93, 108, 121, 125,
    144, 146n, 148, 152
Bellini, Vincenzo, 25
Bender, 124
Benkert, George Felix, 117
Berg, Edward A., 14n
Berlin, Irving, 173
Berlioz, Hector, 25
Berton, Vic, 127n
Binghamton, New York, 159–69

Bird, Arthur, 4
Bizet, Georges, 149
Boehm, Theobald, 124
Bonaparte, Napoleon, 76
Boston Symphony Orchestra, 87, 132
Boyd, Norman A., 160–61
Braham, John Joseph, 3
Brahms, Johannes, 19, 25, 108
Bristow, George Frederick, 4
Buck, Dudley, 4, 26
Bülow [Bulow], Hans von, 29

Cameron, S. T., 67–70
Caruso, Enrico, 65
Chadwick, George Whitefield, 4, 26, 60
Chaminade, Cécile, 98
Chicago, 16–21, 30, 31, 92, 118, 127,
    127n, 129n, 141
    World's Columbian Exposition
        (World's Fair of 1893), 1,
        16–21, 100
Chicago Examiner, 133
Chicago Symphony Orchestra, 127,
    127n
Chicago Tribune, 16
Chopin, Frédéric, 25, 37, 152
Civil War, United States, 8, 108, 135,
    149, 172
Clarke, Herbert L., 33, 129, 129n, 144,
    144n
Claus, 11
Cohan, George M., 172–73
Colonne Orchestra (Édouard
    Colonne), 31, 37

Columbia Phonograph, 128
Congress, United States, xv, xix, 8, 27, 45, 50, 61–70, 66n, 77, 80, 80n, 81, 134, 134n
Conried, Heinrich, 86, 86n
Conway, Patrick, 118, 119–20
Creatore, Giuseppe, 141
Crimean War, 137

Damrosch, Walter, 7, 17–18, 20
David, Félicien, 15
Debussy, Claude, 111
Delahaye, Léon, 34
Delibes, Leo, 29
Delsarte, François, 42n
Distin, Henry, 1–2
Donizetti, Gaetano, 25, 110
Downing, David L., 4
Dunkler, François, 124
Dvořák, Antonín [D'vorak], 93

Edison, Thomas, 85n, 150
Elgar, Edward, 93
Ellington, Duke, 171
Elson, Louis C., 73, 73n
England, see *Great Britain*
Esputa Academy of Music, 117, 117n

Fairbanks, Charles Warren, 115, 115n
Fischer [Fisher], Bud, 140
Fischer, Carl, 118
Fletcher of Saltoun, Andrew, 51, 61, 133–34
Flotow, Friedrich von, 25
Fohs, Alfred D., 3
Foote, Arthur, 60
Ford, Henry, 107n
Forsyth, Cecil, 121
Forsythe, Mary Isabella, 38
Foster, Stephen, 95, 97, 108
Frohman, Daniel, 24

Galli-Curci, Amelita, 152
Ganne, Louis, 34, 60
Garde Républicaine, 25, 34, 36
Garner, Richard Lynch, 73

Gatti, Walter, 38
General Motors, 126
Gilchrist, William, 4
Gilder, John Francis, 4
Gillet, Georges, 34, 60
Gilmore, Patrick Sarsfield, 3, 9, 14, 21–22, 95n, 124
Gluck, Christoph Willibald, 15, 25
Godfrey, Daniel, 10, 124
Goethe, Johann Wolfgang von, 140
Golbel, Adam, 21
Goldmark, Karl, 34
Gounod, Charles, 25, 81, 86, 146n
Grainger, Percy, 143
Grant, Ulysses S., 76
Great Britain, 38–41, 45–52
Green, Joe and George Hamilton, 126–29
Grisar, Albert, 29

Hadley, Henry Kimball, 60
Handel, George Frideric, 25, 146n
Hanslick, Eduard, 29
Harlem, 81, 171
Harney, Ben, 172
Harrison, Benjamin, 2, 18n, 92
Hassler, Simon, 2–4, 3n
Hattstaedt, John James, 21
Haweis, Hugh R., 151
Haydn, Joseph, xx, 82–83, 93, 120, 122, 125, 146n, 173
Hell [Helle], Franz , 33, 38
Henicke, Paul, 10, 11
Herbert, Victor, 60, 61, 65, 68
Hérold [Herold], Ferdinand, 25
Hoffman, Richard, 4
Hogan, Ernest, 171, 171n, 172
Hohenzollern, Wilhelm, 141
Hoover, Herbert, 7
Howe, Julia Ward, 24

Jefferson, Thomas, 115
Johnson, George F., 161–64, 167, 168
Joplin, Scott, 17

Kappey, J. A., 137, 137n
Kéler, Béla, 128
Kelley, Edgar Stillman, 4
Kelvin, William Thomson, 150
Kerker, Gustave, 38
Klose, Friedrich, 124
Krehbiel, Henry, 104
Kreisler, Fritz, 152
Kryl, Bohumir, 127, 127n
Kühner [Kuhner], Conrad, 10

Lassen, Eduard, 38
Lax, 3
Leavitt, Joshua, 38
Lehmann, Liza, 104–105, 104n
Leutner, Albert, 38
Liszt, Franz, 10, 25
London, 38, 39, 45, 46, 47, 50, 51, 59,
    74, 100, 100n, 105, 125
London Daily Mail, 38
London Symphony Orchestra, 98n
Longfellow, Henry Wadsworth, 7n,
    142
Lowell, Robert, 136n
Luther, Martin, 72

Macaulay, Thomas Babington, 135,
    135n
MacCracken, Henry, 24
MacDowell [and McDowell], Edward,
    26, 60
Mantia, Simone, 38
Marconi, Guglielmo, 151
Marine Band, 1, 2–3, 5–6, 12, 14, 16,
    17, 19, 21, 22, 91, 117, 147
Mascagni, Pietro, 84
Massenet, Jules, 11n, 25, 31, 34, 135n
McCoy, William J., 60
McKinley, William, 134
Melzer, Charles Henry, 149
Mendelssohn, Felix, 10, 13, 25, 73,
    110, 138, 139, 140, 141, 147n
Metropolitan Opera (New York), 86,
    86n, 111n
Meyerbeer, Giacomo, 10, 11, 25

Meyrelles, M. C., 3
Middleton, Howard Taylor, 128
Miller, George, 124
Millöcker [Milloecker], Carl, 60
Mormon Tabernacle Choir, 17
Mozart, Wolfgang Amadeus, 25, 73,
    92, 93, 125, 144, 152
Muck, Karl, 132–33, 141
Müller, 3

National League of Musicians, 5–6
NBC Symphony Orchestra, 126
Nessler, Victor, 38
Nevin, 60
New York, 8, 22, 25, 29, 59, 81, 84,
    85, 86, 92, 94, 95, 96, 97, 100, 104,
    105, 127, 128, 131, 158, 159, 161,
    172, 175
New York Herald, 31, 138
New York Music Publishing
    Company, 3
New York Musician and Knocker, 126
New York Philharmonic, 87
New York Phonograph Symphony
    Orchestra, 82
New York Sun, 112
New York Times, 7, 161
New York University, 24
New York World, 24
Nolan, Michael, 11, 11n

Offenbach, Jacques, 38, 60, 135n

Paderewski, Ignacy Jan, 152
Paganini, Niccolò, 33
Paine, John Knowles, 4, 26, 60
Palestrina, Giovanni Pierluigi da, 72,
    121
Paris, 28, 29, 30–34, 72, 100, 105
    Exposition Universelle (World's
    Fair of 1900), 28–38, 100
Parker, Horatio, 60, 104
Parlow, Albert, 92, 124
Parry, C. Hubert H., 104
Paulus, 124

Pepper, J. W., 1–2
Pettit, Horace, 65, 68, 68n
Philadelphia, 1, 2, 4, 5, 14, 18, 100, 173
 Centennial Exposition (1876), 2,
  18, 20
 Philadelphia Symphony Orchestra,
  173
Pond, William A., 3
Pryor, Arthur, 33, 100n, 138, 170
Puccini, Giacomo, 34, 111, 111n
Puerner, Charles, 3, 4, 11

Quigg, John Travis, 2–4, 2n

Rachmaninoff, Sergei, 143–44, 144n
Reeves, David, 10, 11
Reid, Buchanan, 135
Rhodes, Leon C., 160
Richter, Hans, 125
Riemann, Hugo, 121
Riezel, 3
Riley, James Whitcomb, 115, 115n
Riniere, 10
Roberts, Charles J., 119, 119n
Rockstro, William Smith, 122, 122n
Rogers, Walter, 33
Röntgen [Roentgen], Wilhelm, 150
Rossini, Gioachino, 10, 24, 25, 119
Rubinstein, Anton, 25, 147n
Russell, James E., 167

Sabin, W. D., 164
Saenger, Gustav, 118–20, 118n
Safranek, Vincent F., 118, 119, 119n
St. Louis, 22, 17n, 100
St. Louis Republic, 30
Saint-Saëns [and Saint-Saens],
 Camille, 25, 34
Saintis, Armand, 34
Sax, Adolphe, 124
Schaaf, Edward, 141
Schmidt, Arthur P., 10
Schubert, Franz, 10
Schumann, Robert, 25, 144, 146n, 147n
Sellenik, Adolphe-Valentin, 124

Shakespeare, William, 15, 93, 142
Sharp, Cecil, 96
Sherman, William Tecumseh, 135
Smyth, Ethel (Edith Smith), 98n
Songs and hymns (various composers
 excepting Sousa),
 "Abide in Me," 138
 "All Coons Look Alike to Me," 171n
 "Annie Laurie," 76, 138
 "Annie Lisle," 138
 "Auld Lang Syne," 136
 "Baby Mine," 85
 "The Bells of Moscow," 143
 "Beulah Land," 138
 "Charley Is My Darling," 135
 "Climbing up de Golden Stairs," 86
 "Columbia, the Gem of the Ocean,"
  134
 "Dixie," 76, 100n, 102–103, 134,
  136
 "The Cows Are in the Corn," 86
 "The Girl I Left behind Me," 76
 "God Save the Queen," 7
 "Good-bye," 13
 "Hail Columbia" 7, 8, 134
 "Heil dir im Siegerkranz," 132
 "Home, Sweet Home," 138
 "If You Ain't Got No Money," 85
 "Is There Room among the
  Angels," 86
 "John Brown's Body," 172
 "Kuhreihen," 137
 "La Marseillaise," 7, 133
 "Lead, Kindly Light," 138
 "Little Annie Rooney," 11, 14
 "Marching through Georgia," 135
 "McGinty" folksongs, 12
 "The Mocking Bird," 138
 "My Country 'Tis of Thee," 7–8
 "Nearer My God to Thee," 164
 "Oh How I Hate to Get up in the
  Morning," 173
 "Over There," 173
 "La Pas Ma La," 171

"Rock of Ages," 138
"The Song of the Camp," 76, 137
"The Star-Spangled Banner," 7-8, 132, 134
"Suwanee River," 138
"There'll Be a Hot Time in the Old Town To-night," 135, 172
"Three Strikes Two-Step," 106n, 107
"Throw Him Down, McCluskey," 85n
"Yankee Doodle," 134
Sonneck, Oscar, 7
Sousa, Jane (Jane van Middlesworth Bellis), 131–32
Sousa, John Philip musical works
 The Bride Elect, 50
 El Capitan, 38
 Désirée, 1
 The Diplomat, 170
 The Free Lance, 117
 The Gladiator, 1
 Hail to the Spirit of Liberty, 38
 High School Cadets, 117
 King Cotton, 170
 The Last Crusade, 173
 The Last Days of Pompeii, 106
 Music of the Minute, 173–74
 The Smugglers, 1
 The Stars and Stripes Forever, 7, 44
 Washington Post, 117
 Wedding March, 138
Sousa, J. P. prose works
 Airs of All Lands, 7, 18n, 56
 The Fifth String, 38
 Marching Along (autobiography), xiii, xix, 32,
 National, Patriotic and Typical Pipetown Sandy, 38
 Through the Year with Sousa, 89
Sousa, J. P. practices and opinions
 American music, 3–4, 26, 31, 34, 52, 56–60, 71, 73, 81–87, 104–11, 149–50, 171–75

arranging and transcription, 37, 93, 124–26
Biblical and religious references, 49, 72, 91, 104, 120–21, 123, 134, 138, 161, 165, 167–68
blue laws, 159–69
business practices, 5–6, 33, 40–41, 43, 48, 50–53, 55–66, 66, 91, 99–103, 106, 108–109, 147–49, 165–67
classes of music (classical, popular, etc.), 12–16, 20–21, 24, 35–37, 59–60, 71–73, 75, 91, 104–11, 120–26, 140, 144–45, 171, 173
compositional practices, 23, 44, 97, 109–10, 117, 126, 146, 169–70
conducting and leadership, 27, 41–44, 52–58, 117, 145–47
copyright and intellectual property, 21, 45–52, 57, 61–70, 77–87, 133–34
criticism and public opinion, 12–13, 15–16, 20–21, 29, 33, 35–36, 48, 53–54, 81–87, 90, 92, 102–103, 104–11, 146–47, 167–69, 171
cuisine, 158–59
education and upbringing, 89–90, 103, 117, 145, 147–52
ethnicity and nationalism, 42–43, 52, 56–59, 94–97, 105, 110–11, 132–42, 171–72, 175
evolution, 36, 64, 72
government institutions and subsidies, 5–6, 22, 27, 31–38, 91
inspiration and genius, 32, 44, 53–54, 56–57, 73, 81–87, 109, 145–46, 161, 165, 169–70, 173
instruments and instrumentation, 1, 9–11, 25–29, 32, 35–36, 57–58, 90–94, 103, 122–26, 173–74
jazz and ragtime, 52, 103, 144–45, 152–53, 170–75

military, 54–55, 76
programming and repertoire, 3–4,
   11, 13–16, 20, 23, 28, 34–35,
   53–54, 93–94, 109, 132–33,
   164, 171
Prohibition, 113–14, 152–58
recordings and "mechanical music,"
   61–87, 116, 145, 150–52
rehearsals, 11–13, 15, 22
science and industry, 150–51, 175
sight reading, 53–54
social standing, 40–41, 58, 73–74,
   148–52
sports and leisure activities, 71,
   106–108, 112–16, 152
tempo, 118–19
uniforms, 12, 28, 38, 75, 102
women's rights and suffrage,
   97–98, 112, 114, 152–58, 169
Spalding, Warren F., 154–57
Spanish-American War, 172, 172n
Stanford, Charles Villiers, 121
Stewart, 60
Stokowski, Leopold, 143, 170, 173
Stone, Fred, 171
Stransky, Josef, 143
Strauss Jr., Johann, 14, 60, 92, 95, 95n,
   97, 111, 147n
Strauss, Richard, 93, 122, 146n
Sullivan, Arthur, 131, 147n
Suppé [and Suppe], Franz von, 60,
   118, 119n

Taylor, Bayard, 76n, 137
Tchaikovsky [and Tschaikowsky],
   Pyotr Ilyich, xv, 19, 25, 60, 93,
   128, 132
Tennyson, Alfred Lord, 142
Thackeray, William Makepeace, 142
Thomas, Ambroise, 29
Thomas, Theodore, 2, 17–18, 18n, 19,
   31, 118, 128
Timm, Henry Christian, 4
Tosti, Paolo, 128
Transcendentalism, 115

Transvaal War (Second Boer War),
   28, 28n
Twain, Mark (Samuel Clemens), 142

United States Marine Band, see
   Marine Band

Vaudeville, 82, 145, 152
Verdi, Giuseppe, 11, 25, 119
Victor Talking Machine Company,
   65, 67, 68, 68n
Voelkler, George, 4
Voltaire (François-Marie Arouet), 76n

Wagner, Richard, 10, 18, 25, 33–34, 60,
   72–73, 93–96, 104–105, 119, 121,
   123, 125, 132, 135, 138–41, 144
   works
      American Centennial March, 2
      Parsifal, 102, 109
      Tannhäuser [Tannhaeuser,
         Thanhauser], 10, 13, 14,
         146, 146n
      Tristan und Isolde, 108, 109
      Die Walküre [Walkuere], 14
      Lohengrin, 83, 109, 139, 146,
         146n
Warren, Alfred E., 4, 95
Washington, D. C., 1, 2, 3, 7, 8, 9, 12,
   22, 23, 61, 76, 77, 91, 95, 100, 115,
   117, 118, 149, 152
Washington, George, 8
Weber, Carl Maria von, 25
Weber, Joe, 141
Weingarten, G., 4
Whiting, George E., 4, 21, 60
Wiegand, Emil, 3
Wieprecht, Wilhelm Friedrich, 124
Willow Grove, 100, 128
Wilson, Woodrow, 97

Yerkes' Jazzarimba Orchestra, 128
YMCA, 169

Zettelman, Joseph, 127, 127n
Zimmerman, Charles A., 4

About the Editor

Bryan Proksch is associate professor of music history at Lamar University in Beaumont, Texas. His *Reviving Haydn: New Appreciations in the Twentieth Century* (Rochester, 2015) explored Haydn's return to prominence after a century of neglect. Research on Sousa for that study inspired this, his second book. He has published extensively on the history of the trumpet and brass history and serves as a column editor for the *International Trumpet Guild* Journal and editor of the Historic Brass Society's website content.

The Space Between

Also by Antoinette Voûte Roeder

Weaving the Wind

Still Breathing

The Many Singings

Poems for Meditation

The Space Between

Antoinette Voûte Roeder

Design and cover photo by Nicholas Roeder
Author photo by Michael Thomas Roeder

ISBN: 978-1-9993985-0-7

Printed and bound by First Choice Books &
Victoria Bindery, Victoria, BC, Canada

For Elaine and for Lisa

wise women, spiritual companions, dear friends

Contents

The Space Between **11**

The Space Between 12

Quantum Physics 13

Swan 14

Too Much 15

Domanski 16

Double Talk 17

Languages 18

Will 19

Retirement 20

All Is (Not) Well 21

The Fall 22

not a haiku 23

Threshold 24

Late August in the North 25

Two Minutes 26

Awake 27

Water 28

Christmas Morning 29

March Snow 30

Bird Walk 31

A Walk in the Woods 32

Snag 33

Pollinators 34

At Howse Pass 35

Fed 36

Still Life 37

Lane 38

A Koan 39

It Is Said 40

Past 41

then and now 42

A Patriarch's Legacy...43

Fear..44

Maze...45

The Cardiologist...46

Anatomy of Aging or How to Love It................47

Same...48

Grocery List 49

Domesticity 50

Love Affair 51

After Life 52

Husband...53

The poem he never wrote.....................................54

Could Have..55

If You Go Before I Go 56

missing soul 57

Dandelion 58

Observations in a Time of Dying.......................59

You Will Be Met...60

Funeral...61

Ashes..62

When is a poem...63

Prime 64

Light and Dark..65

Poetry...66

In this world 67

Truth 68

Held 69

Anamchara...70

Trudy's Meditation..71

Genjo's Wisdom 72

The Thomas Merton Library 73

More Poems for Meditation 75

Meditation...76

Being faithful 77
Breath Practice 78
Commitment 79
God's Dream 80
YHWH...81
Psalm 23...82
Moonstruck 83
Enter 84
Walking with nostrils flared...85
Quiet...86
Look inside 87
Noticed...88
Beloved...89
When a Gong, a Chime, a Set of Bells, and a Pipe Organ
Are Not Enough to Wake Me Up 90
Westwood Meditation..91
Centre 92
The Liturgy of Meditation 93
The Sit 94
Sometimes..95
I stand at the gate 96
Even when I am absent..97
In a moment..98
The Question 99
When at last..100
Every moment 101
Meditation with Rumi 102
There are times..103
You who are...104
Commandment 105
Once 106
Monk's Cell...107
Writing Breath...108
The perfect poem 109

Imagine the spine 112
Riding my breath 113
Every breath.. 114
Inside me sits.. 115
Word.. 116
The Birds and Francis 117
The Poet's Psalm 139 118
Poet's Meditation.. 119
Mystic 120
Beneath a layer.. 121
When I have filled 122
I want to pass through 123
Meditation.. 124
The end... 125
Acknowledgments.. 126

The Space Between

"The world
suspended
between awareness
and naming
between noticing and labeling
is where life unfolds…"
(*The Sit*)

The Space Between

The space between
beneath, within
the words of a poem is
mysterious passage
threshold and gateway
between the worlds

Words point, words open
to these worlds
but they are not
the worlds themselves

We enter this space
with tremulous breath
slowing step
a still regard
pause to receive
the in between.

Quantum Physics

I have always been alive
you too
in the universe

You could take my life today
for I have always been alive
in muons, gluons, bosons,
other-ons yet to be discovered
or not

In super strings, loops of vibration
the resonance that is the music
of the spheres, of all, of us, and so

I have known you
you have known me
though we've never
met
before

Inspired by Brian Greene's *The Elegant Universe*

Swan

In my dream
you sailed up to me
white, imposing
opened your beak
and offered me
two folded notes with
words of wisdom
I can't decipher.

Today on the banks
of the lagoon you sit
a large white ship marooned
and never even glance my way.

I'll choose my dream.

Too Much

All my life
I have said too much.

I have talked about
the journey inward,
outward to
the universe.

I have said too much.

I have filled the air
with arabesques
with shadowed peaks
cauliflower clouds
red-crested birds

and I have said too much.

Relationships and loves
and lost loves, home and
exile

criticism, protest, praise,
lament found words
and in the end

I have said too much,
I have said nothing
that experience does not
say better.

Domanski

"rainclouds and a scrawl of wind
will be added…"

How does wind scrawl, shawl,
write itself on sky, its fleeting
passage marking nothing?

Only we who venture forth
note its trail as grasses bow
and trees shake branches
as our hair lifts and flies.

No permanence
the scrawl of wind
just passing through
a scribble soon erased

Not unlike us

"Ochre"
All Our Wonder Unavenged
Don Domanski

Double Talk

People have
a great capacity
for words.
Not that they listen,
no, but they produce
an unprecedented volume
of verbiage that hovers over
the natural world like a cloud of gas
veiling the true nature of things,

whereby

the true nature of things
is magically transformed
into something it is not
and never has been:
ours to control.

Languages

There are some languages
into which I make
occasional forays:
a fancy French phrase
tossed aside at the airport,
spicy Spanish in a restaurant,
a story told in Dutch, the dry
tongue of my youth.

There is the body's language,
my own, yours, and ours combined,
the speech of touch; the dialogue of
wind, water, trees, plants,
the song of birds.

The world's alive with languages
emerging from the silence
at the heart of them all.

Will

Who knows
the will of God?
"Ninety percent of barn swallows
have disappeared," *World Birdlife* reports.

Who will report it when ninety percent
of *us* have disappeared, I wonder.

If God willed to save
two of every creature on the ark
are we looking for a repeat performance?

Whose will is it
and where is ours?

Retirement

The planet has announced
it's going to retire. It's tired of
incursions, tunneling, probes,
water forced in, oil forced out
violations causing quakes

the mowing down of forests
exodus of species
the shearing off of mountains
changing rivers' courses

What will retirement mean?
There really is no time to muse,
we've had a taste: cyclones,
hurricanes, droughts,
fires and floods

Not a paradise
of long days
sitting by a pool
sipping cooling drinks
hitting a ball on manicured greens

The earth's retirement spells
          d-i-s-a-s-t-e-r
and she won't be back
to work.

All Is (Not) Well

All is well with the world
(Nothing is well with the world)

With a view akin to a postcard
sent from the Côte d'Azur,
white masts tuck into a small marina
steepled houses lope up hillsides lush
and green and nudging up to
darkly rain-filled clouds

(All is well with the world)
Nothing is well with the world

Up island, days of storm and
deluge, floods and surges,
sandbags and evacuees

A stone's throw, a few miles,
a mountain range or two,
sometimes an ocean separates

what's well with the world
and what is not.

Victoria, Vancouver Island

The Fall

What if this experience of
green-blue earth whirling through
space, spilling oceans and streams,
housing life of all kinds, creeping,
slithering, flying, walking,
visible and in-
the western tanager in its riot
of colors, the ungainly manatee,
the great sequoia, "the human person
fully alive," what if this were
the Garden and the Fall
is still to come?

not a haiku

a blonde breeze
lifts the sweet scent
of clover hovering
over the field

a small love affair

Threshold

Evening wind kicks up
suddenly
sets crowns of spruces
spinning
ushers in that timeless
time
between dusk and dark
day
stepping back
night
waiting to slip in

In between
a threshold moment
a wild stirring
ungraspable
an ache, a longing,
for something…

Late August in the North

Down the lane
the dusty light
of autumn rests
on trees trembling with
the intrusion of
a few yellow leaves,
unwelcome itinerants in
summer foliage.
They will increase soon enough
and trees will burst into bloom
shouting amber and rust.

September waits, drowses in
the wings like Sleeping Beauty,
waiting for the kiss
of frost.

Two Minutes

Two minutes of dawn

Deep swaths of peach and indigo
creep and flow, diffuse
and disappear, leave a dull grey
un-sky.

Two minutes of dawn.
Then it's gone.

You weren't here
to see it.

Awake

The cry of a loon
cuts my sleep short.

In this urban setting
on our puddle of pond
a loon.

There he is in all his
glittering finery, drifting,
dwarfing busy ducks nearby

No sooner here
than gone, he leaves me
longing, looking, hoping for
another glimpse while time flies by

Our lives in transit
our stay but brief
like his.

Water

When days grow short
the towering poplar
casts its bronzed twin
onto the lake
evoking turgid ripples
in reluctant response.

Thick as honey,
water bears the weight of
frosty nights, knows winter
lurking just beneath
the edge of earth.

One day soon
it will come from its lair and
merry movement of wind on water
will sculpt, instead, a
sheet of ice.

Christmas Morning

Wouldn't you love to swoop between
the branches of a spruce, pirouette
in mid-air and sail back to sashay over
the balcony railing, land on its floor
and pick up one, then another
peanut settled snugly in the snow,
testing weight and worthiness, and fly
off to your favorite lair, your booty
wedged into your beak?

Wouldn't you love to be that free,
to be that magpie on this frosty
Christmas morning?

March Snow

Snow flakes
barreling into each other
looking for the perfect place to land
to accumulate

on horizontal shafts of wind
tumbling pell-mell
they fly by in a hurry

Perhaps in March they know
their days are numbered.

Bird Walk

Walking in a late March
friendly snow squall,
tiny pellets misting our sight,
the great-winged redhead of
the woods swoops through
the trees, his call as repetitious
as his food-gathering hammer.

Like a weathervane, a black
lacquered raven sits astride
a sky-scrubbing spruce. He has
mastered a complex musical
score: the audition includes
deep-throated gurgles, caws,
and castanets. A little flamenco, maestro,
please. A trio of woodpeckers, small
and downy, striped backs flashing
chase each other from branch
to branch.

We startle a blue jay, we
spot a magpie, a crow, the
ubiquitous chickadee and
as pellets turn to flakes,
I cannot suppress
the grin on my face,
the bounce in my step,
the snowflakes melting
on my tongue.

A Walk in the Woods

I cannot walk
past a flock of waxwings
in the woods. I have to
stop and watch each one
alight on the tip of a twig
until the spruce bears a crown
of birds, birthday candles live and high
in the sky.

I push back my cap
and free my ears
to hear the whir of their wings
and the buzz of their voices
like tiny beads strung on winter air.

Above our heads
they sail, they float
no weight to their bodies
till one drops like a stone
to a lower branch
and each one follows
in its wake
a whoosh of displaced air.

If the hairs on our heads
are numbered like waxwings
then I am numbered
with an elegant crowd.

Snag

Stand long enough
next to a snag
and it will talk.

Whether felled by fire
or just old age,
with wind whipping up
its long-dead trunk,
you may hear some tall tales
and dry muttering, the occasional
joke when a woodpecker lands;
remembering the old days
when seasons dressed it in green
and gold and life was juicy
and still to be lived.

Pollinators

An itinerant bumblebee
brings his friends to a
Turkish bath, a clutch of
wild roses where they
cavort each in his own
pink cup, rolling in
featherbeds of fine yellow
pollen, dunking their heads
in drunken joy. Like
whirling dervishes in striped
robes they are very small
messengers of global
fertility, furry prophets
easily dismissed.

At Howse Pass

"For me the heritage is superb indeed."
(Psalm 16)

For me the heritage is superb indeed.
Not so much the fruits of the mind
Even less the attraction of mammon

But this wide expanse of native grass beneath
a cobalt sky, glacier river wending through
the grasp of up-thrust mountains still so wild
only bear and cougar, goats and sheep,
elk and deer call them home.

When I stand very still

a breeze quickens
my skin, becomes
my breath

I no longer
know a difference

I am the rush
of river

the shadow
on the mountain

the promise
of the sky

one.

Fed

At the base of this mountain
high over the valley
Stillness drops down
drapes the forest, dresses
us, washes our feet, enters us
with each inhalation.

This is the altar of the Sacred.
This is the bread of the Great Thanksgiving.

Still Life

Gazing through a screen
of yellow tulips, a couple
of purple ones in a vase
the eyes rest on the
giant Olympics rising
from the sea
spring clouds on parade
before them and one single
heron staking out his piece of
sky in slow deliberate flight.

For Margaret and Denis
Victoria

Lane

I would read this book once more
if only for the joy of
rolling on my tongue the name
Stippy-Stappy Lane again,
which I imagine
is a whimsical track
of sand and sun
roughed up by wind
from the nearby sea
a path that does not lead
to village or town
but back to stories
at the knees
of someone dear
hot chocolate and no fear
of tomorrow.

From the Poldark novels by Winston Graham

A Koan

Life is a train

stopped

in the middle of a bridge

flung high over darkened water

on a moonless night

For Ria

It Is Said

There is only now
  so it is said
but *now* is every moment
different, teetering on the edge
of a blade so thin
it is translucent
conducting each wisp
of the before and open
to the next

Sometimes *now* knits itself
into a patch of singleness
a small oasis but even then
it isn't static, something stirs
within the ground

Maybe *now*
is more a wave,
a movement,
always slightly
out of reach

Past

A war I did not fight
even now flows in my blood.

Fear of the enemy is
knitted in my bones.

Pre-birth, birth and every
moment since is woven
into cells too numerous to
count. We do not need

to live our past again
but neither do we shed it.

Our past lives us and
every moment is the locus
and embodiment of every
thing we ever lived.

To be here now means showing
up just as we are, our past
and that of the universe
present and accounted for.

then and now

Sunday-morning-Bach
with a lazy sun filtering in
through the skylight
(there was a skylight,
wasn't there?) and Dad
deep down in his easy chair
half hidden by the morning news
cigar smoke curling into the air

and Bach, then as now,
the jubilant violin concerto,
more joy than a person can hold
rising up to the ceiling
filling the room, was it
Bach or the sun, and what's
the difference anyhow
and though very little
was well with the world,
then as now,
it all felt just
perfect.

A Patriarch's Legacy

It's none of your business,
he said and so
we never knew
why he went away
why he stayed away
  so long
what the war had done
  to him
what powers others exercised
to lure him from his pregnant
wife, 3 children under 12.

There's no one left to ask
  I've tried, and anyway
each told a different tale.

We built our lives
on semi-truths, unspoken
laws, on secrets never shared.

It always felt like quicksand.

Fear

It disappears around
a corner, deep in shadow,
only a tail-tip visible

only to come around
again, bristled nose first
eyes like lanterns

the moment in between
a small oasis
of fearlessness

Maze

The tricky world
between sleep and waking
is a maze, a mesh
of undreamed dreams,
unfinished thoughts, of
plans that will not see
the sun and worries wrestling reason
in the endless restless dark.

When the third train of the night
rumbles in the distance, it's as if
the mind's meanderings hit
a wall. Resolve grows as she gropes
for a book, the light switch, glasses,
and escape.

The Cardiologist

Maundy Thursday
and he enters wearing
a lavender shirt, sleeves rolled up,
tie to match.

He won't be washing my feet.

Sometime into the appointment
he leaves the room
returns with a small device
to place against my heart.
On a tiny hand-held screen
he shows me what's beneath
my ribs: a small live animal
mouth opening, closing
pumping steadily within
the dark cave of my chest.

Awe-struck
curved into the event
as if in prayer my Easter
has just dawned.

Anatomy of Aging or How to Love It

When the skin
pours in rivulets
from wrist to elbow
like silk pleats from
a ruffled cuff

When despite the
hairdresser's skill
glimpses of pink skull
come out of hiding
between strands of grey

When eyes burn and blur
even after eight hours' sleep
(eight hours' sleep? When does *that* occur?)
and conversation turns to a litany
of "I'm sorry," "What was that again?"
"I didn't quite catch that"

When handwriting looks
like hieroglyphics, spiders
crawling on ancient tablets

When landing on the floor
means staying on the floor
in gravity's grip until
help arrives

then the conundrum we face is,
how do I learn to love the slow decline,
this gradual loss, the certainty
of old age?

Same

In the period
of an hour or less
she asks the same question
three times over in
the very same words.

It is as if
her synapses
have dropped into
a track that won't
let go and when
she tries to find another
gravity prevails
dragging her right back.

She clings
to the familiar. Beyond
lies no-man's land
where words mean less
than nothing.

Grocery List

The time came
when some words
had dumped their content.

He would come home
with something else
or maybe nothing at all.

He still liked
to go to market
so she made it easy,
drew a little picture
next to every item.

That's how he shopped
list in hand and still
he'd leave something out.

Then she would work
around it, improvise
a meal he'd soon
forget.

Think of
the love.

Think of
the loss.

For Lisa

Domesticity

I go to clear the table:

> cream-colored roses
> slightly down at the mouth
> wilting in a crystal vase
>
> a basket of yarn
> anonymous knitting
> spilling out
>
> a calendar open
> to a month from now
> various pens and pencils
> in disarray
>
> a half-eaten cookie
> crumbling in a saucer

It could be a Cézanne.

Love Affair

I love my piano
   and the ease with which my fingers find
   the keys, their pattern, and the conversation
   that ensues

I love the keys
   their intimacy cool
   beneath my hands
   mapped since childhood
   like others might have mapped
   the stars

I love their black and white
   geography, stair steps long
   more felt than seen, a
   disciplined maze through which
   my fingers weave, in and out and over,
   smoothing sounds or spanking them,
   sparking them or sending them like messages
   into the world and whether there's
   another listening ear or not,
   no matter, that is all
   I have become.

After Life

If there is to be
no music
I wish you'd tell me now

'cause I'll be lining up
to catch a train
to a different destination.

Husband

When they walked
in snow, on ice,
he offered his arm,
his hand took hers

as if it were
automatic

but she knew better.

It was love.

For Michael

The poem he never wrote

was the one that planted kisses
along her spine, the one whose
crested waves bore her along
disarmed her totally.

What he wrote was
countless love notes, scraps
of different colored paper
crazy cartoons of himself, a
full moon face, cockeyed,
glasses crooked, hair all scruffy.

Florist cards with conventional text
followed by his loving scrawl and cards
with photographs sublime his eye had framed
opening on printed words that cast a trail of years
together, the poem he never wrote but lived
with her.

Could Have

I could have lived
  unfettered and free
  to delve deep, to
  explore the soul map
  granted me

I could have gone and
  lived alone with solitude
  created home for thought
  and words, for language lyric
  and reflective

I could have
  but
I would have
  missed
  you.

If You Go Before I Go

I will be lost
        for a time

I will not know
        the way or
what to reach for
        for a time

Time will be
        endless
Space will be
        empty

For a time

Perhaps I'll grow
new skin in time

But tell me,
how will I know me
without you?

missing soul

When I've been living
                             outside
myself

it becomes
                             intensely
necessary

to climb back in
                             though it
is

like trying to clamber
through a high window
                             left part-
way open

in a house
that turns out to be
                             my own

I have to do it
despite scrapes and bruises

It's a matter
of life and death.

Dandelion

How many poems have been written
about that perfect globe of
eiderdown poised on a stem,
tens of tiny snowy pinpricks
left by a petalled sunburst?

If so much care
is spent on a plant,
a milk-white miracle,
surely we can ask
a miracle for you,
so ill in your hospital bed?

For Glenda

Observations in a Time of Dying

This thin time
delicate membrane
that life has become

Through it we experience
life's borrowed nature
our gradual stepping back
from the fray.

What remains is
a filament, fine thread,
diminishing flame
burning cleaner
falling back
to its source.

For Deanie

You Will Be Met

You *will* be met

Like the pelican
in the clouds
come to meet
its mate rising
from the lake
below

You will be met
when you depart
at last

Funeral

The service was long
and tearful, filled with
words, more words, and then
still more.

The crowd was mixed
more old than young
and dear and filled
with memories.

We filed into the basement later
lined up at a table laden

As if these suit-clad gentlemen
and high-heeled ladies had walked
the backroads of Uganda, starving,
this crowd loaded up their plates,
sat down munching buns and squares
midst a deafening din of talk.

Is it grief that makes us hungry?
Are we hungry? Or could we gather,
share our stories, hold the one
who's gone before us in the silence
when the words give out
and eyes fill up?

Ashes

His ashes in a gorgeous box
rest on the dresser
quite serene.

At times she takes the pouch
out, lays it on her belly,
warms it with her hands.

We talk about *our* ashes.
I want to fly,
my ashes on the wind.

You will not hold me back.

Will you?

When is a poem

not a poem?

When words pile up
like stacks of stuff
at a rummage sale

when music has fled
and cadence is tattered

when space and breath
are nowhere in sight
and all has been said
that can be said

when mystery has packed
her bags and left
for more receptive climes.

Prime

This, she says reluctantly,
is one of those books by
a poet past his prime
someone who has said it
all before, is now fishing in
static water. Because he once
had something to say
a publisher graciously
printed his words, granted
him one more book.

Even poets reach the end,
the place where the bottom gives way
and after that it is all
just air.

Light and Dark

The poem that appears
behind closed lids
quick and alive

fades to nothing
in the light of day
where voices scurry

from dusty corners
point out its faults
its lack of luster.

The poem appears
poor and little
eyes cast down
an orphan child
waiting for rescue
in the thick rich dark
where the poet finds
her voice once more.

Poetry

It's the words themselves
that open their doors
and let me fall in
with all my heart,
fall in and through
into something else
something else
that has no words
at all.

In this world

of lies and unrest,
of malicious mischief,
what matters a poem?

And if a poem
bears no weight
has no power
to transform

what has?

Truth

The language of poetry
may prove to be
the only bastion left standing against
alternative facts, misinformation.

Trust a poet
to choose each word
for its power of truth
to convey life as lived
on planet earth.

Held

She leans in
eyes alive
body alert

Already she has extended
her heart, holds it
open, holds it
towards you
holds your words
with tender care.

Do you know
how rare that is?

Anamchara

When I sit with you
quiet and open
nothing remains but

a clean threshing floor
fundament
bedrock.

Pour what you will
into this space.
It will hold
and hold fast.

It isn't my doing
It's not my space.

I only hold it.

Grace.

The ministry of spiritual accompaniment

Trudy's Meditation

After the silence
her eyes   soft and misty
reflect far-away places
other lands
foreign shores

the wholly, holy other
within

Genjo's Wisdom

I came to him
with a question.

"You know that already,"
he said.

He knew I knew
but until that moment
of being known
I had not known
that I truly knew.

The Thomas Merton Library

is a small book-lined room
upstairs that has been our
home some eighteen years.
In this cavernous convent
one cozy cell that's held our group-
in-prayer on dark snowy nights
and sun-stifling eves in June
and this June we will depart and
it will return to what it was,
a library.

More Poems for Meditation

"My Beloved lifts up his voice, he says to me,
'Come then, my love, my lovely one, come.'"
(*The Songs of Songs* 2:10)

Meditation

June mornings are easy
I sit on the floor
cross-legged before
my prayer table

The window is open
The walls fall away to
the traffic's swish-swish
a dog's chant-like bark

I sit in the world

    - - - -

January is hard
I struggle to come
to my cushion
sit huddled in fleece
The cold is a fortress

My breath breaches
the battlements
Breathes life to
the homeless, the old

I sit in the world

    - - - -

I sit on the floor
cross-legged
in a muddle of contrasts
in a world
where opposites meet
and where they meet
dualities
       drop
         away

Being faithful
to daily sitting
is not easy

Still
even when I
fail to show up

Someone sits
Is faithful

Breath Practice

Incredibly simple
Terribly hard

Can you
watch your breath
and not jump in
to change it?

Watch your breath

It changes you.

Commitment

You have to be willing
to bear the pain

or you will miss
the ecstasy

God's Dream

It is as if God
asleep in Elijah's cave
dreams of me while
Elijah paces up and down
in front

and I teeter
on the lip of the cave
afraid of both
the prophet and God
unable to believe
God's dream
of me.

YHWH

You have been courting me
for years by way of Bach,
of Brahms, of lovely friends,
of loves that flowered and some
not. By way of great
sequoias, frost-tipped grass
the shell-eared pika,
the red-necked grebe

You have been courting me
for years, always the flow
of life toward me. Now
at last I turn to face you
fully, no holds barred.

The answer is yes,
can only be yes.

Psalm 23

"Yahweh is my Beloved
I lack nothing."

*How many worlds
break open before me
spilling their treasures
at my feet*

"Yahweh is my Beloved
I lack nothing."

*What is your desire?
What do you need?*

Yahweh is my Beloved
I lack nothing.

Moonstruck

A sliver of moon peel hangs
in a tangle of naked branches
among shriveled apples
black with winter's kiss.

So light, so bright, so other
is this crisp crescent in a night- tree
as it meets the modulations
of a pre-dawn sky.

Inside my house
I sit suspended
on this lemon-wedge of time
and pray the stillness
and the waiting.

Earth, awake or dreaming
holds me for you
Beloved.

Enter
the silence
of their icy
contemplation

mountain peak
and taut blue sky

not a thought
to the human

O blessed liberation

Walking with nostrils flared
scent-memory of yesterday's roses
drunk on a different smell today
moldering leaves, damply brown
trampled down beneath my feet.

Sun dapples through forest canopy
bounces off bright berries
scarlet, white, aubergine.

September day
lifted out
of the strife
of a conflicted world
and who's to say
this is not
meditation.

Quiet

I am very happy
to be home and
very quiet, quietness
that sizzles in my
ears, spreads its folded
wings around my limbs
and keeps me close, asks
nothing of me, does not
urge or argue, plan tomorrow,
organize or publicize. She settles
down within me and illuminates
the darkness with her subtle light
until I know myself once more
whole and child-like
at the world's beginning.

Look inside
Who is home?

Nobody is home
Nobody is not home

Noticed

My mind ranged far away
diffused, unfocused when all
of a sudden I dropped into
this moment, heard you practicing,
exploring highs and lows of your
instrument, noticed the gnawing in
my back, the still container of this house,
my faithful heart's beat, my lungs' long breath,
noticed the noticing.

Beloved
  inside
   my breath, my
   bones, throughout
   my body

Beloved
  outside
   in the day's noise
   busyness and fragrance

everywhere
Beloved

When a Gong, a Chime, a Set of Bells, and a Pipe Organ Are Not Enough to Wake Me Up

but the sound of silence
weighty and full
has me in its thrall
alert
to all that is.

Westwood Meditation

She rings the bell
three times

The furnace wheezes to
a stop

We close our eyes
Sounds grow large

The tick-tick of
the cooling ducts

the swish of cars
on a rainy street

We settle into
silence
dropping to a place
where neither sight nor sound
is spoken

Centre

This pool at the centre is
deep, is timeless
unfathomable and
unchanging, always
available

it lives alongside
terrible misery
hideous agony
exhilarating joy
and ordinariness

always available
at the centre

The Liturgy of Meditation

Eyes close.
Step into bliss.

Before all thought,
sense and sound
are what they are,
rising, passing,

step into bliss.

Slowly, surely
naming happens,
language darkens
the horizon.

Worship:
What does it mean
if not this,
not this?

The Sit

The world
suspended
between awareness
and naming
between noticing and labeling
is where life unfolds
in all multiplicity
all one
unblemished
and even the one
who sits knows nothing
about it

Sometimes
between observations
I am merely
the gaze

one moment of eternity
between the structures of the mind

unaware
of the Beloved

yet not

I stand at the gate
today

It will not open to me

No matter where I start
it will not let me
in

though somewhere in
the deepest dark
a seed of certainty
blooms, declares
you are never
out

Even when I am absent
You are not

I dream away
You hold me

You live life
through me, in me

hold me together
send me love notes

"Come back, come back"

In a moment
of time
I wander the cosmos
looking for You

What if You
are not there?

The Question

Who is God for you now,
she asked.

The unexpected
the un-awaited
the no-show

never absent

When at last
the gate slips open
disappears,
has never been there
I stand alone
in a field
vast and spacious

Behind me life
in all its richness
buoys me forward
into the unknown of
the ahead

Every moment
breaks open
in meditation

holds past,
present, future

it's all ours
now

Meditation with Rumi

Do not call on
the Beloved

Do not grasp for
what is yours

already

There are times
I come to sit
You are here
already

I am welcomed
I am held
Then I wander
stray away
searching through
my yesterdays
looking to
tomorrow

And you sigh
arms still open
eyes still full
of me

You who are
no-thing

I am come.

Commandment

"This is my breath
which is given to you

Breathe into the world
Breathe into your heart

Fill the void with
my life-giving breath

Weave it throughout
each day, each night

A cloud, a fire
steady companion
on the way"

Once
I knew
were this breath
to descend still further
down
down
I would find my Self
face to face
with You

Monk's Cell

As dawn edges darkness back
I make my way to prayer

Silence sizzles in my ears
breath settles in my body

Dawn-filled
Quiet-filled
room

Nobody there

Writing Breath

I want to write
breath

If only I could

When I close my eyes
she appears full-grown
full-blown

It
is
her
right
It
is
her
gift

I want to write breath

She takes my pen.
Breath writes me.

The perfect poem
a blank page

pure
awareness

Imagine the spine
like that of a fish
slender white bones
raying outward
perfect structure
to carry breath

Riding my breath
Riding a rainbow

At my feet
A pot of gold

Every breath
opens up
to new terrain

Like a scout
who moves ahead
pointing out
the open sky
the profile of
the hills ahead

See that, feel this

This too
is yours

Inside me sits
a small monk
deep in
contemplation

while the me
that meets the world
runs around
a mind maze

I claim them both

Word

He breathed on them.
It was his Word.

His Word gave life
like they'd not had
before.

They opened before him
turned to the world

The Word in the world.

Where is it now?

The Birds and Francis

Don't you think
instead of sermonizing
Francis listened
to the birds' interpretation
of the sacred light of dawn
the holy shadows of the
evening, all creation's
travail in between?

Then perhaps and in
conclusion Francis whispered,
"Little sisters, tell me more.
Tell me more."

The Poet's Psalm 139

"Even before a word is on my tongue...."

The words appear
soft
hard
hovering behind
beckoning in front

Always just
out of reach
as they should be

They belong
to You.

Poet's Meditation

Will it ever be thus?

It will ever be thus.

May it ever be thus

the words that nestle
upon my tongue
known to you
before they emerge
given
received
held
in the most sacred
of containers.

Psalm 139
"even before a word is on my tongue
lo, oh Lord, thou knowest it altogether."

Mystic

There's something so profane
about language that attempts
to describe mystical experience.
Words taste like ashes
in my mouth,
dry, less than nothing.
I spit them out
to make room
for the Only Word.

Beneath a layer
of incessant talk

the quiet surface of
a pond lies transparent
in its depth

at its center
sheer awareness

No sign
of thee or me

When I have filled
the room with words
there comes a time
when words crave silence

One by one
words drop away
uncover Silence
the great container

Non-word sounds
reveal themselves:
dawn wind sweeping
through spring leaves
a distant bell

Below that,
Silence
holding all
until all disappears
and Silence
holds
Itself
alone

I want to pass through
words
watch them split and splinter
fall away
as I glide
into
nothingness

into
everything

Meditation

I will sit alone

and in the sitting

begin to learn

the lonely way

the way that leads

to my demise

the death that I

alone can die.

The end

will be
like a child
blindfolded
led by
an adult

Surprise!
Surprise!

And it will be

It will be

Acknowledgments

Heartfelt thanks to Nicholas Roeder for his beautiful cover photo and patience with putting this volume together. Also to my husband Michael Roeder who has helped me negotiate the labyrinth of computer folders and files. And to the lovely people who support and encourage my work, those very special people who commit some poems to memory and recite them back to me, deep gratitude.

The following poems were published previously:

"The Fall" in *Presence: An International Journal of Spiritual Direction*, Vol. 21, No. 4 (December 2015).

"Quantum Physics" in *Saging: The Journal of Creative Aging*, Issue 18 (Winter 2016).

"The Cardiologist" in *Focus: The Canadian Medical and Dental Society Magazine*, Issue 2, (August 2017) and in *Saging: The Journal of Creative Aging*, Issue 24 (Fall 2017).

"In this world" and "Too Much" in *Saging: The Journal of Creative Aging*, Issue 24 (Fall 2017).

"The poem he never wrote" in *The Stroll of Poets Anthology*, (2018).

"Color Me Empty" and "Anamchara" on the Pacific Jubilee website, http://www.jubileeassociates.ca.